The "G" is for Guts

Cover: Six glider pilots of the 87th squadron in Britain.
Clockwise from top left (Arnold A. Best, Harrison McVey,
Fredrick M. Winkler, Lee A. Wheelock, Eddie Allen, Charles
Stephens).

To order additional copies, please contact us.
BookSurge, LLC
www.booksurge.com
1-866-308-6235
orders@booksurge.com

The "G" is for Guts
An American Glider Pilot's Story

S.W. Maynes

2006

The "G" is for Guts

_____

Acknowledgments

Where to begin? I can't thank my Uncle Charles enough for regaling me with his powerful and inspiring stories. My life is richer because of his shared experiences. Many thanks as well to Aunt VeNona for her great stories and ability to remember and fill-in necessary details. She was the perfect grandmother to my children during our audio-taped sessions together, playing with them (she even learned to play chess to please them) and plying them with popsicles and chocolates. Her tremendous faith and spirit is remarkable.

In addition I must thank Uncle Charles's wonderful Idaho friend and fellow glider pilot, G.L. Williams. What a delight it was to visit this good man in his home. He welcomed my mother and me as long-time friends and kept us on the edge of our seats fascinated by his stories. He is an impressive individual. Very physically fit, he is definitely not someone that I would want to challenge in a 10k race.

Glider pilot Douglas Wilmer also deserves many thanks for responding so quickly and effectively to questions and concerns that I had about the project. He was abundantly kind and encouraging and an excellent source of information.

I admire greatly his dedicated work in quietly writing his column for so many years and as custodian of the glider pilot film and video library.

Thanks also to glider pilot Miles Wagner for our pleasant conversation together. I appreciated his sharing some of his wartime experiences with me and felt uplifted by the humility that this man expressed in his remembrances.

It was a joy to speak to Mary Lou McVey, the widow of glider pilot Harrison McVey. She very graciously fielded my questions per telephone and then went above and beyond by sending me several different printed articles about World War II glider pilots. I am grateful for her help and support.

The fantastic staff at the Silent Wings Glider Museum in Lubbock, Texas should be thanked as well. Research assistant Benjamin Clark spent a whole day cheerfully carting box after box of pictures and memorabilia for me to look through. World War II glider pilots and museum volunteers, Doug Flynn and Otto Lyons, sat down with my son and me and spoke to us of their experiences and explained what was going on in a lot of the pictures we saw. It was a truly great experience to visit the museum, and I hope that many people will walk through its doors.

The folks at BookSurge have done a great job of shepherding me through the book publishing process. I appreciate the help of John Mark Schuster, Reagan Stafford and Pamela Snow-Prince.

Last but not least thank you to my ever patient husband Todd and to my children. Todd made it possible for me to travel to Las Vegas several times to interview Uncle Charles and to make the trip to Lubbock. I greatly appreciate his love and support. I wouldn't have been able to do this without him.

For my sweet mother

PREFACE
The "G" is for Guts

This book tells the story of a young man growing up in the American west in the pre-World War II era, his experiences as a military glider pilot, and the story of the glider pilots and program itself, as viewed through his eyes. For those with a fondness for exciting wartime literature and not much patience for folksy home-life descriptions—and wishing that the narrative would just cut to the chase—this writer at least believes that some knowledge of upbringing and background is essential to understanding the motivations and character of anyone that was part of what Tom Brokaw has called "The Greatest Generation." Don't worry, the battle scenes will come. But World War I, the great Depression and the nature of life in the United States during these times all contributed to the development of the intrepid men and women of this generation.

The man featured in this story is my uncle, Charles Stephens. For as long as I can remember I loved hearing stories about him. A couple of years ago when he agreed at my mother's insistence (and I mean insistence, she wasn't taking no for an answer) to have his experiences recorded I was thrilled to be asked to be part of that process. It has been wonderful to listen and to learn about World War II from one who was there. This is Charles Stephens's story as he told it to me; supplemented by his own writings, conversations with other glider pilots, and various books about World War II military glider pilots.

Charles Stephens is one of my heroes, along with the other glider pilots and all the men and women who served our country during World War II. One cannot help but marvel at their sacrifices. They gave their best when our country needed them the most, and for that we should be forever grateful.

World War II glider pilots are for the most part forgotten heroes, or as one glider pilot said "they were the unsung heroes of World War II." Many people don't know that the military used gliders and that gliders were flown in all of the major campaigns of the war and were generally, along with the paratroopers, the first invasion forces to go in. They were in the vanguard.

At the risk of their lives glider pilots delivered badly needed supplies and manpower behind enemy lines. They flew engineless airplane-shaped wooden crates attached like kites on strings to tow planes. The American gliders, the CG-4A's (unlike the British gliders which the Americans sometimes flew), weren't even made of wood; they were framed with steel girding covered in canvas. According to many accounts glider pilots didn't receive the medals or the credit they were due for their wartime contributions. It was suggested by a glider pilot that maybe they didn't receive much recognition because they operated mostly behind enemy lines. There weren't a lot of witnesses to their valor; they operated quietly behind the scenes. Glider pilots were often recommended by the airborne officers for citations because of their bravery but these requests for commendations were frequently ignored.

Some of the glider pilots had a reputation for being "bad boys." When the need for glider pilots was great and the air force couldn't find enough pilots to meet their expanding quotas they took some "washed out" power pilots and made them glider pilots. They weren't washed out because of their inability to fly the planes; they were a talented lot, but mainly because of bad attitudes or reputations as rule breakers. As one glider pilot put it: "They broke the hearts of these guys (by not letting them fly), but flying a glider gave them a second chance. Most did a better job of piloting than did the power pilots. They were uncut diamonds. They did everything that was asked of them and did it well."

The glider pilots were a different kind of men. They were both gutsy daredevils and skilled technicians that relied on a blend of intuition and the ability to think and act quickly under pressure to preserve their lives, the lives of the men they carried and the loads they were transporting. They flew unprotected in what was essentially a plywood box or canvas tent across miles of land and ocean to pocket-sized target areas behind enemy lines where they dove and crash landed under intense fire. At times they were under fire for miles flying over enemy territory. They did this carrying jeeps, troops, trailers, howitzers, and supplies of all kinds including in some cases numerous gasoline tanks. One glider pilot described this by saying: "Imagine, flying a motorless, fabric-covered CG4-A glider, violently bouncing and jerking on a one-inch thick nylon rope 300 feet back of the C-47 tow plane. You see the nervous infantrymen behind you, some vomiting, many in prayer, as you hedge-hop along at tree-top level instinctively jumping up in your seat every time you hear bullets and flak tearing thru the glider. You try not to think about the explosives aboard. It's like flying a stick of dynamite thru the gates of Hell." [1]

Because the gliders carried heavy loads the landings had to be swift and short or the gliders might stall and plummet to the ground after being cut loose from their tow planes. The trailers and jeeps could sometimes be jarred loose at landing and come crashing through the glider and the men in the front of it. If gasoline was carried it could ignite if the glider was hit, and trees, large rocks, walls, and buildings could cut a glider in half or dash it to splinters if in the seconds a pilot had to find his landing zone and dive, he missed seeing something or couldn't stop as quickly as he had anticipated. And as if that wasn't enough to contend with many of the landing zones were flooded or laced with deadly obstacles by the Germans as was particularly the case in Normandy.

The glider pilots had exhausting flights to their landing zones. A glider pilot stated "there was no automatic pilot. The glider pilot flew his glider every second of the way. You had to fly in a certain spot behind the C-47 (tow plane) or you could mess up the tow plane. You were in prop wash constantly. It was tossing you like a cork in the ocean; it beat you from one side to the other." Then after the marathon flights and roller-coaster landings the glider pilots had to be prepared to fight. They were trained fighters. They fought to deliver their loads and to get safely out from behind enemy lines so that they could do it again.

The history of the 101st Airborne describes the glider pilots as "the most uninhibited individualists in the Army," and further states: "There seemed to be something about flying a glider, or being selected for that job, that freed a man from the ordinary restraints of Army life. Those who wanted to fight, fought like lions. Those who wanted to go back... managed to get there before anyone else... [The glider pilots] were usually right up front during those crucial hours when the need for men is greatest. But they successfully defied all attempts at organization."[2]

When the glider program was in full swing the American glider pilots numbered just under 6,000. The casualty rate for World War II glider pilots was "one of the highest of any combat specialty" because of the hazards in battle and training accidents. "Their casualty rate was 16.4 percent (987 glider pilots) and roughly 20 percent of the number who flew in each combat mission." According to the *Tribute to the American Combat Glider Pilots of World War II*, "military doctrine typically holds that 10% casualties are unacceptable and will render a unit ineffective for further combat.[3]

Estimated casualties for glider pilots and riders were as much as 40 percent for some missions. In Operation Varsity (the Rhine River crossing) alone, "less than 25 percent of the gliders landed unscathed, and seventy glider pilots were killed and 114 wounded or injured."[4]

Military gliders and large-scale glider operations are obsolete now, a thing of the past. They have been replaced by helicopters and other transport aircraft that are safer, more reliable and technologically advanced. But because gliders are outdated and no longer in use does not mean that we should forget the service of the glider pilots or the need they filled in their day.

John L. Lowden, the author of *Silent Wings at War: Combat Gliders in World War II*, spoke of receiving an offer from the Air Force Association for "a spectacular book filled with dramatic photographs... which capture the magnificent legacy of the U.S. military aircraft from WWII." He lamented that "the aircraft I piloted were nowhere to be found in the book." He wrote to the AFA saying, "Some of us who flew during World War II did not 'feel the tug of g-forces' in a hurtling fighter. Nor did we fly to war in a vast armada of multi-engine bombers. We were combat glider pilots who collectively, participated in every major invasion of the war. Yet the aircraft we flew, the American Waco CG-4A and the British Airspeed Horsa gliders, are never included in the visual anthologies that have been published since the war's end."[5] In response the AFA replied that he was correct and admitted that this was an error on their part. The glider program and its pilots have been forgotten as by the AFA in this instance, and this is a very sad and ungrateful thing.

General Omar Bradley, the senior American ground commander in Europe, refused to attack Utah beach during the Normandy invasion without airborne troops, the gliders and the paratroopers. He felt that an attack would be impossible without airborne support and was able to persuade Eisenhower of his opinion. Huge numbers of casualties were predicted among the airborne, but it was thought that the risk was necessary to the success of the mission.[6] "They didn't think we'd be comin' back," said one glider pilot. The glider pilots were expendable. It's not certain that the glider pilots themselves really comprehended the risks, but they were men just the same who would do whatever they were asked for their country. While it is true that most of them loved flying and many would have done just about anything to fly, including flying a glider, there were a lot of other things, as young men in the prime of life, they could have been doing rather than flying straight into enemy territory in a "flying coffin," as gliders came to be called.

A glider pilot said to me when I was asking him some questions, "You should have been doing this ten years ago." His point was that many of the glider pilots have passed away and there are not so many left to speak to anymore. He was right of course, but I am just glad that there are glider pilots around to speak to at this writing. Striking too was another comment made by a glider pilot. We were discussing an event that he had witnessed and I explained to him how a glider pilot from a different vantage point had described it and he said that "if you weren't right next to each other or in the same field even though you were involved in the same operation it could be as if you were in a different battle altogether." Each of the glider pilots has a story to tell from his own unique experience and perspective.

The glider pilots that I have spoken to have been gracious and kind and have all shared interestingly enough, a kind of understated modesty. I think of eighty-eight-year-old Miles Wagner saying simply "I got banged up," in speaking of his last glider mission into Southern France when a jeep he was carrying broke loose and smashed him and another man into the front end of the glider. Mr. Wagner had been "a flyboy" as he put it but said that the air force wouldn't take him as a power pilot because he was too old; but he was not too old to be a glider pilot, and he was glad. And I think of eighty-four-year-old Douglas Wilmer who said that "he felt good about being a glider pilot." He didn't have much as a boy and couldn't have afforded to be a pilot or to have an advanced education if he hadn't enlisted in the army. He had dreamed of being a pilot and built model airplanes in his childhood. He joined the army in 1939 and was on active duty when Pearl Harbor was attacked. He'd been training to be a power pilot when about halfway through the program he was "washed out" and made a glider pilot. They "put us into gliders," he said, "they didn't ask us." Sad at first, he soon adjusted and worked hard to be a good glider pilot.

Doug said that "I made myself a promise as I was being flown home from Europe and on my way to the Japanese War; that I would never forget my glider pilot brothers that didn't make it." Currently he is the custodian of the glider pilot film and video archives. His main project is working to transfer all of the glider videos to DVD's. In addition he has written the Glider Soldier column of the airborne newspaper (*Static Line*) for twenty years.

G.L. Williams, "Wizard Williams" as he was called, received dual orders as a power pilot cadet and a glider pilot about midway through the power pilot program. He had intended to be a fighter pilot. He received a transfer to a power pilot school in Arizona and the next day received unexpected orders to report to glider training in Texas. This turn of events stunned him, but because he'd had only one year of college and it was a requirement that power pilots have two he felt that must have been the reason for his having been shifted to gliders. Crushed and disheartened he moved on to Texas. He said that though he later found that he could have continued in the power pilot program because the dual orders had been a mistake, he never looked back. He said "There were a lot of fellows in my predicament, a lot of really good fellows." He immediately bonded with the glider pilots that he met and developed a strong sense of kinship with them that overrode any desire to be a power pilot. Today Mr. Williams, a torch runner at the '84 Olympics in Los Angeles, at eighty-three is still going strong, so strong in fact, that he often runs six miles a day. The day after I met and spoke with him he was to run in a ten mile race.

Reflected in the life of my Uncle Charles is the story of the lives of these very human, but great men that were the glider pilots of World War II. Despite disappointments and set-backs they met new challenges head on. They were fearless in doing their duty and many of them were able to defy the odds and accomplish the seemingly impossible. To all of the glider pilots we owe a debt of gratitude and it is hoped that we will learn from their examples how to live lives of value and honor.

The burning ruins of an American CG-4A cargo glider. Photo courtesy of the Silent Wings Glider Museum in Lubbock, Texas.

Chapter 1
Peace Destroyed

On the afternoon of Sunday, December 7, 1941 the warm festival of brilliant autumnal color that had just weeks ago adorned the forests of Logan Canyon was now only a memory. The cheerful, riotous feast of fall's burnished reds, oranges and yellows had been replaced by a more simple, Spartan landscape. Still as college sophomore Charles Stephens and his friend Dick Aegerter glanced out the window of Charles's shiny, blue '35 Chevy on their way back to Utah State University they couldn't help but feel a rush of appreciation for the cold, stark beauty of the glittering snow-capped peaks and the glistening frost on the pines; Logan Canyon was magnificent in any season.

Charles was comfortable and confident behind the wheel of his Chevy. He had a love for all things mechanical. He could take a car apart piece by piece and doctor any automotive problem if need be. He'd been driving, you might say, since he was in fifth grade. He had his mother's permission to drive when he first climbed excitedly behind the wheel, but it had taken some real lawyering. She'd been bottling fruit one day in her sweet, steamy aromatically charged kitchen and was all caught up in the process of slicing, sugaring and boiling when it came time to pick up her husband and older sons at the ranch. Charles volunteered to drive and assured his mother that he could do it alone.

A cook of some local renown, Louisa Stephens's preserves along with her cakes (sour cream chocolate was a favorite) and pies were legendary, and had won as many awards as there were fairs in Bear Lake County. Louisa didn't want to leave home with the pots bubbling and the ripe, ready fruit spread before her in the legions. She'd risk ruining the precious harvest if she left midway through the bottling (which to this frugal mother of nine would be so wasteful as to constitute a serious sin). To her mind she didn't have much choice but to entrust Charles with the errand. Although Charles had always proven trustworthy it was with some trepidation that she dispatched him.

Charles was thrilled as only a young boy can be to have the opportunity to drive but somewhat daunted when he discovered that he could hardly reach the pedals of the family's '29 Chevy. He would have to almost stand in order to drive it. But not of a disposition to be discouraged, he propped himself into a driving stance and gave the car the go. He proceeded haltingly up 4th street (also called the upper road, which mercifully was not heavily trafficked) gradually familiarizing himself with the gas and the brake and easing his stubborn lead foot. As he drove further along the quiet, shady streets of Montpelier, Idaho his ride became smoother and he started to really feel that he was getting the hang of it. Why he had this thing licked, he was thinking to himself. Anybody could drive. Charles was disappointed then when he drove past his Uncles Bert and Dell and graced them with a proud, little wave and a smile and in return they greeted him with horrified looks of shock and surprise. They acted like they'd seen a ghost.

Charles was relieved to finally get out of town into the broad, sunny fields and to relax and enjoy the ride. When he got to the ranch he turned off the car and stiffly climbed out (it felt good to move) and opened the gate at the upper end of the field— from there it was just a short drive across the fields to where his Dad and brothers were. Unfortunately there was one very big obstacle blocking his path that he hadn't anticipated. His Dad had water running in the upper ditch that snaked clear through the ranch. There was only one way to avoid the ditch and that was to drive all the way around to the other side of the property along Joe's Gap road and onto the highway. Charles didn't dare do it. He knew he wasn't ready to drive in traffic. He would have to take on the ditch. He might get stuck in it, but that was better than causing a huge accident out on the highway.

He forced himself back into the car and into his jockey position. Charles jerked the car into reverse so he could get a run on the ditch and then pressed his foot to the accelerator as hard as he could. His teeth were bared and his young muscles ached as he held the pedal to the metal, clenched the steering wheel and launched the car precipitously over the ditch. Whoosh, he felt the wind whistle by his ears as the car left the dusty ground. He leaned forward into the dive. Then there was the rough bumping of the wheels on the dirt. He'd made it! Very nearly pitched out of the car in the attempt, there was just enough force to carry him over the ditch and safely on to the other side. With white knuckles still clinging to the steering wheel he left the gate wide open and kept right on going bouncing across the field without so much as a backwards glance until he reached the yard where his Dad and brothers Earl and Dean were waiting.

His Dad and brothers were so astonished they didn't know what to think. They were surprised to see the car coming from the direction of the ditch and even more surprised to see Charles driving it. From then on, in Charles's mind anyway, he was a veteran driver.

Twenty-one year old Charles traveling to school was truly a veteran driver having spent many years driving and fiddling with cars. As Charles motored along through Logan Canyon with his friend Dick he listened contently to the steady hum of the engine and thought about the fun he'd had on his weekend visit home (it was always good to see the folks) and about school at Utah State. He and Dick talked about their classes, girls, guys and family news. Dick was practically a seventh brother to Charles; they had grown up together and there wasn't anything that one didn't know about the other.

Dick was tinkering with the radio channel trying to improve the reception when all of a sudden they heard broadcast loud and clear, "We interrupt this program to give the following news bulletin; the Japanese have attacked Pearl Harbor!" Upon hearing this news Charles felt as if he'd received a crushing blow to the chest. As he and Dick listened in rapt attention and soaked up every bit of information that they could glean about the attack they felt at once intense anger and a paralyzing chill; they felt chilled to the bone. It was as if the freezing wind and the fierce December cold had somehow penetrated the body of the heated car. Instinctively they both knew that from here on out their lives would never be the same.

Charles silently pulled the car over to the side of the road and said to Dick "I don't know about you but I think I'll forget this going to school and go back home and join the service." Dick said "Well I've got to finish my schooling. I can't join the service now. Why don't you take me on to Logan and then go back?" Charles would have liked for his buddy to say "Yah let's join up," but he didn't try and convince Dick to ditch school and enlist with him. Dick had lost his mother only a few years before and his father earned a meager wage employed as the high school janitor. They couldn't afford a car and Dick's Dad walked the considerable distance from the high school to his home every working day in rain, sleet or snow. Charles knew what Dick's attending college meant to his family.

Charles nodded and carefully steered the car back onto the road headed southwest towards Logan. They would proceed on to Tilly Kunz's boarding house for young men where Charles and Dick lodged at Utah State. When they arrived at Tilly's they found every boarder in the place assembled in Tilly's neat, homey, lace doily covered living room. The men were pacing the floral carpeted floor nervously and saying "What are we going to do about this?" Charles spoke up immediately and said, "I'm ready to go now. Let's join the service!" There seemed to be almost universal agreement that this was the thing to do. Every man was ready and willing to support the country's war effort in any way that he could. By the time they'd finished discussing their plans it was late in the evening. Their minds were made up but for this night it would be lights out and they'd have to sleep on it.

The next morning no one attended classes at Utah State. A shaken and grieving nation listened as President Franklin D. Roosevelt powerfully proclaimed December 7, 1941, "A date that will live in infamy…" Charles was electrified by these stirring words; they were from that moment forever etched in his memory. He felt a surge of patriotic pride as Roosevelt in his impassioned speech to Congress pressed for support to declare war on Japan and called for a massive build-up of men and materials. Roosevelt demanded more airplanes than had ever before been produced in the United States. Instinctively he knew this was going to be a new kind of war; a war for the skies as well as the land and sea. Roosevelt thundered a call to arms.

En masse almost every eligible male at Utah State decided to enlist immediately. Alarmed, the President of the University, Elmer Peterson, called a special assembly. In a room packed to capacity and then some President Peterson told the student body that he understood the feelings of those who wanted to enlist straightway and respected them, but he counseled the students not to quit school and throw away a whole quarter's worth of work with only a few more weeks left to complete the term. He said to finish the quarter and then join the service after the holidays. President Peterson said that if the students wanted to enlist his heart was with them. He was able to persuade the majority to stay. Most felt that if they didn't enlist soon they would be drafted; one way or the other they would be serving in the armed forces. Charles was anxious to sign up but determined to do as the President advised. He buckled down and completed his studies for the quarter with the intent that he would join the air force after the Christmas holidays.

Chapter 2
Some Good Advice

Charles Culver Stephens was born July 20, 1920, the fifth in a family of seven boys and two girls. His parents were John Edwin Stephens and Louisa Perkins Stephens. Their children were: Ruth, La Grande, Earl, Dean, Charles, Glenn, Sterling, Shirley, and Roger. Friendly, ever-smiling Glenn died mysteriously as a youth several weeks after having his appendix removed. He and Charles, at only twenty months apart, had been inseparable. The family was devastated.

Charles was named after his grandfather Stephens. His middle name, Culver, came from a drifter that had boarded with the family. Mr. Culver had come to the Stephens ranch asking for food and shelter which he was given in exchange for work. He was a hard worker and John and Louisa liked him and wanted him to stay, but he had the wanderlust and couldn't abide staying in one place for too long. A short time after he left the ranch the Stephens learned that he had been killed in Pocatello, Idaho while trying to climb on the rods of a moving freight train. Charles was given the middle name of Culver in his memory.

John and Louisa often helped folks that were in need. One

day when Charles, his older brother Dean and his Dad, John, were out on the ranch and had just finished the milking and were headed home in a pounding rainstorm, they passed an old truck off to the side of the road. It was unusual to see a truck sitting there out in the country and after they passed it John told Dean (who was driving) to stop and go back so that they could get a better look at it. It was dark and difficult to make out but on closer observation they saw an open truck with a man and a woman and five or six kids ranging from about age nineteen to one or two years huddled in the flat-bed. The family had slipped off the road into the deep mud and had broken an axel just south of the old house, barn and corral (the Stephens had moved off the ranch into a house in town several years before) where the slough crossed the road. John pulled his hat down over his head and hurried over to the truck. Knowing that there was nothing that they could do to fix the truck that evening John told the family that if they wanted to get out of the weather they could stay in the house at the ranch which they readily accepted. From conversation it was learned that the family was on their way to Oregon having driven all the way from Oklahoma. They were travel worn and tired not to mention cold and soaked They had abandoned their dusty Oklahoma home in hopes of making a new start, but at that moment they were sopping wet and in some serious trouble.

Charles and Dean drove back to the ranch with the family's oldest boy just older than Dean, harnessed a team and with the horses tugging and straining and water pouring down their backs, muscled the truck out of the mire and to the old house while John and the man made a fire and prepared the house so that the family could move in out of the rain.

The family hadn't eaten all day and only had a couple of dented cans of pork and beans for provisions. John gave them a large bucket of fresh milk and then drove home to see what Louisa could spare from their kitchen. She had just baked bread so back John and the boys went to deliver loaves

of her crusty, delicious, never one slice will do potato bread.
In addition there was a jar of fruit, newly-picked vegetables
from the garden, eggs, flour and enough of everything to give
them a fine meal or two.

The next morning John set to work helping the man repair
his broken-down truck. They soon discovered that they would
need some new parts to get it running. Dean drove the man
and his son to town while John and Charles did the milking.
Washington Irving at the garage chipped in a few parts and
in a week's time the family was ready to set out again on their
journey. While they were waiting the man and his older son
helped in the hayfield and the girls and the younger boys
had a thrill a minute riding the ponies, Peggy and Doll, all
around the ranch. John paid the family for the work they did
and continued supplying them with all the milk, vegetables,
eggs, etc., that they could use—then they were gone and the
Stephens didn't hear another word about them.

In the early 50's John was pruning bushes in his yard when
a big, black Cadillac pulled into the driveway. A man got
out and approached John with his arm out-stretched saying
"Mr. Stephens, do you remember me?" John looked him over
carefully and said frankly, that he was sorry but that he didn't
know him. The man said "Well, I remember you. You saved
my family back in the 30's." Then the man told John about
the bad condition that he and his family had been in when
their truck broke down in Montpelier in a rainstorm and how
grateful the family had been for his help. The man said that
his children still loved to talk about riding the ponies and
how much fun they'd had at the ranch. He said that they'd
had some more hard times before they arrived in Oregon. In
Oregon they found work at a lumber mill. After they learned
the trade they got into it by themselves and when the war came
along they got some government contracts and prospered.
The man said that they were now in a position that if there
was anything they could do for John that he should just name
it. He said that he remembered everything about the place.

The only thing that was different was the old house and the barn on the west side of the highway were gone, and that the roads were not as muddy. John refused to take anything but was tickled to see the man. It made him feel good to know that after so many years that he still remembered him and was grateful enough to stop and tell him so.

John hadn't done anything unusual. It was the same thing that his neighbors would have done. That was the way of folks at that time in the little town of Montpelier. Most of the town was made up of Mormon pioneer stock. Louisa's mother, Isabelle, and her sister Janette, had the dubious honor of being reputed to be the first set of identical twins born in the Salt Lake Valley, and that wasn't in a clean, comfortable hospital with a physician attending. Their ancestors had known practically every privation conceivable in traversing the plains and the mountainous West. Pioneer stories were told and retold for generations and fostered in most an understanding of and sensitivity for those who were in need.

Now his country was in need and Charles was eager to serve as almost all the young men he knew were. Another part of him couldn't help but be excited by the prospect of soldierly adventure and daring. Charles had always dreamed of being a pilot but hadn't ever really believed that he'd have the opportunity to be one and here staring him in the face was a chance to fly for his country.

Thanks to a good friend and a series of fortuitous events he had become a licensed civilian pilot in the fall of '41. After his first year at Utah State Charles's Dad became ill and needed surgery. Charles took a year off to help out on the ranch feeding the cattle and lending a hand with the chores. He grew and matured in that year. He'd wasted time his first year blindly hopping from subject to subject. He was sure that he wanted to be a forest ranger and then a prison warden after his sociology teacher preached prison reform—he really didn't have any idea what he wanted. Back at school for his second year he'd barely stepped foot on campus when along came a buddy of his older brother La Grande and Charles's sister Ruth. Lowell Peterson was an old family friend and Charles's former high school shop and algebra teacher, not to mention his scoutmaster as well (that's how it was in small towns).

Lowell's first words to Charles were about the draft. He wanted to know what Charles was going to do about the draft. Charles told him that he hadn't been drafted and hadn't signed up for the draft. He was twenty-one years old but he hoped to complete his studies. Lowell said "When you go into the service and there is no doubt that you will after so long because this thing is getting serious overseas, what branch would you want to belong to?" Charles replied without any hesitation that he'd been thinking of trying to get into the air force to become a pilot. Charles too felt as most people did that war was inevitable and that it was just a matter of time before he would be called into the service. He wanted to have an edge on flying if he was going to war. Lowell smiled brightly and said "You want to be a pilot? I teach at the civilian pilot training school at Utah State (there wasn't anything that man couldn't do)." He was a professor. Lowell told Charles that if he wanted him to he would put his name down and try and sign him up for pilot training. Charles said yes and the next thing he knew he was studying to be a pilot.

In flight training Charles flew every morning from seven to eight to complete his thirty hours of solo time and then attended ground school flying courses for three hours. He took his other college classes in the afternoon. By the end of fall quarter and shortly after Pearl Harbor he'd received his private pilot's license.

Charles's dream of flying had initially taken flight when he was about eight. He'd delighted in designing paper airplanes and whittled wooden airplanes with moveable props that he held out of the window on car trips to see them spin. He logged many an hour imagining he was flying sitting on an old rake seat that he mounted on the outhouse overlooking the chicken coop roof for wings. He even had a stick to control two boards on hinges fixed onto the edge of the roof for ailerons.

It was partly because of this desire to be airborne that Charles and Dick Aegerter tried to parachute off their neighbor Mumford's barn one day. They had a six-foot-square piece of canvas and they trimmed the corners and tied ropes in different spots around it to make a parachute. They took a log that weighed about thirty or forty pounds and tied it to the chute and tossed it off from the lowest point on the lower roof of the barn (about twelve feet high). The log floated gracefully to the ground so the boys were feeling good about their homemade parachute. They then crawled up to the highest point on the lower barn and shoved the log off. The chute flared and the wind blew the log off to the side a bit but it landed okay if not quite so smoothly as in the first attempt. Then Dick was keen to try out the parachute for himself. The parachute was deemed worthy of a human test subject and Dick readied for the jump. He moved down to the low end of the lower barn and Charles tied him tightly to the chute. Dick jumped and the chute went "rmrmrm," and he just about "hit the silk" (got tangled in the unopened canvas). Fortunately the parachute flared just before impact and Dick hit the ground hard but was intact. Nothing was broken. Dick was raring to go again and told Charles, "I'll jump off the top if you will." Charles who was just relieved that the chute had opened and that Dick hadn't broken both of his legs said, "I'm not about to jump off that." He knew that they didn't have enough canvas for a parachute jump off the top of the barn to be safe. They were lucky to have the six-feet of canvas, but the jumping would have to stop there. Dick kept needling him trying to convince Charles to do some more test jumps, but that was the end of their parachuting.

Charles had read so many books about flying a plane (all the books that he could get his hands on from the school library and the Montpelier city library) and play acted flying

so much up on the outhouse roof that when in flight school
he was able to fly for the first time he was completely at ease
and at home in the air. His flight instructor kept asking him
if he'd ever flown a plane before. To Charles it seemed the
most natural thing.

Chapter 3
Serving Uncle Sam

Charles enlisted on January 2, 1942. He said a tearful good-bye to his family and boarded a bus headed for Pocatello, Idaho and the enlistment center. Alfred Kunz, Richard Hughes, Mickey Gilligen, and Frank Sakamoto, all old friends from home rode along with him. There was really no time to feel sad or homesick with so many good buddies together jawing and teasing. At the enlistment center there were about twenty-five men assembled to be inducted into the service. Charles made friends there with Alan Valente from just outside of Pocatello and an Indian fellow off the Fort Hall reservation that the men dubbed "Chief." The name fit him so well that no one even bothered to learn his real name, and he seemed to like it. Most were draftees except for the five from Montpelier and a few others. Draftees were assigned wherever there was the most need but enlistees could choose their branch of service.

Charles and Richard Hughes chose cadet pilot training school and the air force; Mickey Gilligen chose officers' training school; Frank Sakamoto chose artillery school, and Alfred Kunz thought he wanted to be a mechanic in the air force. They were sworn into the service and asked if they had any prior military service or ROTC. Because Charles had ROTC at Utah State he was instructed to report to the Recruiting Officer. Their group of twenty-five was being transferred to Fort Douglas in Salt Lake City, Utah.

Charles was placed in command of the group as they entrained from Pocatello to Salt Lake with stops in McCammon, Idaho and Ogden, Utah. The assignment was an easy one. Charles didn't so much as have an opportunity to flex his executive command muscles. He was supposed to block any escape attempts and discourage juvenile or foolish behavior, but no one was any trouble. They were a pretty disappointing bunch. In Salt Lake they met a sergeant at the train depot who transported them by truck to Fort Douglas.

At Fort Douglas uniforms were issued. The men were told to ship their civilian clothes home; that from now on they were strictly GI. There were so many men coming in all at once that they just threw them their clothes, it didn't seem to matter if they fit. The men were issued the standard uniform and had their arms loaded with two pairs of itchy, woolen long handled underwear, an extra heavy GI full length overcoat, heavy work shoes, heavy leather gloves (nothing was light, they were going to get stronger just wearing the clothes), socks, underwear and a slick, rubber raincoat.

The twenty-five young men from Pocatello now merged with a much larger group of men from the region. Again the question was asked, "Has anyone had any prior service?" Two or three guys raised their hands—they'd had a hitch in Panama or somewhere and they were ordered to "Fall out and report to the orderly room." Then those with ROTC and anything remotely having to do with the service were asked to do the same. Charles went to the orderly room. Because they were short of instructors at Fort Douglas he was asked to help call the roll for the barracks, and to see that the men assembled in formation for shots and training and indoctrination classes. Barracks were assigned by branch of service and/or future destination as could best be determined. There were approximately sixty men to a barracks and fifteen to twenty barracks at the base, filled to capacity with men still wet behind the ears who had only just joined the service.

The men sometimes felt like big, aching pincushions they received so many shots, and then there was a battery of tests to determine which school candidates were best suited for. Enlistees were asked to decide on a branch of service or if they had already chosen whether they wanted to reconsider and choose something else. They were free to choose whatever branch interested them the most: the navy, field artillery, infantry, cadet pilot school, whatever they wanted.

Dozens of men were being shipped out each day and more and more came to replace them. After ten days of helping with the men in his barracks Charles was asked if he would like to stay at Fort Douglas for the duration of the war as an instructor. "No," he said, "I didn't join your army to be an instructor." He was told that he would be shipped out in due time. In the meantime the men were busy drilling and taking tests and being indoctrinated.

Finally it was time for the friends from Idaho to leave Fort Douglas. "Chief" was the first to go with an all Indian division and then Frank Sakamoto was taken soon after by an all Japanese division. Frank fought in Italy but that was all Charles ever heard again about him after their parting. Alfred Kunz, Alan Valente and Charles were shipped out together for Sheppard Field in Wichita Falls, Texas. Dick Hughes and Mickey Gilligen were both kept in Salt Lake for another month typing forms for new recruits. Mickey later went to officer candidate school and received his commission. He was assigned as an executive officer of a troop carrier group in England where Charles was eventually stationed (in a different group), but they never did see each other. Dick Hughes joined Alfred, Charles and Alan in Wichita Falls.

When Charles received his orders to go to Sheppard Field he was asked once again, "You've had prior service, would you

be in command of a carload of men on your train, cadets
going to Sheppard Field? Keep them from cutting in and out
of rail cars, scattering all over and from trying to run home
to mama? Will you report to a lieutenant who is in command
of the whole troop train and help him check the men in when
you reach your destination?" There had to be somebody in
charge of each of the cars. Charles agreed to be responsible
for his group and it was another cake walk. No one seemed
inclined to cause any trouble. For the most part the men just
sat and talked in their seats.

Immediately upon arriving at Sheppard Field Charles
was called into headquarters and asked if he would be a
permanent instructor. Charles said "No," that he was sorry,
but that he didn't want to stay and be an instructor. At
Sheppard Field it was a "Groundhog Day" kind of experience;
they started everything over again. There were more shots,
written and oral tests, another physical and the same tired
indoctrination films and lectures that the men had listened
to at Fort Douglas.

Sheppard Field was much larger than Fort Douglas. There
were about 50,000 new GIs there assigned to groups according
to which school they would attend. There was still a lot of
shuffling between the groups and patriotic persuasion and
arm twisting behind the scenes. Minds were constantly being
changed. If there was a need for extra men in any branch
of the service, and a service man met the qualifications he
was called in and asked if he didn't want to volunteer for
that duty. Charles was asked to go to navigation school,
radio operator school, mechanic school, gunnery school and
officer's training school since he'd had two years of college.
He turned them all down and remained committed to pilot
training school. He knew that he wanted to fly.

Alfred Kunz volunteered to be an air class mechanic but
he was told that he would have to wait awhile for an opening
in mechanic's school. In the meantime an immediate opening
in gunnery school was offered to him and weary of waiting

he said "I'll take it," and switched to gunnery school. He was transferred to a school in Baton Rouge, Louisiana and became a gunner on a B-17. He was assigned to England and was shot down and killed on his first fighter mission

Dick Hughes wanted desperately to attend pilot training school, but every time he'd go in for the qualifying physical his blood pressure would spike. After the physical it would drop down to normal. It was the strangest thing. Dick became obsessed with trying to get his blood pressure down for the physical. He scheduled several appointments attempting to catch his blood pressure when it was low, but it never worked. When an opening came up in radio specialty school Dick took it. He resigned himself to accept that for whatever reason he was never going to be a pilot. He went to radio school in Illinois and then spent the duration of the war in China.

Charles and Alan Valente were accepted for pilot training. However there were not enough schools to accommodate the burgeoning ranks of prospective air force cadets so they were told that they would have to be transferred to a training squadron. There they would wait their turn to attend flight school. After six weeks in Wichita Falls, Texas, Charles and Alan were forwarded on to New Orleans Army Air Base in New Orleans, Louisiana to do some more waiting. Many men were in their same situation; they were qualified to be pilots but there was no place for them to receive their training. In New Orleans these men were given whatever menial jobs could be assigned to keep them busy: janitorial, clerical, anything that no one else wanted to do.

Fortunately because of his ROTC experience Charles was asked to do something a bit more interesting than toilet duty. He was requested to take new groups of enlistees and draftees to indoctrination classes and to march them to meals, shots, lectures, and to teach them close order drill and some weaponry training. He was to give these new recruits their first taste of the service. He had some of them for two weeks, three weeks, four weeks and longer; it all depended on when they were called up for duty.

Charles had learned from his ROTC training to be comfortable using a variety of different weapons. Some of his training had been downright fun as well as educational. Among other things they'd run toy battleships and planes across the room and practiced taking readings for field artillery and antiaircraft practice in his classes at Utah State. They'd had firing practice without live ammunition, but they learned to aim their guns and pull the triggers just as any marksmen would. His college training was very helpful to him. Because of his knowledge and performance with the recruits he was told that if he wished he could stay in New Orleans and teach basic training. "You'll end up as a drill sergeant," he was told cheerfully. As tempting an offer as that was he said, "Thanks, but no thanks."

Charles had additional experience with weaponry that went way back. As boys he and his friends were always monkeying around making things. Weapons were their specialty. They played cops and robbers in the barn with clothespins to shoot rubber bands. If the boys weren't fast on their feet or didn't dodge quickly the sting of the rubber bands could really smart. They got so they could even shoot the bands up through the cracks in the barn and hit their marks. They were pretty effective firearms. They made a variety of guns and weapons, but one gun stood out in particular as being the most sophisticated. It was Charles and his old buddy Dick Aegerter that designed it with a specific purpose in mind. They were going to teach some lazy, trespassing cows a lesson.

Cows at that time were allowed in town and often wandered from yard to yard. Louisa Stephens's lush, blooming backyard garden with its neat rows of vegetables, rainbows of delicate flowers, rosy berry-filled bushes, grassy expanses and gurgling brook with a little wooden step bridge seemed to draw cows like a magnet. Charles was tired of chasing cows out of the yard and told Dick "I am gonna sting one of those old biddies so they'll stay away." He and Dick determinedly set to work making a gun that would have a little more fire power than

any they had previously made. They used Dick's father's
railroad drill and fashioned a gun over in Mumford's garage.
They found a ball bearing and rolled it deep into the barrel
with a wad of paper stuffed in with it. For the crowning touch
they stuck a three-inch firecracker with a little wallop in the
gun and put the fuse through a hole that they had made in
a pipe cap. They were ready for the cows! They'd think twice
about trespassing in the Stephens's garden again.

It didn't take long for the cows to come. Even when the
boys would chase them out they'd come tromping in another
way. It just seemed to go on and on. Here were the Lurcher's
cows, let loose on the street again prancing in "a chomping
and a chewing." In seconds they'd be on Louisa Stephens's
verdant lawn and in her fragrant garden, anywhere they could
find something to munch. Charles was in a corner of the yard
concealed behind some greenery and prepared to take aim.
Dick chased a cow down into Charles's range and as she was
just crawling through the fence to try and make her get away
Charles put the bead on the gun and readied to pull the
trigger. "I'm gonna sting that ol' cow," he muttered fiercely.
He had her well within his sights. But just as he was putting
his finger to the trigger and commencing to fire something
held him back. He began to have doubts about the gun. He
paused for a moment thinking. Dick was furious. He had the
cow all poised and ready to be shot and there was Charles not
doing anything, in some kind of trance. While Dick fumed
and fussed Charles thought "Well now, wait a minute, what if
I do more than sting her? I just want to scare her, not hurt her.
Maybe I'd better see what this gun can do."

In the background Charles could hear his cousin, Merle
Stephens, driving by as he was hauling wheat from the dry
farm to be cut and shoveled into the granary. It occurred to
Charles that before he shot the cow he could shoot the granary
door and test the gun out. The granary was two thirds full at
the time and there was a lock on the door to keep the kids
from playing in it and sliding down the heaping piles of grain.

Charles took aim at the granary door, pulled the trigger and "BOOM," the explosion shattered the door. The boards were split where the firecracker hit and wheat poured out of the broken door.

Charles ran to the granary at breakneck speed and in a frenzy of activity tried to shove the wheat back in. About five bushels of wheat spilled out before he could plug up the hole. He grabbed gunny sacks and stuffed them inside to stop the flow of wheat. Charles gathered up the clean wheat and put it back into the bin and took a broom and swept up the soiled wheat as best as he could and fed it to the pigs. He and Dick decided not to shoot any cows that day, and Charles went out to the ranch to do his chores.

When Charles returned home in the evening his Dad was angry. He'd found out about the granary door. "For hell's sake look what Merle did to that door!" he bellowed. "Backed into that door and broke it. And he never said a word about it. That bothers me more than his breaking it." John Stephens paced the floor and finally said resignedly, "Let's go and see if we can fix that door." There was a pile of lumber near the granary and Charles got the boards and helped saw the wood. He and John sawed the boards and nailed them together to patch up the door. John didn't say anything more though everyone could see that he was upset with Merle.

Charles managed to keep the gun out of sight for awhile. His parents didn't approve of children having guns. It didn't help matters that some kid they'd heard of had been blinded by a bee-bee gun. But a few days later he had the gun around by the rabbit pens, sitting on top of the pens as Charles did his chores. His Dad came in and saw the gun and took hold of it and said worriedly, "What's this?" Charles said proudly, "I made a gun."

"What did you do with that?"

"Oh nothing, I just made it."

John said, "You tear that up! That's as bad as any rifle. Don't you dare shoot that or you'll blow yourself to pieces!" That was the end of that gun.

Charles did what he was told and never said another word about it until years later. When he finally had the courage to speak to his Dad about it he said, "Do you remember when Merle backed into the door and spilled the wheat?"

"Yes," said John and stiffened involuntarily, "And Merle never said a word to me about that."

"Well, there's a reason that Merle never said a word to you about it."

"What do you mean," said John looking puzzled.

"Merle didn't do that."

"What do you mean Merle didn't do that? How'd that happen then?"

"Remember that gun you found and made me tear up?"

"Yah," said John.

"Well, I shot that door and that's what it did, destroyed the door."

"YOU SHOT THAT GUN! Good hell, son you could have been killed! And all these years I thought it was Merle." It was lucky for Charles that with the passage of years John could see the humor in the situation and just had a good laugh over it all. Strangely enough he never had said a word to his nephew Merle about the door. This was just the first of many experiences that Charles was to have with guns.

Chapter 4
What Do You Want Me to Fly?

It was while Charles was in a waiting state in New Orleans, a kind of military purgatory confined to base and not allowed any passes or leaves, that a very unusual thing happened. The name "Charles Stephens," was blasted over the troop's loudspeaker. "Charles Stephens, report immediately to the base commander!" Charles instantly started to anxiously wonder what in the world he could possibly have done for good or bad to merit an interview with the base commander. When he reported to the base commander, a colonel, first one he'd ever seen in the service, he was told that the colonel had received an urgent telegram from General Hap Arnold in Washington that concerned Charles. They had been instructed to check their rosters for qualified personnel for a new glider program that was being introduced. "Military gliders," thought Charles, "Why I've never heard of such a thing."

General Henry H. "Hap" Arnold, chief of the U.S. Army Air Forces, was the driving force behind the development of the United States' military glider program, with Adolf Hitler's glider exploits as his inspiration. After the invasion of Poland, Hitler was greedy for more conquest and set his sights on France. In order for Hitler to invade France he had to breach the heavily fortified Maginot Line. Instead of storming the line as expected, Hitler decided to attack north of the line through Belgium. In a stroke of military genius Hitler used gliders to seize control of the notorious and supposedly impregnable underground fortress of Eben Emael in Belgium. The exterior of deeply-rooted Eben Emael perched above the steep side of the Albert Canal and the Geer River with domed steel cupolas, enormous concrete casemates and powerful antiaircraft guns.

A force of seventy-seven highly trained men and ten gliders swooped silently down on the grassy field atop the fort and in just over a day took Eben Emael and defeated the 780 men guarding it. Granted Hitler had developed a formidable new weapon for the attack, a "Hohlladung," or hollow charge that imploded rather than exploded, and blew right through the concrete walls of the fort and deep down into its belly. But what the German glider force accomplished on that day was truly extraordinary.

Even more remarkable was that the Germans suffered the deaths of only six men and twenty wounded at Eben Emael. Prior to this no one would have believed that Eben Emael could have fallen without a long, protracted and bloody battle at a tremendous cost to the Germans in men and materials. The German success was due largely to the cloak of secrecy that the quiet flight of the gliders provided. The attack was fully engaged before the Belgians had any idea what had hit them. Belgian defenses at Eben Emael were designed to repulse conventional enemy attacks, not to guard against an enemy already atop the fort itself. The fall of Eben Emael burst the flood gates into France with the speed and the force of the crack of a mighty sledgehammer. Virtually unimpeded the full strength of the Third Reich thrust itself upon unwitting France like a swollen, angry river surging through the breach.

One of the best kept secrets of the war, so hush, hush was

operation "Granite," as the Germans called the capture of Eben Emael, that it took the United States months to unravel the mystery of the invasion. The United States simply didn't know how the Germans had defeated the Belgians at Eben Emael. It wasn't until nearly a year later when in the battle for Crete the Germans used gliders as part of an enormous airborne invasion force that the Allies really became aware of the use of gliders in war.

Seventy-four German DFS 230 gliders packed with men and armaments plunged into the rocky, uneven terrain of the tiny island of Crete. A total of 13,000 men made up the German airborne attack force of paratroopers and glidermen. Over 5,000 German airborne ultimately became invasion casualties. The Germans won the battle for Crete but faulty planning that failed to consider the landscape, and provide the element of surprise (the defenseless gliders were seen and readily targeted) caused them to suffer heavy casualties and catastrophic glider and tow planes losses. The Allies however, didn't know about the massive German losses. They just knew that the Axis powers had scored a complete victory. That set the American brass to thinking (a dangerous thing).

Hitler on the other hand, stung by the gross inefficiency and the enormous cost of his triumph in Crete, vowed never again to use gliders on such a large scale. He did employ gliders in several smaller missions including a dramatic mountaintop rescue of Mussolini who was being held by the Italian police atop the highest peak of the Abruzzi Mountains. But Hitler did not use gliders again as part of a special invasion force.

Hitler had expert teams of glider pilots to work with in the war effort. Since World War I and the Treaty of Versailles Germany was prohibited from maintaining or developing an air force. As a way of circumventing the treaty, civilian glider clubs proliferated. There were even German high schools that offered courses in gliding as part of the regular curriculum. Hermann Goering, the Chief of the Luftwaffe, said in 1922, "Our Germany's whole future is in the air, and it is by air power that we are going to recapture the German Empire. To accomplish this we will do three things. First, we will teach gliding as a sport to all our young men. Then we will build up commercial aviation. Finally, we will create the skeleton of a military air force. When the time comes, we will put all three together—and the German Empire will be reborn."[7]

Hap Arnold too looked to civilian glider clubs for expertise in developing an American glider force. Arnold reportedly had "a quirk to his character, most unusual in a professional soldier: he firmly believed that a civilian expert knew more on a given subject than any military man."[8] He recruited a civilian glider pilot, Lewin Barringer, the first general manager of the U. S. Soaring Society, to head the glider program and gave him the rank of major in the air force. In addition, John Robinson, winner of the national gliding championships in 1940, and members of his gliding school in Elmira, New York were asked to design a gliding course for instructors.

Even then with all of the assembled civilian talent the glider program had its critics. Not everybody thought that the creation of a military glider program was such a good idea. It was difficult for Arnold and Barringer to mobilize support for an officer's rank for glider pilots, and incredibly it demanded a hard fought struggle to actually commission the building of gliders. A colonel who was charged with procuring the gliders said crustily, "The man who sold General Arnold on gliders is Hitler's best friend in the United States."[9]

From its inception the American glider program suffered the slams and jars of severe turbulence. In March of 1943 Major Barringer was killed in a plane crash over the Caribbean Sea. He was returning home from England where he had attended meetings concerning the progress of the British and American glider programs. Richard C. DuPont was appointed to take his place. About a month after Dupont took charge a glider demonstration was conducted in Kershaw, South Carolina to show how gliders could be used safely and effectively. The demonstration was intended to ease the fears of certain generals who had doubts about the glider program. Paratroopers from the 101st airborne were dropped in to secure an area and then gliders swooped in with heavy equipment and supplies. Fortunately the demonstration went smoothly and the generals' misgivings were at least temporarily alleviated.

Then came Operation Husky in Sicily, the Allies' first bold step in an aggressive hopscotch assault into Italy, which Churchill referred to as "the soft under-belly of the Axis."[10] Just before the attack the British General, Montgomery, called for gliders to land in Sicily at night to spearhead the invasion despite the vociferous objections of many on his staff. Only British pilots manned the gliders with the exception of twenty-eight Americans who volunteered to copilot. The British pilots had no night gliding experience and little understanding of how to pilot the American CG-4A gliders that were provided for the mission. To make matters worse "the landing terrain was bad in the extreme," with "boulder-strewn fields, high stone walls, olive groves, and deep ravines."[11] Sicily was liberated in five weeks and the operation was dubbed a success but in the fray few of the gliders made it to their targeted landing zones. Many gliders were released early over the ocean by skittish tow plane pilots who became anxious under enemy fire and some gliders were even destroyed by friendly fire. Eighty-eight British glider pilots and thirteen American copilots perished.

Even though it was administrative planning and preparation errors that caused the tremendous glider losses, it was inevitably the glider program itself that came under fire. After this debacle supporters of the glider program had a tough sell, and things were only going to get worse in the short term.

In August 1943, Robertson Aircraft Company in St. Louis, one of sixteen companies under contract with the government to build gliders, staged a glider demonstration. The mayor of St. Louis, the state prosecutor, the president of the Chamber of Commerce, Robertson's CEO, his deputy and five others were all on board a Waco CG4-A for an exhibition flight over St. Louis's Lambert Field. The tow plane and glider soared gracefully into the sky but shortly after the glider released from the tow plane at a height of 2,000 feet disaster struck. While a crowd of horrified spectators looked on the glider's wing ripped off the fuselage as if cruelly seized by some angry, mythical god of the skies, and the glider plummeted to the ground killing all of the passengers.

Speculation ran high as to the cause of the crash and sabotage was feared, but an investigation revealed that a faulty wing-strut fitting which had been subcontracted out to a former coffin maker caused the accident. Because of this incident gliders were dubbed "flying coffins." Furniture manufacturers, piano companies, makers of pool tables and canoes, and coffin manufacturers had all gotten involved in the process of making parts for gliders.[12] There was such an urgent need for the gliders that quality control and coordination as especially concerned the subcontractors, was virtually ignored in the rush to produce gliders.

After the avalanche of negative publicity following the St. Louis tragedy General Arnold knew he had to do something dramatic to restore faith and build confidence in the glider program. He staged another series of glider demonstrations for the generals at Laurinburg-Maxton Army Air Force Base. With the generals looking on flying C-47's successfully snatched grounded gliders into the air showing how wounded troops could be evacuated from a combat zone and equipment and gliders recovered. For the "*piece de resistance*," the generals were taken at night to an open, floodlit field surrounded by trees. The lights were turned off and a military band played. A few minutes later the lights were turned on and incredibly only thirty feet away from the generals the field was filled with gliders and soldiers already out and "ready for action!" [13] The generals were amazed and "once again convinced of the value of this new weapon."

But still there was more bad news in store for the glider

program. The head of the program, Richard C. DuPont, was killed during test flights in September for a new glider, the XCG-16. The glider went into a spin and although two men were able to survive by bailing out, DuPont did not jump in time for his parachute to fill and he plunged to his death. His brother, Major A. Felix DuPont, was appointed in his place.

Chapter 5
Who Needs an Engine?

The glider program was off to a rocky start. But much of this hadn't happened yet when Charles was considering signing up as a new, green glider pilot. He really didn't know anything about military gliders. The colonel said that he met the qualifications for glider pilots as did one other man on base. In order to qualify to be a glider pilot it was necessary to hold a private pilot's license or be a commissioned officer with a pilot's rating. The colonel asked Charles if he was interested. Charles, his curiosity piqued, said that so long as it was flying he would be.

The colonel assured him that he would be flying so Charles said "It's flying and it's now, so I'm interested." He was eager to fly and tired of waiting around for a slot in cadet pilot training. "How long would it be before I could get into cadet pilot training school if I decided to stick with it, and not become a glider pilot?" questioned Charles. "Well, we don't know, all the fields are loaded up." With that Charles said "Yah, I'll do it. I'll be a glider pilot."

The next thing Charles knew the base commander was telling him "Pack your bag. We don't know the full extent of all this, the orders just say Rush, Rush, Rush…, no further orders. Pack your bag and be ready to go at a minute's notice." Charles packed his bag that morning. In the early afternoon his name was announced over the loudspeaker again, "Charles Stephens report to the orderly room immediately, Charles Stephens…" He went to the orderly room and waited, and waited, for about three hours without hearing anything. Finally he left and went to dinner and a USO show.

Two hours later his name was called and he reported back to the orderly room. A lieutenant in charge of company transfers said that he had received expedited orders for Charles to receive immediate field clearance and be shipped by train to a glider pilot training school in Twenty-Nine Palms, California. The lieutenant assigned him a jeep and a driver and sent him on his way. The other man on base who met the qualifications, Anderson from Ohio, was also going to Twenty-Nine Palms. They were under special orders and were routed on a serpentine course through Baton Rouge, Little Rock, Texarkana, San Antonio, El Paso, Albuquerque, and finally on to Palm Springs.

After about three days of travel they arrived at the Palm Springs, California train station in the wee hours of the morning. Since there wasn't any kind of welcoming committee and they were exhausted, they bunked out on the station's wooden benches. Around seven o'clock that morning Charles arose and asked the station master where Twenty-Nine Palms Army Air Base was. The station master said that he'd never heard of it and that he had no idea where Twenty-Nine Palms was. But taking pity on the displaced soldiers he took the trouble to look the name up on the map and found a site marked Twenty-Nine Palms about thirty miles out in the desert. "Ain't nothin' out there" he said in disbelief. Charles said earnestly that there had to be something out there. That's why they'd come. The station master wanting to be helpful said "We'll see," and got out the telephone book and searched for Twenty-Nine Palms Army Air Base. Soon he'd found a listing and was scratching his head and saying "Well, I'll be darned there's a phone out there. Try this number and see what happens." A Captain Sweet grumpily answered the phone and said yes, that this was the air base and that he would send a man out to fetch Stephens and Anderson. Charles and Anderson had some more time to rest on the benches and then transportation arrived (a guy in a jeep yelling "Are you the ones who called about Twenty-Nine Palms?)

At Twenty-Nine Palms Captain Sweet gruffly demanded, "Who are you and what do you want?" Slightly taken aback, Stephens and Anderson tendered him their orders. Captain Sweet was surprised and said that he had not been expecting anyone for at least a week. Charles said that they were supposed to be going to glider pilot school. Sweet said that they hadn't gotten anything going yet and that he'd only arrived there two days ago. He said "We've got a tent here that we sleep in and another one that we cook in and that's it." Charles said "Well, our orders were to go to Twenty-Nine Palms."

Captain Sweet got on the phone and put in a call to Washington. "Thirty cadets?" he was protesting. "We don't have any school here!" The next thing Charles knew Captain Sweet was asking him if he could drive a truck. Charles said yes, he'd driven a truck on the ranch at home. "Well," said Captain Sweet, "We're supposed to go to March field (in the San Bernardino area) and load about six of their trucks with tents and supplies and start a glider pilot school here." Charles, Anderson and Captain Sweet and the four men that he had brought with him to Twenty-Nine Palms set out for March field.

They drove to March field in a weapons carrier (A truck larger than a jeep about the size of a pickup with one long seat in front and a cargo space in back. In battle they'd mount fifty caliber machine guns on them and use them to haul supplies and ammunition.) They loaded the six trucks with supplies: food, tents, cots, everything that they'd need to get the base up and going, and back they went to Twenty-Nine Palms.

There wasn't much to start a glider school with at Twenty-Nine Palms: just the tents, a couple of decrepit old shacks, two Schwitzer sailplanes, an L one observation plane, and an ancient Model A Ford along with 100 feet of rope and some side winder rattlers. The men were impressed that one of their sailplanes was donated to the air force by Douglas Fairbanks Jr. to help train glider pilots. Everybody wanted to be the first to fly that plane.

The sailplanes were gliders proper but the L one observation plane was a power plane with a single engine. It was really just a seat in the sky to direct artillery shells from. It was a light aircraft that was typically sent up to spot enemy locations and send readings back to the guns. It was a slow flying plane, but generally speed was not essential when spotting on each other or taking photographs.

The L one tiny as it was, was still about two times the size of another small airplane that was popular and would be used in later training, the Piper Cub. Other small planes that were used in glider training were the Aeronca and the Taylorcraft. When there weren't enough sailplanes, power planes were used for training glider pilots in their stead.

Many of the small airplanes of that era like the Piper Cub, did not have a start button to get the engine going. If the pilot was alone he would have to step out of the plane and turn the prop and try and fire the engine and jump inside before it took off without him. The pilot's task was a little easier in some of the small planes with parking brakes; there wasn't the excitement of the mad dash and the fear of being dragged along the runway halfway in and halfway out the door. A pilot couldn't have jumped in the L one for take-off if he'd wanted to. The cockpit sat high enough that it took a ladder to climb inside and get it started. The L one and the Taylorcraft had push button starts.

In order to glide in a power plane the pilot pulls the throttle back in flight to cut the engine. Cutting the engine is like taking one's foot off the gas in an automobile; the engine is slowed and idles, barely running. Then in order to be truly gliding, after cutting the engine the pilot pulls the plane up adding a little load. The extra stress on the engine from the effort of moving upward kills the engine completely.

If the pilot dives the airplane fast enough wind resistance automatically turns the prop and starts the plane's engine again. Only problem with that is that most of the time glider pilots had to fly at such low altitudes, six hundred feet or so, that even if a glider was in a straight dive the plane would probably run into the ground before it would start up. Restarting the engine in the air wasn't something that glider pilots attempted.

If a pilot was nervous about gliding he didn't stall the engine to kill it and would just let the engine idle and the propeller windmill on his flight. Then when he wanted power he could press the ignition and start the engine as long as the propeller was still rotating. Bigger planes could be trickier in the windmill mode. If a pilot was windmilling in a large plane wind resistance could cause vibrations and turbulence that would pert near tear the engines off unless the pilot feathered the prop. Feathering the prop was like driving a car in the right gear. Instead of forcing the prop to push through the air the prop could be turned the other way to cut through the air. Feathering the prop allowed the pilot to float through the air with minimal resistance.

Initially there were no programs or schedules at Twenty-Nine Palms. The camp had to be set up and that required everyone's full attention and assistance. A slit trench was dug for the latrine, tents were assembled, the beds were fixed, tarps were laid down, and the portable cook stove was set up; all that was necessary to get the base up and running was done. During this time more men kept on coming in a steady trickle until there were thirty glider pilot cadets on base. The base also received more tow planes, four additional gliders, and more of the necessary rope for towing.

It was several weeks before the eager cadets had their first glider rides and then along with the flying they attended ground school every day. It was nearly identical to the training that Charles had completed at Utah State so it was easy for him. He ranked high on all of the tests. He was asked to teach but declined; he wanted to fly.

The cadets did mostly thermal soaring over the desert. Thermals, rising bodies of hot air, were abundant in the desert. The cadets recognized them as whirly dusters. There was always a wind going up the side of a mountain. A pilot could get on top of that and sail back and forth on it getting boosted further and further up. The cadets took turns taking flights of a half hour to three quarters of an hour in duration. To become airborne they used either the Model A Ford driving along with the tow rope attached to a sailplane or the L one observation plane towing two sailplanes. They'd jump on a thermal like a cowboy on a wild horse and glide around for as long as they could ride it.

Near the end of training at Twenty-Nine Palms Charles got a good high altitude tow and rode thermals until he was well beyond the usual height. When he'd had enough he dove the glider and did a couple of graceful loops on his way down. Upon landing a captain who was the acting flight commander went through the motions of chewing him out for encroaching on another man's flight time. Charles's ride had taken two and a half hours! He'd been so intent on riding the thermal and milking all the altitude he could out of it that he lost all concept of time. Fortunately no one really seemed to mind. They kind of enjoyed the show.

Chapter 6
Southern Beach Boy

When the cadets completed thirty hours of glider training at Twenty-Nine Palms they were to proceed to another base. Once again Charles was asked to stay on as an instructor. He said thank you, but no. Since the training facilities for the second phase were not yet ready Charles was shipped back to New Orleans for more waiting.

The lieutenant in charge of transfers in New Orleans looked perplexed when Charles walked into his office. He blurted out "What happened? Why have you returned?" The lieutenant didn't have much for Charles to do other than more of the ever popular toilet detail. He advised Charles to remain close to the barracks during most of the day because he could be called up at any time; his orders after all had been rush, rush. After two o'clock in the afternoon each day not knowing what else to do with him, the lieutenant excused Charles to go off and do whatever he wanted to within regulations.

Charles became the envy of the barracks. Often in the afternoon he'd go to Lake Pontchartrain on the outskirts of New Orleans and swim and sunbathe or go to the big funhouse on the shores of the lake. There were large merry-go-rounds and giant slides that the people rode down on gunny sacks. There were rotating tables that a person could climb on moving at slow speed and then they'd speed them up and whoosh—that fellow would be scooted right off or he'd give another guy a nudge and off he'd go. They'd clean house that way clearing the tables. These kind of funhouses don't exist anymore.

If he wasn't at the beach or the funhouse Charles would go to a park or tour the city; he had no duties of any kind in the late afternoon. He'd never had it so good. Waiting didn't seem so bad. He could get used to this. Soaking in the radiant sun lounging on a beach towel, or splashing around in the sparkling water at Lake Pontchartrain life seemed pretty nice, but Charles was not to be a man of leisure for long. He hardly had time to get comfortable and then he was transferred.

Just before he left New Orleans he had a very disquieting experience that reminded him of his commitment to the service and the risks it entailed. He witnessed the first airplane crash that he'd ever seen. He'd gone with a group to Audubon Park on a Saturday. While there he and a friend decided to walk over to Tulane University and tour the campus. They were strolling through a beautiful tree-lined neighborhood with elegant southern homes when all of a sudden two P-39 Bell-Air Cobras appeared flying at only about 300 feet of altitude. The men could hear the sputtering of an engine and then both planes went into a turn. One of the fighters fell out of the turn and plummeted straight down not more than a half a block from the open-mouthed soldiers. With a loud explosion the airplane hit between two houses and less than forty feet from the sidewalk.

Charles and his friend ran to the crash site as fast as they could. They were about the first to arrive. Any hopes that they'd had for the survival of the pilot vanished upon viewing the wreckage. The top of the cockpit wasn't even visible. It had been smashed about three feet into the ground and the rest of the airplane covered it in a crumpled heap. The tip of the plane's wing had sliced into one of the adjoining houses and the owner had grabbed a hose and was showering the area but there was no fire. In just a few minutes the police and firemen arrived and they chased everyone away. This brought the war home to Charles early on.

Chapter 7
Soaring to New Heights

A short time later Charles had traveling orders; he was moving on to Hays, Kansas. It didn't take long to discover that there was no air force base in Hays, Kansas or anywhere near. The men were stationed at Kansas State Teacher's College. This assignment proved a boon to morale as summer school was in session and most of the students, in fact almost all of the students, were of the female gender studying to be Home Economics teachers and secretaries. The cadets bunked in the field house under the stadium bleachers and all their meals were lovingly prepared by the pretty Home Economics students. The food was very well received, and there was a fair amount of meal-time eye-batting and flirtation.

Seeing as they were the only soldiers in town the cadets' company was much sought after. There were dances, swimming parties, picnics—some kind of social event was going on almost every night, and there was plenty of romance. Several of the cadets hooked up with the hometown gals. Charles enthusiastically joined in the activities but didn't get serious with anyone. There was a girl back home that he was sweet on. The town's people were very kind to the soldiers; they treated each one as though they were really going to make a big dent in the war effort. Every Sunday there was a dinner invitation to one home or another which made the stay in Hays quite pleasant.

The cadets attended a full menu of ground school courses just as they had at Twenty-Nine Palms. They took navigation, meteorology, theory of flight, etc, at the college and then traveled about ten miles to a private civilian flying school under contract with the government to train pilots, the Hart Flying Service School. They had about twenty Piper Cubs so the thirty glider cadets had plenty of flying time.

Flight training consisted of dead-stick landings, spot glide landings, some longer navigational flights, night flying, and finally night dead-stick landings. When a glider pilot executed a dead-stick landing he'd take off on full power. He'd then fly for a bit, cut the engine off and without power he'd sail down and land.

Spot landings were like target practice. The instructor would put a sheet out on the runway and the cadet would try and land on it without power. Green grass pilots' landings were usually about one hundred yards off in any direction. With practice the cadets learned to "slip a glider" so that they could be more accurate in their landings. Gliders in a landing dive gain speed rapidly but if the pilot "slips the glider" by turning it and sliding down at an angle and tipping the glider slightly up this acts as an air break and gives the pilot more control on the landing. He can then more easily straighten the glider out when he gets to the right altitude and land smoothly. Some gliders that the cadets would fly later in their training had spoilers that would help to automatically drop the glider down to where it needed to be on the landing, but for now the cadets had to learn to do it manually.

After the cadets had thirty hours of flying under their belts they could start night flying. The first night Charles was scheduled for a dead-stick landing he buzzed the darkened airfield along with his instructor getting a feel for flying in obscurity. Only the lights from three flares on a wind tee could be seen. They were on the downwind leg when the instructor advised "Here's about where I'd cut the switch." Charles obediently reached over to cut the power. To his amazement his instructor barked threateningly "You damned fool, not with me in here," and refused to let him cut the switch. Charles could sense that this probably wasn't going to be a good time for him to practice his dead-stick landings with his reluctant, civilian instructor kicking and screaming all the way so he didn't try to argue and landed his plane on full power.

The nervous instructor jumped out with the engine still idling and said "If you're crazy enough to do that go ahead, but it's not for me. Life's too short. They can have this [blankety blank] job!" Then he stomped into the hanger, slammed the door and quit his job as an instructor.

Charles still had scheduled flying time so he took the plane for a spin around the field. When he got to the spot where the instructor had said to cut power and was ready to pull back on the throttle he thought, "Now wait a doggone minute, my instructor wouldn't do this, what the hell am I doing?" He then had a short discussion with himself which ended by his deciding that he had to do this to be a glider pilot, risky or not. He then very deliberately cut the engine, stalled the propeller, glided down, and landed on the marker alongside the tee just as if he'd done it a million times before. Feeling confident at his success he stepped out of the plane, gave the propeller a twirl to get it started and repeated the process all over again. Back on the ground for try number three, here came the manager of the airfield driving up in a jeep. The manager hollered: "What happened? Where is your instructor?"

"My instructor quit on me."

"Well, then you did it yourself. How was it? Were you worried?"

"Not particularly."

"Did it scare you?"

"No, what do you mean by scared? I hesitated about whether I wanted to do it or not. My instructor wouldn't do it, so why was I going to do it?"

"Did it bother you?"

"Not really. Don't want to make a practice of it."

He persisted, "Would you do it again?"

"Sure I would."

"Let's see yah."

The manager gave the prop a push and up Charles went. There were no problems; the third ride was as smooth as the first two. The manager repeated "Would you do it again?" Charles said that he surely would and did it again and again at least four or five times until the manager was satisfied that he was proficient

The manager said that Charles had been the only one to do a night dead-stick landing—no one else had gone through with it. He wanted everyone to try but ordered the men not to start their own engines. He instructed them to wait in their cockpits until someone came to kick the prop.

The whole cadet class did their dead-stick landings at night without an instructor. They really didn't need any lengthy instructions; they already knew how to execute dead-stick landings. It was just a question of doing the glide landing at night. What's more, most of the cadets had more flying time than their civilian instructors at Hart Flying School. They could have been instructing the instructors.

The next morning Charles was told that they wanted to see him in the flying school office. Hart himself spoke to him and said: "You've flown before, haven't you?"

"Yes, I have a private pilot's license."

"We've got an opening here. If you want to stay here for the war I think we can get you on detached service. You can stay right here during the war and instruct."

"No, I'm sorry sir I don't want to be an instructor. I didn't join the army to be an instructor."

"Well," said Hart, "I thought I'd give you a chance."

Charles for the most part was pretty quiet and unassuming, and had not the slightest desire to seek recognition or notice, but he had a history of being picked out for his special skills and abilities. In high school he'd been athletic-minded but kind of small and scrawny. In his sophomore year they'd lined the boys up from tallest to shortest, and Charles was second from the shortest (only Max Weaver from Bennington was one half inch shorter). By his junior year things had changed. He was sixth from the tallest at a "towering" 5'10" and a hulk compared to what he'd been at a hefty new weight of 125 pounds. Seeing Charles playing intramurals the high school basketball coach, Jerry Taylor, tried to get him to go out for the team but Charles refused saying that he had too many chores to make it to all the games and practices.

Then on a bright, clear day in the early spring of his senior year Charles was out herding the cows and calves on horseback. He was moving the big brown-eyed spotted cattle from pasture in town to the ranch. One of the spunky calves feeling frisky scrambled underneath the five-foot fence around the track field where there was a space just small enough for a saucy, little calf to squeeze through. Enjoying its freedom, the calf was set to amble and skip all over the field. Feeling lazy and not wanting to go all the way around to the field gate so he could fetch the calf, Charles got off his horse, backed up so he could get a running start, and gazelle-like jumped the fence. He then sped around the calf, chased it under the fence, and sprang leisurely over the fence again. Charles then mounted his horse and rode on with the cattle.

The next day at school he received a note saying that Coach Taylor wanted to see him right away. Charles left class immediately to report to the coach. A friendly Coach Taylor told Charles that he'd seen him leap the track field fence and "How high can you jump?" was his question. Charles said seriously "It depends on how mad I am at the calf I guess." The coach chuckled a bit and then looked Charles squarely in the eye and said "We'd like to have you come out for the track team." Charles shook his head and said "No, sir I can't. I have chores to do." Coach Taylor replied, "I know you do. That's what you told me about basketball, but if I could get you excused from your sixth period study hall would you come out and practice during that period?" Charles couldn't see anything wrong with that and said that yes, he would.

In the afternoon Charles was called into the principal's office. Charles was wondering what in the dickens the principal wanted. Hadn't he already been called out of school once that day? How did they expect a person to get any school work done? In A.G. Winter, the high school principal's office, a stony-faced Principal Winter started to give him a hard time saying "So, I hear you want to skip sixth period and go out for track?" Charles said honestly "No, I don't want to particularly, but the track coach wants me to." Principal Winter seemed taken aback by his response and before Charles could say anything further he quickly added that it would be just fine with him. He advised Charles to try and find an extra hour each evening when he could study so that missing study hall wouldn't affect his grades, and then he sent him on his way.

The following Friday was the sub-district track meet. Charles won first place in the high jump and set a new record at 5'10 ½". That record stood for many years. Charles also took second place in the high hurdles. The following week at a cold and rainy district meet in Pocatello, Idaho Charles jumped 5'8" for first place. The next week was the state meet in Pocatello and also Senior Class Day there at Idaho State University. Charles earned a gold medal and won first in state with a jump of 5'10". The high jump was the only event that Pocatello High School didn't win first place in that year. When the winner of the high jump was announced at the Senior Day Dance the kids from Montpelier nearly went wild. They hoisted Charles onto their shoulders and paraded him all around like he was royalty.

The following year at Utah State Charles took a track class

and jumped 6'0" for second place in the spring meet. That was the last time he ever high jumped. He enjoyed it but his second year in college he stayed home to help his Dad on the ranch, and later when he went back to school he felt that he just didn't have the time to spare. Developing his jumping ability seemed a luxury that he could ill afford. It was just one of the many talents Charles had.

Chapter 8
What's the "G" for?

Every now and then in cadet training a check pilot would fly in from Randolph Field in San Antonio, Texas to evaluate the cadets' progress. All of the cadets in Hays passed the check pilot screening and half-way through the program they were advanced in rank to staff sergeants with a nice pay increase. They went from earning thirty dollars a month to receiving $140 a month plus 50 percent additional for flying status. After being used to thirty dollars a month they felt like they had money galore.

At graduation from Hays the cadets were awarded their wings, pilot's wings with a large "G" in the center shield. The "G" constantly provoked conversation. The cadets were the first flying sergeants that anybody had ever seen and everybody wanted to know what the "G" stood for. People would ask, "What's that "G" for? Are you a gunner?" The cadets would answer that they were glider pilots and that the "G" stood for guts. "Well what's a glider? I didn't know we had gliders," they'd hear. The gilder pilots were amazed by the number of people who didn't believe that a plane could fly without an engine.

After graduating from glider training in Hays, Kansas the cadets were sent to English Field in Amarillo, Texas to await the next phase of their schooling. Three classes of glider pilots were formed with about thirty to a class, around ninety to one hundred men in total. There weren't many planes to fly there initially. Glider pilots were being trained much more quickly than gliders were being built for them. There was an airfield in Amarillo but not much else to go with it. Finally they did get some sail planes and a training plane for the fighters, a BT6. It was a high-powered, speed plane that could tow three gliders. Most trips it only towed two, however. The cadets flew Cubs and sail planes just enough to keep their hands in it; they got a few flying hours and were shipped out.

Charles's class moved on as a unit to Blacklund Army Flying School in Waco, Texas. They were the first troops to set foot on the base. Practically everything was brand new there except for the planes. They removed the engines from some Piper Cubs and remodeled the front of the Cubs to make them into three place gliders. The glider pilots were used to making do with whatever they had, and the Cubs worked fine as gliders.

One day they were going through the chow line, and Charles's buddy, Best (he was a sweet, strumming guitar player who took his guitar with him wherever he could and really livened things up), suddenly became angry and started yelling threateningly at the chief cook, a big, tough, battle-hardened 1st sergeant with a uniform covered in stripes from his service hitches. Charles thought Best had gone crazy and so did the enraged sergeant who with his face beet red, looked like a volcano about to erupt. Best was yelling "Take off my coveralls! Look they've even got my name on 'em, A.A. Best!"

The sergeant hollered back, "What do you mean talking to me that way? I'm Albert Auston Best and these are my coveralls? Who do you think you are cadet?"

Best puffed himself up and growled "Well, I'm Arnold A.

Best and where do you get off havin' the same initials and last name as I do!"

It was quiet and tense there for a moment as they menacingly stared each other down, but soon a slight smile of understanding brightened the sergeant's swarthy face and he began to laugh and laugh and they both laughed together like brothers. They, the "Best" men, ended up being quite friendly after that.

In Waco they had some BT13 airplanes that could tow Piper Cubs two at a time. The pilots were able to get some good, long rides there. The gliders picked up altitude during the day from the warm rising air as they coasted over the super-heated highways and parking lots around the area. Right at the end of the airbase was Lake Waco, and at night if a pilot wanted an altitude boost he'd fly over the lake. As the land temperature dropped at night, the water still retaining some of the heat from the day became warmer than the land. The pilots could get a nice rise in altitude from flying over the lake at night, and had a lot of fun doing it.

The cadets were becoming increasingly adept at gliding and the training seemed to be going well until one night there was a terrible accident. Alongside the runway in Waco was an office building and a big tower with a bright red light—a warning light. The pilots were instructed to always stay to the left of the light. There was a large open field to the left of the light that was a designated landing zone as well as the runway. It was extremely dark at night with the base lights blacked out. The warning light was about all that the glider pilots could see of the base on a dark night. The pilots were warned over and over not to land to the right of the light, but this one young kid was flying around at night and nobody knew why or how but he flew right into the warning light knocking it out completely. His death was the first in Charles's close-knit, glider group. He was a newlywed who had married one of the girls from Hays, Kansas. It was an awful shock for all of the men.

If they didn't know before they all sensed now that this was serious business. The men were being pushed to exhaustion in their glider training. They flew day and night for as much as ten hours a day with no time off on the weekends. They kept up this rigorous schedule for four weeks sometimes taking single flights that lasted up to five hours. After this training was complete there was another graduation exercise and the men were told that they were ready to fly the large cargo gliders. However, none were off the assembly line. They didn't have any big gliders at all. It was always in the future. We're getting them, they'd say, they're just not here yet. Charles and his group got through with their flying at Waco and they had another thirty cadets coming in to take their places. It was hurry, hurry, hurry, only to wait, wait, wait.

On a rare Sunday when they had some free time Charles went with a friend to the USO. An older couple approached them there and said "We'd like to take you out to our home to dinner, won't you please come?" The cadets were thrilled at the prospect of a home cooked meal and said an enthusiastic "Yes!" "Sessions" was the name of the family they visited. The Sessions had two sons in the service about the same age as the cadets. Their boys were homesick, they said. They served the two grateful cadets a fancy dinner and then pampered and fussed over them all evening. Charles and his friend, well-fed and contented, couldn't remember when they'd been doted on so.

Weeks later Charles was surprised to receive a letter from his mother saying "How do you know the Sessions?" Mrs. Sessions had written to the cadets' parents to tell them how much they'd enjoyed their visit. At that point in time Charles couldn't even remember immediately who the Sessions were. He had to think "Who were the Sessions and why were they in contact with his mother?" Then when it dawned on him and he recalled the lovely evening he'd spent with them and their many kindnesses he felt another infusion of gratitude. He just hoped that at least for a little while they'd helped the Sessions to forget about missing their sons.

Chapter 9
Yeehaw! An Introduction to the Rodeo

The night of the Waco graduation the cadets had their first Saturday night off in a month. They all headed to town in a stampede. One guy said, "Boy, I've had enough of this! Let's go to town and relax. I gotta get away from here. Let's go to the show and sleep all the way through it. We'll get seats in the corner and nobody will be waking us up. We'll sleep through both features and let'em kick us out when it's done. Forget about this—we'll come back when we wake up!" Everyone agreed that this was the thing to do. All the cadets were tired but they just wanted to get away from the base.

The cadets went into town with the intention of going to a picture show but when Charles spotted a rodeo advertised on a billboard in Waco he said "That's where I'm goin'!" The other guys disapprovingly murmured, "Oh, who wants to go to the rodeo? We don't want to do that, never heard of anybody wanting to do that. What's a rodeo, a cow and horse show. Let's stay together and go to the movies." Despite Charles's protestations no one else seemed to share his enthusiasm for the western cowboy show.

"Well you guys go where you want. I'm gonna go to that rodeo!"

"You ornery thing," they hollered at Charles, but when they saw how determined he was they broke down and begrudgingly agreed, "All right we'll go to the rodeo too." They didn't really want to, but rather than split up they decided to go along.

"This had better be good," they growled at Charles. They had never, any of them, been to a rodeo. Charles's friend Best had been around a little; he'd ridden a horse a time or two, but the rest of them well, they'd never even sat on a horse and maybe never even seen one for real the way they acted. They threatened Charles that if they didn't get a good sleep at the rodeo they'd beat him all the way home.

As luck would have it, they had tickets for one humdinger of a rodeo! It was one of the best and the meanest that Charles had ever seen. The animals were out of this world! The cadets nearly went crazy.

It started out calm enough with horses and riders parading around the center ring and the guys were already complaining, "Is this a rodeo? Gee, look at them 'pretty' horses."

"Ah, that was just a prelude," Charles said. Then they turned out the bucking horses with guys on bareback holding on for dear life being toppled off left and right.

"What the devil is going on here," they squealed. They were on the edge of their seats. They'd never seen such a show.

They'd just gotten settled down after the bucking horses when they commenced the bull riding. One of the big Brahma bulls rushed out like a massive whirling dervish and in a powerful bucking and kicking frenzy hurled off his rider. When a clown steered him away from the cowering rider the bull charged and jumped through the fence. He then barreled under the grandstand and ploughed through a couple of concession stands. The crowd went wild! Clowns fought with and teased the bulls routinely and could usually control them fairly well, but for this bull to be corralled it took four cowboys on horses with ropes to hog-tie him and get him back in the stadium. That bull came close to dropping part of the grandstand before he was through. The fellahs howled with delight and said, "What kind of a show you got here? Hell, that bull could have killed us!" They could hardly believe it could be so wild. Afterwards they told Charles that they wouldn't have traded that experience for anything in the world. They declared that it was the best night of entertainment that they'd ever had. They talked about it for months. From then on everyplace they went together they begged Charles to find out if there was going to be rodeo in town. "Steve, (Charles's nickname)" they'd say "You watch if there is a rodeo and let us know. We want to go to another one." They just had to get to the rodeo!

Some of the guys even had a new-found respect for Charles. Flynn, who Charles often kidded, would say, "Do you ride horses like that?"

"No, not that kind," said Charles.

"Well, do yours buck?"

"Yah, once in awhile you break one that way and take a ride. But they don't buck that hard. The horses that you see in the rodeo are trained to buck."

"My heavens," he said, "I'd never seen anything like that."

Chapter 10
Horsing Around

Charles had plenty of experience with horses and cattle and the cowboy life. Horses had been his family's bread and butter. When John and Louisa Stephens first married John farmed a piece of land with his brother George. He and George had worked hard to scrape up enough money to buy the land.

Later John ambitiously set his sights on the Covine place, 340 prime acres between Bennington and Montpelier with dry farm, rich irrigated land and pasture. John went to the bank for a loan of $10,000 to buy the farm, an unheard of sum in those days. Even though John had always paid his debts the bank managers scratched their heads and looked askance. When the bank finally did agree to loan him the money he was warned that he would have "a heavy load," and that it would take "some real strong shoulders to carry that debt." There were many including some bank advisors, who thought that John was making a huge mistake; that he'd never be able to pay the debt off, and told him so. Without wasting a second thought as to the naysayers in three years time John paid the entire amount off by selling oats and horses to the army during World War I, and was able to pay cash for a new house for the family in town.

John Stephens liked to trade horses, and was a good judge of horses and other farm stock. Trading was one of the things he enjoyed most about farm life. He could talk trade and visit for hours over a dollar or two of making a deal. He traded often and took pleasure in his dealings, always hoping to get the better of the deal.

One beautiful spring day John and Charles had finished feeding the cattle and had a few rare hours of idle time. They went for a ride and ended up at the Riley Hoops ranch in Afton, Wyoming about thirty miles from Montpelier. John said "Let's go and trade horses," and he and Charles rode expectantly into the yard finding Riley and his brother at the corral with a three-year-old mare. They'd just broken the mare and were getting her tied to the fence and unharnessed.

After the customary hellos and hearty handshakes John announced that he'd come to trade horses. Riley said tauntingly "What have I got to trade you?"

John replied "What about that mare?"

"What about that mare?" John looked over the mare and then Riley showed him a two year old Holstein heifer. They chatted for some time before Riley asked curiously "What have you got to trade?" Riley offered that he could use a mate to a big brown horse that he had in the barn. John took a gander at the brown horse and said "I've got one to match him and he's a good horse except he won't walk." Riley said his horse didn't walk well either. It was agreed that the next time Riley came to Montpelier he'd come and size up John's horse. Then if Riley wanted him they'd negotiate a trade.

A few days later Riley and his brother came to the Stephens's ranch to see the horse. Charles jumped on a pony to bring "Barney" in off the range. The Hoops brothers eyed him critically and checked to see if he was "balky." John told them to hook him up and try him any way that they wanted to see how he minded. John and Charles harnessed a team with Barney and hooked them to a wagon. The horses settled easily into pulling the load and dragged it around the yard and through the field. Barney as usual wouldn't walk but did a kind of jog trot. John pointed this out to the Hoops brothers again and said it was the only fault that the horse had.

After a couple of hours of talk it was decided that they'd make a trade. Since Barney was the larger of the two horses some boot had to be involved. The Hoops's mare was worth about fifty dollars and the heifer about thirty-five. It was decided that John would get the mare and the heifer for Barney. The Hoops had a big truck and would make the exchange. Barney was loaded into the truck and two days later the mare and the heifer were delivered to the Stephens.

That fall at the fair was the next time they saw the Hoops brothers. They came over and started talking and the subject finally got around to horse trading and Riley said "I can't trade horses with you anymore." John, surprised, asked why and Riley continued "That SOB of a horse you traded me was no good." John wanted to know what was wrong with Barney and Riley said in a discouraged tone, "That horse won't walk." John said incredulously "You knew that before we traded, I told you so."

"Yeah, but I thought after you'd get him worked down, he'd walk then, but he just can't walk."

"Well, I've still got the mare and the heifer and you've had three months work out of that horse, but you load him up and bring him back and I'll pay you five dollars for gas to trade back." Riley was taken aback by the offer and only half agreed to make the exchange. Two weeks later at the fair in Logan, Utah, the Hoops brothers came over to talk. John said "I thought you were going to bring that horse back?"

"Well we got to thinking maybe we hadn't seen Barney's best points so we started to look him over a little better and now we wouldn't trade that horse for any horse you've got!"

On the way home from Logan Charles asked his Dad why he'd traded in the first place if he thought he got beat, and

John said "I didn't get beat. The mare alone is better than Barney, and the heifer will grow into more than the both of them, but if I would have let them know I got the best of the deal, they'd never trade horses again." John traded horses with the Hoops many more times over the years. He eventually traded the mare for a team which they later sold for $225. They milked the heifer for three years and got three calves from her and finally sold her as a full grown cow for $400.

Horses were something special to John Stephens. He appreciated them for what they were and what they could become. It wasn't surprising that the family from Oklahoma upon returning for a visit spoke fondly of riding the Stephens's horses. Charles had many pleasant memories of working with the horses in the fields and of horseback rides with his Dad and his brothers, taking the cattle and horses into the hills, and/or chasing after the stock and bringing the prodigals home. The Stephens brothers (John and his brothers) were known for having some of the best horses in the Bear Lake Valley.

The Bear Lake County Fair was one of the highlights of the year for the residents of southeastern Idaho. The Stephens especially looked forward to the equine competitions. Whenever they entered horses for judging they won a ribbon. Their horses also excelled in the pulling contests and races. If Charles and his brothers weren't riding for their Dad they were usually pulling or racing for someone else, and those contests could get mighty exciting. One time Dean was jockeying a horse for a man from Wyoming. He was riding hard in the lead when his horse suddenly stumbled and fell rolling completely over him. Then the whole field came over the top of them. There ended up being a large pile up with horses and jockeys splayed out in a disorganized mess. The Stephens family was holding their collective breath and fearing the worst for Dean. But as it turned out Farrel Gardner broke his arm, but Dean being in the thickest of it didn't get a scratch.

The Stephens boys were unafraid and completely at home

in the saddle. From the time he was big enough to sit on a horse Charles rode. He drove a team of horses on a pull-up (used to throw hay onto the stacks) when he was six. The pull-up was the starter job on the ranch, then as the Stephens boys grew older the mower, the plow hay rake (to turn the hay to dry), push rake (for gathering up the hay), the disk (for planting seeds after the fields were plowed), and other work was done, all using horses for power. John didn't get a tractor until after World War II.

It was not uncommon for even the best horses to get a little wild sometimes and it could be like a Stephens's day at the rodeo. Charles had his share of runaways. John bought a horse from Arnold Tueller that he used to drive around town on a single buggy. They named the horse Bill because that was Arnold's boy's name. Bill would get all flighty and shy away whenever a car passed him. One day Charles and his brother Dean drove into town with Bill pulling the buggy. They stopped at the house for a minute while Dean ran in to do some things. Charles was waiting patiently in the buggy holding the reins when a truck came whizzing by and frightened Bill and boy, howdy they were off to the races. Bill dashed off jerking the reins from Charles's hands. He sprang over the ditch in front of the house taking the buggy with him and tossing Charles like a rag doll out of his seat and spilling him over into the box at the back of the buggy. Bill then sprinted along the side of the house towards the garden and the corral. Fortunately Dean caught a glimpse of their flight through the kitchen window. He sped out through the backdoor and setting off at an angle to the run-away buggy managed to get in front of Bill, crowding him into the fence where Dean firmly grabbed him by the bit and halted his spree.

Their big brother La Grande did not have such luck when he was younger and playing with the family horse, Bally. George Stewart and a gang of rowdy neighborhood boys had been over and George had thrown a rope across the top of the swing-set and pulled it down until he had equal rope ends on either side of the swing-set. He tied one end of the rope to Bally's saddle horn and handed the other end of the rope to the first in line in a row of jostling, eager, excited boys. The boys were going to take turns getting rides. Bally would advance and pull a boy into the air and then go backwards and lower him down. It seemed like a grand idea. It was all going very smoothly and a great time was had by all until it was La Grande's turn. With an expectant La Grande clutching the rope in his youthful hands Bally suddenly and inexplicably went on a tear. She rushed forward and yanked poor La Grande up until he smacked into the top pole of the swing-set, was knocked loose and came tumbling down, breaking his arm in the fall.

It was not unusual for a group of kids from the neighborhood to visit the ranch and while the Stephens boys were milking or doing their chores they'd help a bit and then ride the ponies. Russell Schopper and Harry Speirs went out one time with Charles's brothers, La Grande and Earl, and while they were doing all the milking Russell and Harry were enjoying the ponies. Russell was on old Buck showing off and pretending to be a jockey. He kept picking on Buck and complaining about how lazy he was. Harry got tired of hearing about what a good rider Russell was and how lazy Buck was, and slipped a curry comb under Buck's tail. Upon feeling that curry comb bristling his hindquarters old Buck exploded. He threw Schopper about ten feet into the air and whinnied and bucked (true to his name) all around the yard, like he'd gone mad. A shocked and humbled Russell didn't know what had hit him.

Once Charles was out riding with his brothers and going after the cows. Dean was breaking a colt on the ride. The colt started to run and Dean though determined couldn't hold him. The rebel colt tore down a hill towards a gate with pole bars set at about six feet high. Dean breathed a sign of relief, confident that the colt would have to stop there, but next thing they knew the colt was still running at full speed and soaring over the fence with a white-faced Dean clinging to her for dear life. A triumphant colt then ran all the way around the pasture and through the cows like he was doing his victory lap. Dean was considerably shaken, but the colt acted as if nothing unusual had occurred. After that he developed the bad habit of taking the bit in his teeth and taking off anytime he felt like it. He did it with Johnny Aegerter riding him one time. He bolted and ran to the corral gate at breakneck speed but this time instead of leaping over the gate he put the brakes on hard and catapulted Johnny over the gate head first.

Charles's roommate in college, Lewis Sadder, 6'4", lean and lanky, came to visit and ride the horses. Charles had just broken Peggy's colt, a nimble, little black pony that was full of life. Long-legged Sadder wanted to ride her so Charles helped him on and instructed him to wrap his legs tightly around her so that he wouldn't fall. Sadder did and things started out fine but because his legs were so long the pony kicked his feet as she ran and jarred him loose. As he tried desperately to rein her in Sadder flew over her head and the pony galloped over the top of him rolling him in the mud and manure. When the colt was finished with Sadder he looked like he'd been run over by a whole herd. Charles and his Dad laughed until they were nearly sick and Sadder had all the riding that he wanted.

The worst runaways that Charles ever had were Strip and Bally on the push rake when they were four-year-old geldings full of nip. They were hooked up to the push rake and left standing while Charles was driving the pull-up. They were fine for awhile until they got the notion to go walking. The walk soon became a trot and Charles seeing their flight set out after them at a good clip. When Charles got close enough to the rake to grab a line Bally glanced back and spying Charles on his heels nervously swerved to the inside and nearly onto the teeth of the rake. This frightened him so that he whirled over to the outside and broke the sweep jerking the rake away from Strip who then lunged to the side and broke his sweep. Away they went through the yard scattering pieces of the push rake from here to kingdom come. John jumped off the haystack where he was working and rushed over to see what was causing all the commotion.

Together John and Charles were able to stop the horses. John instructed Charles to immediately hook Bally and Strip up to the other push rake. They were to go back to work until they quieted down. When Charles first hooked them up they were itching to run again and as jumpy as a man with red ants up his pants. John left to do the milking and Charles and the wayward horses began their task of gathering up the hay. They bunched hay until it was dark. The team was dripping with sweat and exhausted when Charles unhooked them. The next morning Bally and Strip were easy as could be to lead and control. They never ran away again.

A year later when Charles rode out to the range to gather in the horses he was horrified to find Strip lying in a crimson pool of blood on the field. He had been shot through the front leg. The family thought that since deer season had just opened that it was probably some crazy, short-sighted hunter. There wasn't anything they could do for Strip. He had to be destroyed.

Chapter 11
Boys Will Be Boys

The next stop for Charles was Lubbock, Texas. In Lubbock Charles enthusiastically set out to find an old friend. Leslie Smith from Montpelier was stationed there as a cadet flight instructor. Charles went to his outfit and asked the orderly room clerk for Captain Smith. The clerk said "He's Lieutenant Smith."

"Oh is that right, I knew him when he was a captain. Can I see him?"

"Well, he's in confinement."

"What do you mean? What's happened?"

"He's in confinement. You'll have to talk to the CO before you can see him." Then the clerk said tentatively "Just a minute," and seeing that there was no one else that needed his help he escorted Charles to the commanding officer, a lieutenant colonel's office.

The lieutenant colonel wanted to know what business Charles had with Lieutenant Smith. Charles said forthrightly that he was from his hometown, that he and Leslie had gone to high school together and that he had come by to say hello. The CO replied that unless it was an emergency he couldn't let

Charles see him. Lieutenant Smith was confined to quarters awaiting company court-martial for bouncing his wheels off a moving freight train with a cadet (that must have been some ride for the cadet thought Charles). Charles did not get to see his friend Captain/Lieutenant Smith—they court-martialed him and busted one rank. Charles felt sympathy for his friend knowing that he probably could have been court-martialed a dozen times for things he'd done. This kind of thing was not unusual, not unusual at all. It didn't end up being a permanent blot on Lieutenant Smith's record though. By the end of the war he was a lieutenant colonel himself.

At Lubbock the glider pilots were in for some more waiting because as yet there were no combat gliders. But pilots were in ready supply. They were arriving daily and soon there were about 1,500 at the field. The pilots had some combat training, rifle range, bayonet and grenade practice, formations and classes, anything the commanders could think of to keep them busy. There were about 150 small planes for the pilots to train in: Aeroncas, Taylorcraft and Piper Cubs, split up onto three auxiliary fields.

Finally the long heralded fifteen passenger CG-4A gliders arrived! There were only twelve of the hot (in terms of popularity, definitely not in terms of looks), new gliders, but eventually everybody got a turn at flying them behind C-47's. They kept them flying nearly twenty-four hours a day. It wasn't enough time for the glider pilots to get a good feel for them—nobody was mastering the art. They were still relying on small planes for the bulk of their flight training, but it was a start.

Gliders were something of a novelty to most folk. Civilian crowds lined the fences at the fields in Lubbock to see the glider take-offs, and the glider flights became a bit of a show.

One Sunday morning Charles was scheduled for an early flight at an auxiliary field. After his flight instead of waiting a couple of hours for a truck ride back to the base he hitched a ride with a pilot who was flying to the base. As they approached Lubbock they could see the gliders flying off the runway so they decided to land on the taxi strip alongside the runway. The teeming crowd at the fence was much larger than normal on this particular day. Seeing this the pilot said to Charles conspiratorially, "I'm going to really give them a show, and make them duck by landing right over them on the very end of the strip under full power." Since he wasn't the pilot Charles didn't argue.

Unbeknownst to them the field crew had left a mound of dirt about fourteen inches high at a right angle to the end of the strip. Flying low the pilot couldn't see the mound over the tall weeds on the field. He cleared the fence at about ten feet high and the nervous crowd dived to the ground just as the pilot hoped they would. However there was no time to celebrate—within a second or two the pilot was blindly ramming squarely into the pile of dirt tearing both wheels off the plane. The fast moving plane scooted painfully on its belly and then one wing tip hit the ground and folded. The second wing tip also hit and collapsed. Then the prop crashed against the ground and smashed into pieces. The engine veered sideways with a jolt that nearly stood the plane on its nose. The plane then flipped back jamming the tail section into the ground and bending the frame. Then there was quiet.

An astonished Charles immediately turned towards the pilot and asked him if he was hurt. The pilot said "No, no, how about you?" Charles said he was fine; so they climbed gingerly out of the wreckage (there wasn't much to climb out of). Dumbfounded they both sat down in the grass a little distance from the plane, half expecting the plane to burst into flames at any moment. It didn't catch fire but crash trucks and an ambulance came screaming onto the field just the same. A crowd had gathered around the perimeter of the wreckage and hushed as the rescue workers started sifting through the broken and twisted remains of the plane to find the pilots.

With no bodies in sight a bewildered crash officer finally asked the crowd if they knew what had happened to the pilots. Charles and the pilot then walked over and identified themselves. The officer wanted to know if they were okay and they assured him that they were perfectly fine. The flight surgeon from the ambulance insisted however that they be rushed to the hospital for a complete check-up. He fussed and fretted over them and was sure that they'd go into shock. The attendants put them both on litters and loaded them into the ambulance and then before Charles and the pilot could say "Boo" plunged shots into their arms. Charles spent the next day in the hospital.

Nobody could believe that they could walk away from a plane so thoroughly demolished without being injured in some way. A tow truck hauled the wreck over to the hanger where the awful looking spectacle was on display for a couple of weeks. People wanted to know, "How'd you survive that?"

While at Lubbock Charles had his only furlough in the service; he had a girlfriend at home that he was eager to visit. When a soldier put in for a leave of absence he never knew when or if he'd get it. He had to pack his bags and be ready to go whenever it was approved. Charles had been corresponding with VeNona ever since he entered the military. He'd first met her when she was a skinny, little slip of a girl. She was a fourth-grade student of his older sister Ruth. Ruth was teaching in Georgetown, Idaho and Charles and his brother Earl traveled by buggy or sleigh to bring her home to Montpelier every weekend. Once when they went to gather up Ruth they met VeNona—to Charles then she was just one of a bunch of "pesky, damn nuisance kids" hanging around his sister. That's what boys his age thought of girls.

Charles didn't hear about VeNona again until one summer in high school when he worked at the Mumford ranch in a place called Border just across the Idaho/Wyoming state line. There wasn't really a town there, just a popular local dance hall and ranches. He and several other boys worked from sunrise to sun-set milking cows, working in the fields, feeding the stock, rounding up horses, and the like for six days of the week. He went home from Saturday night to Monday morning. At night at the ranch they only had a coal oil lamp for light and so usually went to bed pretty early. But one activity became an evening ritual. A fellow farmhand named Jerold Clark called a girl named VeNona from Georgetown at exactly 7:15 p.m. every night. About all he'd say was "What's yah doin'?" This about sent the other boys into hysterics. They'd do their best to fight back the giggles and heckle him a bit and pressure him to, "Ask her what she's doin'?" and he'd ask her again and again. Jerold's wooing of VeNona kept the boys in stitches.

Charles hadn't thought much of VeNona from his two previous encounters but when he saw her a few years later he was stunned. He was home from college and attended a dance where he spied VeNona from across the room. She'd changed so much why he could hardly recognize her, and boy could she dance! Charles had changed too and was no longer so indifferent to girlish charms. She was soon his favorite dancing partner and though they didn't have much occasion to date; she was the best date he'd ever had.

When Charles was granted a seven-day furlough he threw his clothes into a duffle bag and set out for Montpelier. Four days would be spent in travel but it would be worth it just to see the look on VeNona's face. He wasn't going to tell her that he was coming. He wanted it to be a surprise! And it ended up being a surprise, a disappointing surprise for Charles. VeNona had gone to visit family in Utah and was not present for Charles's visit. La Pril Irving discovered Charles was home though and planned a big party at the church for him and Darren Stephens who had just been drafted. Nearly everyone he knew from church was there.

During his visit Charles also drove to Logan to see some college friends. He was walking through the Utah State quadrangle when he heard someone yelling "Sergeant Stephens, Sergeant Stephens!" He turned around to see his old ROTC instructor, Sergeant Daley. The sergeant was amazed at Charles's staff sergeant stripes! He wondered by what magic Charles had been able to make staff sergeant in less than two years while he had been in the army for over twenty-five years and had only made buck sergeant. Sergeant Daley good-naturedly gave Charles some serious grief for his rapid advancement. They had a nice visit over at the new military service building on campus. It seemed that Charles had only just gotten settled at home and seen a few friends, and it was time to report back to Lubbock.

Chapter 12
Rank Has Its Privileges

Halfway through his training at Lubbock injury was added to insult for Charles's ROTC instructor, Sergeant Daley, when the glider pilots were promoted from flying sergeants to flight officers. This was something totally new. There had never been such a rank before. People would ask "What's a flight officer, never heard of it." Being a glider pilot was strange enough but now they even had a special rank invented for them. After World War II they did away with the rank of flight officer. This made it tough for the glider pilots to explain what they did and what their standing was—to some it was as if they'd never existed. People didn't know what to think of them.

In order to change from an enlisted man to an officer a pilot had to receive a discharge for the good of the service. For one glorious day the glider pilots were civilians! They spent that day purchasing their officers' uniforms and sowing their wild oats in town. They were given a clothing allowance instead of being issued everything; they could pick out what they wanted and make sure it fit.

A soldier had to experience that marvelous change to

fully understand it—so many more privileges and freedoms. It was like stepping into another world with about double the pay. The flight officer rank was a warrant rather than a commission, the closest thing to being a civilian that there was in the military. Charles thought that it was the best rank that ever was!

Charles later turned down a commission on three different occasions rather than give up his rank as a flight officer. He was offered a promotion to second lieutenant and told that in time he would probably advance to the rank of captain, but he wasn't interested. Flight officers received 10 percent more for overseas pay than some other officers and didn't have to accept many duties like officer of the day or court-martial duty, yet they enjoyed all the privileges of being an officer. When glider pilots left the base after scheduled flights they could stay out and just call in for their next assignment. It was hard for Charles to believe that he was in the same army—everything was changed with his rank advancement.

After one month at the Lubbock Army Flying School, Charles was shifted over to the South Plains Army Flying School, also in Lubbock. Men were pouring into Lubbock from all the different basic flying schools and fields. The CG-4A fifteen-place gliders were in constant use. Fortunately they were finally starting to get more of them.

The glider pilots were taught how to execute "the Snatch," a rescue plan to retrieve landed gliders from the combat zone. The pilots would attach a rope to the glider and string the rope across two big uprights several feet apart. A tow plane, usually a C-47 trailing a hook on a cable, would then dive down and catch the glider rope between the poles with its hook. Once the rope was hooked the tow plane pilot winched it in and pulled the glider up fast maintaining the tow plane's air speed. It gave the glider pilots butterflies to be sitting in the glider waiting to be snatched. It didn't matter how many times they practiced it, it was unnerving to be suddenly jerked hard into the air. Sometimes the rope would break or the hooks would be yanked out of the plane or the glider. It was risky business. They worked on the snatch sporadically up until D-Day, but they weren't very successful. In the European Theatre the idea was pretty much abandoned. In Burma and Southeast Asia the technique was used with greater success, particularly to transport the wounded.

Any glider Charles flew he figured had a one way ticket into combat. There were no airfields and no easy ways to get flyable gliders out. Ninety percent of the gliders that landed overseas in the airborne invasions made their last flights there. After crash landing into enemy territory under fire most of the gliders weren't in any kind of shape to be salvaged anyway.

The glider program as a whole was rapidly moving into full gear at this time. It was beyond the experimental stage and there was a huge need for more recruits. Initially the goal had been to train 1,000 glider pilots. In April 1942 General Hap Arnold asked for 4,200 glider pilots. A few weeks later the number was raised to 6,000.

Efforts were made to recruit civilian pilots of either power or glider craft and many responded to the call to duty, but not enough to fill the growing need. Glider pilot standards were relaxed so that more men could be recruited. Candidates without any prior flying experience were eligible. The maximum age was edged up to thirty-five rather than twenty-six, the age for power pilots, and 20/20 vision was not required if vision could be corrected to 20/20 with eyeglasses. In addition, glider pilots only had to pass a basic physical and mental exam.

Because of his ROTC training Charles was called into the CO's office and asked if he would take sixty raw recruits and make soldiers out of them. He was assigned private quarters in a room in the recruits' barracks and for thirty days took the men under his wing. He marched them to get their shots, uniforms and chow and worked to get them fit with calisthenics and marching drills. If it rained they'd hold classes in the barracks and Charles would teach them how to care for their weapons. They'd take rifles and pistols apart and clean them. He taught them everything he knew to prepare them for flight training and to be good soldiers. In the end Charles felt that he probably learned more from teaching the recruits than they did from him.

The field got so crowded with all the new men that the brass finally started shipping out those who had been there the longest. For some reason Charles never entirely understood, he was transferred to Alliance, Nebraska and assigned to a troop carrier unit. They were supposedly forming overseas units there but Charles couldn't help but wonder with the temperatures in Alliance if they were just sent there for some kind of extreme weather conditioning. It was February and living in Texas Charles had hardly noticed that it was winter. This all changed rather abruptly when he was shipped to Alliance, a small town in the northwest corner of Nebraska not far from the Wyoming border. He couldn't believe it could get so cold outside of the Antarctic!

At Alliance they had a full complement of gliders and tow planes and would fly about three times a week. One time Charles was flying in the midst of a fierce blizzard and didn't dare cut off tow to land for fear he'd he be swept away and unable to see where to land—so he landed while on tow. As he rolled to a stop twenty men dressed like Eskimos rushed out and grabbed the struts to keep the wind from blowing the glider away. It was a wind like Charles had never seen! Weather-wise it was the toughest place he had ever flown in. They nearly froze their feet and hands in the frigid weather even though they had fleece-lined flying suits and sheep-skin caps and boots. They'd try and put on all the uniform that they could. When it snowed, which was most of the time, it seemed to snow horizontally. Oftentimes the glider pilots couldn't see the tow plane flying in front of them. They'd watch for any sign of the tow rope and try and determine which direction it was coming from.

Charles was only in Alliance for about a month when his group was transferred to Ardmore, Oklahoma. Ardmore, located just north of the Texas border, was hometown to Gene Autry, the cowboy/movie star, and the glider pilots had a lot of fun with that. Because the glider program was so new and a bit of a novelty, sometimes people would give the pilots a hard time; they'd say "There are no gliders here, what yah doin' here?"

"Oh," the pilots would say, "We come down to bail Gene Autry out."

Since Charles had taken his buddies to the rodeo everybody thought he was some kind of expert on cowboys, rodeos, the West, and the like. Charles's friend Flynn was a huge fan of Gene Autry's. Charles would say to Flynn to provoke him "Ah, Gene Autry's no cowboy, he's a drugstore cowboy." Flynn would pout and say loyally, "You're wrong, he's a genuine cowboy!" Then Charles would say "He can't rope a steer, and he ain't never ridden a bronc. How can he be a cowboy?" He'd tease and tease Flynn until he was fighting mad and had steam pouring out of his ears. Gene Autry had a genuine fan in Flynn.

Chapter 13
Best Looking Officers Charles Ever Trained

Charles's group wasn't in Ardmore for very long before they were moved on to Bowman Field in Louisville, Kentucky. Bowman Field was a commercial airfield with about 300 light planes and a small number of gliders. There were about 1,500 ready and eager glider pilots there, all of them officers. The pilots were scheduled to fly two to four hours a day and then to attend classes and lectures for another couple of hours. The rest of the time they were free to do what they wanted.

Bowman Field was also the flight nurse training field and had about 1,000 nurses there at all times. These women were straight from nursing school. They'd volunteered for the service and hadn't as yet had any military training. They were on flying status and had to spend four hours in a plane each month to collect their pay. Anytime the pilots went out to fly there was a line of a half a dozen nurses waiting to hitch a ride. The glider pilots usually took at least one nurse on every flight.

The pilots would often go up with about fifty planes in the air and play follow the leader. They were allowed to fly 100 miles in any direction from the base but prohibited from landing anywhere outside of the base. They got to know the area around Louisville like the backs of their hands. If they had a navigational flight scheduled they didn't even need to take a map.

Paratroopers stationed on base had flight requirements the same as the nurses. They had to make one jump or accumulate four hours in rides and so many landings so that they could get their jump pay in addition to their regular army pay. In order to draw their 50 percent flight pay glider pilots had to fly four hours a month actual flying time or three hours and ten landings and take-offs. That was pretty easy to do with their schedule. The planes were quite in demand however with so many glider pilots and nurses and paratroopers needing flight hours.

As soon as the nurses joined the service they had wings put on them and were given a second lieutenant's commission. If they qualified for air evacuation they would receive special training. Because they were going overseas they were all required to have combat training. There was a shortage of instructors for the nurses so Charles was called on to teach due to prior service. "Would you take a flight of these nurses and be their den mother?" he was asked. "Yah, I'll do it," he responded. He was assigned a flight of sixty nurses from one barracks and another buddy of his was assigned to another nurses' barracks close by. Their job was to teach the nurses the army. They were straight from civilian life. It was a little odd however since the second lieutenant nurses outranked the flight officers. It was kind of funny to be outranked and putting the women through the paces.

Charles taught his nurses everything they needed to know about army life. They drilled, tore down weapons, hurled grenades, dashed through obstacle courses, went on marches, and shot at the rifle range, as part of their training. It proved to be a terrific weight loss program. Some of the girls lost as much as twenty-five pounds in three weeks!

The nurses had to be prepared to meet certain combat-ready standards and to qualify in all the specific skill areas. It was regular combat training just like for the men, but Charles had to admit that training the women was really different; he was having a ball! Nothing was quite the same.

When Charles took the nurses out to the rifle range to teach them how to shoot a round clip from a Springfield 30-06 he asked them if anyone had shot a gun before.

"I've shot a gun," offered one of the nurses, "A .22."

"Lot of difference between a .22 and this rifle," said Charles. "This rifle packs a wallop."

The Springfield 30-06 was a big eight-pound gun and when it was fired the force could jar a man's whole body. Charles showed the nurses how to sling the rifle to their shoulders so it wouldn't kick so hard, and told them to hold the rifle tight against their shoulders. All of the army rifles had straps so that the soldiers could sling them over their shoulders and move with their arms free, and it was possible to rig the straps so that they held the rifles in place when they shot and there wasn't so much jarring.

"This is what it feels like when you pull the trigger," said Charles and then he'd pull on the gun and jam it back into their shoulders. "Oh, ow," they'd holler. "That hurts!"

"Yah, wait until you shoot this one; it will really hurt!" Even with Charles's best advice after the first day on the rifle range the nurses all had black and blue shoulders and were so sore that the next day they couldn't bear to shoot. Practice was postponed for a week on account of injury. When they met on the rifle range the following week Charles had a plan. He called his nurses to attention and ordered them to adjust their shoulder pads to take the impact.

"What shoulder pads?" they questioned.

"Why the ones you have on to cushion the blow!" said Charles looking perturbed.

"Oh, we can do that?" and they left to find something to stuff up by their shoulders to use as a protective shield. When the nurses returned two or three held up small towels, "Will these work?" they wanted to know. Charles said that they would do nicely and advised them to place the towels inside their uniforms in the right spot—the spot that already hurt. The rest of the nurses shuffled around looking for some kind of guard but turned up empty-handed. Seeing them lacking Charles finally said sheepishly "Well, now look, I know that you've got some excellent pads for this, and you all wear them every thirty days. So go get them."

"Do you mean…?" they blushed and tittered.

"That's what I mean," Charles said shortly, and sent them back to the barracks to fetch their feminine pads.

They ran back waving them like flags and singing out: "This do, Flight Officer Stephens? This do?"

Charles taking a hasty look around to check for onlookers said curtly "Yah, put in your shoulder pads—those should work." Those makeshift pads saved a lot of nurses from having sore arms. They'd pin the pads in by their shoulders and put the rifle butt right up next to them and it made a comfy little cushion. The nurses did do all that they could do to embarrass Charles about his choice of shoulder pads, but he didn't regret it.

Charles could hardly keep from laughing watching some of the gals shoot the big rifles. A shot would almost knock some of them down. They'd groan "Oh, that hurts," and he'd say "Pull that sling tighter—get it solid on your shoulder. Don't let it go on the arm. Keep it on the shoulder." In the end the nurses got through pretty well and felt quite proud of themselves. Many of the nurses from other barracks complained of bruised and aching shoulders for a long time after the training. Those nurses would say to Charles's gals "How come you're not hurtin'? How did they let you do that?" and "Who told you to do that?" when they found out about their homemade shoulder pads.

For Charles training the nurses was often quite amusing. Bayonet practice with a wooden rifle and a stick stuck in the end for poking was a laugh a minute with the women jousting furiously and losing their sticks (they'd halt combat to try and recover their sticks). The obstacle courses were fun too. The nurses would grab a rope and swing out over a water obstacle and often they couldn't hold on and whoops, down they'd go into the drink. The nurses continued their training with Charles for about thirty days and then it was time for the final march.

The final march was a ten-mile hike with a full field pack. A full field pack weighed around forty pounds and Charles knew that there probably wasn't a nurse in his command that could carry that weight for ten miles. He instructed the nurses to report to the hike with a full pack. They replied, "Well how do we carry that?"

"Don't make it too heavy."

"What do you mean? It has got to be forty pounds."

"Doesn't say that, it says full pack." The nurses walked away looking confused.

The next morning Charles blew the whistle and the nurses came tumbling and lurching out for the hike with their heavy packs—some still loading as they moved along. Many could hardly lift their packs. Carrying them on their shoulders for ten miles was clearly going to be an impossibility. Charles could imagine his sixty desperate nurses dragging their packs by their shoulder straps roughly over rocks and hills to try and make the ten-mile distance. They could be seriously injured hefting forty pound packs.

He called them to attention and said "There's about nine tenths of you that are not going to make two miles let alone ten. This says full pack," and he pointed to the instruction sheet. "I have a full pack. That is what I intended for you to carry, a full pack. I've got all I can put in it; it's stuffed full. Now I am going to tear my pack apart and show you what a full pack is to me." Charles unzipped and unstuffed his backpack tearing out wads and wads of crumpled newspaper. The nurses were at once hugely relieved and amazed. "Oh," they stammered gratefully.

"Fall out!" Charles gave them five minutes to come back with a full pack. Back they skipped much more quickly than the first time. Charles then said "Okay now a lot of you have your combat boots on for the first time. You have to have your combat boots on to make this march. We've got two trucks following behind us and sixty people here ready to make this hike. Don't be ashamed to jump onto that truck if you get a blister on your foot or a real sore spot. Don't be afraid to get on the truck, that's what we bring them along for." The nurses confidently shook their heads and said "We can make it."

About a mile and a half down the trail Charles heard some meek little voices saying, "Can we just go and get into that truck?"

"Well, sure you can," said Charles, but made certain that he teased them about it afterwards.

At the finish of the hike the nurses had to go to the camp swimming pool, jump off the ten-foot-high board with their full packs and swim to the other end and climb out. Charles about got drowned sixty times. The nurses would jump in okay, but they couldn't swim with their packs on. They'd weigh them down even just filled with paper so Charles would have to fish them out. He was sure that some of them would have drowned wearing the forty-pound packs. It was one big swimming party with everybody dripping wet and having fun. And there was nothing doing but the nurses had to throw the instructor in; against sixty of them there wasn't anything that Charles could do to resist.

The nurses invited Charles to the officers' club that night to cap off the party, but he thanked them kindly and said no, that he'd had enough partying for one day. They were great gals and he had thoroughly enjoyed being their instructor but they had exhausted him and he needed to get some rest.

Charles felt that he learned and benefited from being an instructor. It was a privilege to teach the recruits. One evening when he had some free time and was walking down a street in Louisville some guy started hollering, "Sergeant Stephens,

Sergeant Stephens, hold up there!" Charles turned to see a man come galloping across the street towards him.

"Do you remember me?" the man said.

"I don't think so," Charles answered, "Why should I?"

"I was one of the raw recruits that you taught back a few months ago. You gave us a good basic training that I appreciate now that I am a flight officer. I just wanted you to know that I appreciated what you did for us." Charles was mightily embarrassed at not recognizing him, but was happy that the man had stopped him. It made him feel like all that work was for something.

Chapter 14
Myhan and Wright

While he was in Louisville Charles met a bitter and discontented man by the name of Myhan. When Myhan was under twenty-one he had attempted to join the U.S. Air Force but was declared ineligible. He didn't want to accept no for an answer so he ran off to Canada and signed on with the Royal Canadian Air Force. He was assigned to the original Eagle Squadron of Americans and received his wings. Before he was sent overseas with the Eagle Squadron he was granted a furlough. He went home to the States to visit his family. The draft board got wind of his presence and since Myhan was now twenty-one they contacted him saying, "Hey, you're going to fight alright, but you're gonna fight for the Americans." Despite his pleas and arguments to the contrary the board refused to let him return to Canada or go overseas with the Eagle Squadron.

Myhan was mad as a hornet. He said that the Canadians had trained him when the Americans wouldn't and now the Americans wouldn't let him go over and do his duty. He vowed that he would never go into combat for the United States. Myhan said that he would take the training right up to the dock, but that was as far as it went. He would not fly in battle for the United States because of what they did to him.

Myhan kept his Canadian uniform and every once in a while he'd proudly dress as a second lieutenant in the Canadian Air Force. He'd walk out as a Canadian officer one day and change into his American uniform the next. Only those whom he confided in, his close friends, really understood why he did that, everybody else thought he was some kind of an eccentric. He went through flight training, but when the time came to split the squadrons to go overseas he told the CO, "I don't want to fly anymore. Take my rating away from me."

"Well, we'll have to cashier you out of the service for dereliction of duty and draft you into the infantry," was the response.

"Okay, that's fine, but I'll never go overseas to fight with 'em. I'd shoot my own foot off or something before I'd do that."

"We hate to waste your training and everything. Would you take another job then?"

"Yah I'll do that, but I won't fight for the United States after what they've done to me."

They offered him a position as an instructor in link trainers, a stationary training where the cadets put a plane through all the maneuvers on the ground. Another fellow, Wright, joined him—said he didn't want to go overseas either.

Wright had a story of his own. He wasn't a really big, powerful guy but he liked to talk tough. When he was drafted they put him in an outfit and told him that they were going to make a soldier out of him. Wright had trouble marching and kept getting out of step. His drill sergeant noticing him stumbling along one day called a halt to the marching. The sergeant then proceeded to chew Wright out for not knowing how to march. While giving him a verbal beating the sergeant put his angry face right in Wright's and spit on him in his fury. Wright wiping the spittle off his face said indignantly, "You don't spit on me. I didn't do anything wrong that you have to spit on me." The sergeant even more provoked replied, "I'll spit on you any damn time I want." Then he spit on Wright to prove his point. Wright incensed, pulled a small knife out of his pocket and jabbed the sergeant in the chin, knocking him cold.

Assaulting a senior officer was no trivial offense. The brass threatened to court-martial Wright and threw him in the brig. The probate officer visited Wright and said "What's goin' on? How did this happen?" A disgruntled Wright said "Nobody spits in my face. I don't care who he is." The officer said "But he's your drill sergeant. He's the superior officer in charge of you."

"Yup, but that doesn't give him the right to spit in my face."

"What do you mean spit in your face?" questioned the officer.

"He spit in my face. He was cussin' me out and drooling and spitting so I told him please don't do that. He said he'd spit on me any damn time he wanted to. So he spit on me and I decked him."

They gave Wright a week in the brig to cool down. The provost officer said "We're not going to court-martial you for this. Go on back to your unit and stay out of trouble." Wright went back and his sergeant never so much as looked at him funny let alone spit on him again. He wasn't an imposing fellow but with that pocket knife in his hand he could make up the difference.

Chapter 15
Invasion of the Enemy American Base

It was at Louisville that Charles had one of the most comical experiences of his wartime service. The CO of Stout Field in Indianapolis and Charles's CO at Bowman Field got together and hatched a plan to try and capture each other's fields. There was real concern at the time over possible enemy attacks in the United States and it was thought that this exercise would improve troop readiness. Many areas of the country already had evening blackouts so that the enemy would not be able to readily identify targets.

The two COs had said—you know there's a chance that we'll have an invasion from Germany. There are German submarines off the East Coast. The CO of Stout Field said "We ought to make sure that we do something to alert these people that there is a war on." The COs put their heads together and decided to raid each other's bases and take prisoners and everything else that would make the attacks as realistic as possible.

The commanders left it up to the men to decide how best to conduct the raids. There was a big brainstorming meeting at Bowman Field with all of the glider pilots. The pilots were saying, "Okay, we've got to raid Stout Field. How are we gonna do it?"

"Let's bomb 'em!"

"Bomb them with what?"

"We can bomb them with flour bags and Piper Cubs. Send up about one hundred and twenty Piper Cubs, fly over Stout Field and drop two pound sacks of flour on them. Ka boom! A bag of flour squashes and explodes just like a bomb."

"We can't do that, somebody might get hurt with all those sacks of flour hurdling to the ground. Let's just invade them."

"Yah," said a whole bunch of the pilots, and so the invasion began.

The Bowman pilots flew photo reconnaissance missions in Cubs over Stout Field. They mapped out the entire area and put together an invasion plan from the photos. They knew where all the buildings were on base and their purpose. Each pilot was assigned a specific drop area. Charles's assignment was to capture Building No. 4 just behind Operations. There was a parking lot alongside it with access from an airplane taxi strip.

On the day of the invasion the attack force lifted off before daybreak for a two and a half hour flight to Stout Field. The force would arrive around seven just as the field was becoming active. Three hundred light planes flying in formation, descending on Stout Field like a swarm of hungry grasshoppers. Charles was close to the front of the formation. The first four planes in front of him were to take the airport itself and the Stout command post. The pilots had painted faces like they were great, war heroes going into battle, were clothed in full battle dress and equipped with gas masks, tear gas bombs, and guns with blank ammunition. Charles had a little carbine that went "POP, POP" when fired and sounded like a rifle, but there was no lead in the barrel. The only people on the base who had live ammunition were the Stout MPs and they had advance notice of the invasion. They were

sworn to secrecy as was the CO and his staff—for everyone
else it would seem like the real thing.

Charles landed on the taxi strip as near to the parking lot
as he could and then taxied across the lot to Building No. 4.
His copilot was to take Building No. 5 right next door. They
jumped out of the plane and ran to their separate buildings.
There were a few people around, early birds off to work.
Some even stopped and stared at the plane in the parking
lot. Charles pulled on his gas mask and burst open the door
of Building No. 4 throwing a tear gas bomb canister in and
hollering, "All out, all out with your hands up!" He then rapid
fired two rounds of blank ammunition into the ceiling.

Amid a whirling chaos of gas and high-pitched screams
Charles looked around to find that he was in the reception
room for WAC inductions and that there were about fifty girls
there all in some state of undress from totally nude to semi-
nude. They were in the process of changing from civilian
clothes to WAC uniforms. Reconnaissance, not to mention
officer training, hadn't prepared Charles for this! He didn't
know who was more embarrassed, him or them. "Oh hell," he
thought, "why me?"

The tear gas bomb had completely caught them off guard
and they couldn't see or hardly breathe and then the rifle fire
had sent them into hysterics. Some were groping in the dark
for something to cover themselves with, others were crying
pitifully, "Help me, help me," and nearly all were scared to
death.

Charles yelled through the mask for them to fall out
outside and fired another round or two and they moved out
like a flittering flock of frightened chickens. All the while
trying to maintain his threatening posture Charles quickly
searched around to help grab some clothing for the women
to cover up in. Oh, he was sorry to be there.

When they were outside, the women with tear gas
streaming from their eyes finished dressing with whatever

they could throw on. Charles marched his prisoners past the administration building to the center of the quadrangle. The pilots in the first four planes had taken the airport and stopped all traffic and communications. They tied it all up. Stout Field had been captured in only twenty minutes. The Stout MPs just watched it all.

Charles's copilot in Building No. 5 didn't have quite the same luck, if one could call it that. A gal saw him coming and ducked behind the door. When he busted in she jumped him from behind and took him prisoner. "You're my prisoner buddy," she yelled in triumph. So much for his conquest—she hauled him out to the quadrangle for show.

While the invasion was in full swing one of the commercial airline pilots at Stout came stomping out onto the airfield and said "I've seen what you are doing. I'm not part of this fiasco. Just step aside and let me taxi out and I'll take off and be out of your way. I've got a schedule to keep." The pilot assigned to capture his plane and halt all traffic said "You don't move!"

"You don't kid me," said the commercial pilot. "I know you're not going to shoot me. You've got nothing but blank ammunition there. Just make sure that you don't get hit with the props, coz' I'm leavin." The invading pilot undiscouraged pulled out the bayonet on his rifle and propped it on one of the plane's tires. He said daring his foe, "Let's see you move now!" The commercial pilot thought better of it and halted in his tracks. Nothing had moved from Stout Field since the invasion. The Stout Field CO congratulated the invaders from Bowman Field and then announced to his people that being ready for an alert was going to be the order of the day.

Post invasion the first assignment was to help clean up, particularly where blanks had been fired. Then the Bowman pilots went to their planes and headed for home. In the parking lot Charles found that he had been boxed in and had to ask several people to move their cars. It was amazing what a rifle on a guy's shoulder could do to establish authority and initiate action. All Charles got was, "Yes sir, I'll do it now sir," when he requested that people move their cars.

The Bowman invaders took some heat when they returned to base. The men who had stormed the PX stole a bunch of candy bars (cases of them that they passed out to everybody) so there was a lecture about that. They weren't supposed to loot the place. If in actual combat a soldier saw a souvenir it was understood that he'd probably take it, but the men had been instructed not to in this case.

The Bowman CO informed his men that they should expect Stout Field to attempt a retaliatory attack. The pilots set up a patrol so that they would be on guard. They didn't want their field taken as quickly as they captured Stout Field. From the air they watched for convoys or any extra activity. They waited and flew the roads and air routes regularly watching for Stout to try and attack.

About ten days after the Stout invasion a column of trucks was spotted heading toward Bowman Field with a white flag jeep as a referee. Bowman was ready for them! Defending pilots cheerily loaded three one pound flour bags onto each of their planes and set off after the column. When the enemy was about twenty miles from the base the planes flew down the road and released their payloads from about four or five hundred feet up. When the flour bags hit the ground or a truck they exploded in a white cloud and soon there was only a long white column visible from the air. It was a white out— they were totally bombed out! Stout never even got to the base. The referees declared Stout wiped out and they turned around and went home with their tails between their legs. Bowman gave them hell from the air, and put them out of business!

As well as planning enemy attacks and counteroffensives many of the pilots at Louisville got swept up in the excitement of Kentucky horse racing. Charles was in Louisville for the start of the season. He and his buddies would try to fly in the mornings so that they could have their afternoons free to go to the races. Leo Frances Flynn and usually a couple of others, Best and Fitch, would go every afternoon they could to Churchill Downs. Servicemen were free so if they didn't bet too heavy it was pretty cheap entertainment. This was the year Count Fleet won the Kentucky Derby. The races leading up to the Derby were every bit as interesting as the Derby itself if not more so, and the pilots couldn't help but be fascinated by it all.

Charles was in good company in Louisville. The movie star Jackie Coogan was there for training. He had enlisted and was a glider pilot. Coogan was also famous for having been married to Betty Grable. Charles never ran into him. He heard that he was sent to Southeast Asia, Burma he thought.

Chapter 16
Life with VeNona

In the spring of 1943, once Charles was an officer and had saved enough money that he felt he could afford to be married, he sent VeNona a diamond ring and asked her to be his bride. He had dated sporadically while in New Orleans, Hays and Lubbock, but had never met anyone who he fell so deeply for as VeNona.

It took VeNona about three months to get to the train, but she must have liked the diamond ring because she immediately said yes to Charles's proposal. She'd been dating other guys just as friends. There was this one fellow she was seeing named Johnny that her typing teacher couldn't abide. When her teacher saw a ring on her finger he'd said abruptly "Who's that from?" VeNona answered coyly "Someone you don't know."

"That's okay then," was his reply. Charles didn't know Johnny or the typing teacher, but the teacher was definitely in his camp.

In July VeNona and her sister Thelda came to Louisville for the wedding. They left chilly Montpelier dressed in coats and woolens because of a late spring and nearly melted when they got off the train with the temperature at 112 degrees with 80 percent humidity. Kentucky welcomed them warmly.

It took three days to get the blood tests and the marriage license and Thelda broke out in life-threatening hives from a shrimp dinner they ate, but other than that things went pretty smoothly. Charles and VeNona were married on July 10, 1943.

Charles had asked for a honeymoon leave and was told that he could have three days subject to recall. He and VeNona had one night together before the base called and canceled his pass. He spent the next five days on field maneuvers on the outskirts of Louisville near the Ohio River. A kind woman named Vicky Jenny whose husband was in Charles's outfit befriended VeNona and drove her out to see Charles where he was bivouacked. VeNona was so grateful and happy to see Charles that she vowed that if she ever had a daughter she would name her Vicky.

After Charles got back to base he and VeNona rented an apartment over a garage in the backyard of long-time Kentucky senator, Alben Barkley. Mr. Barkley was in Washington, so they didn't get to know him, but they slept above his garage. Later he became Truman's vice-president and once told the following story about the vice presidency: "A man had two sons. One son went to sea, the other was elected Vice President. Neither was ever heard from again."[14]

A curious thing happened to Charles while staying in the Barkley apartment. The little kids in the neighborhood kept pelting him with rocks, then they'd run off before he could speak to them. He couldn't figure out what was going on. He thought that they must have been some real ornery rascals to be attacking people in that way. Charles later learned the soldier that had lived in his apartment before had beaten his wife. The kids had somehow gotten the story confused and either thought that Charles was the wife beater or had decided that all soldiers were guilty by association, and that was the reason for his being under siege. At any rate Charles wasn't too popular with the little folk for awhile. It made him feel bad on several levels to step outside and have rocks flying at him.

Many things were difficult for Charles at that time, but being married wasn't one of them. It was a wonderful thing to go from being an enlisted man to an officer but it was even more wonderful to go from being single to married. What a difference it made to come home after flying and training to be greeted by VeNona's warm, friendly smile. Charles felt complete with VeNona at his side.

VeNona was becoming anxious about Charles's overseas departure and wanted to make sure that he was spiritually as well as mentally and physically prepared. She encouraged him to advance in the priesthood of their church. She made all of the necessary arrangements so that he could have a recommend for advancement from his Bishop back home. The mission president in Louisville then ordained him as an elder in the priesthood. As the president ordained him he felt impressed to tell Charles that he would "Walk through the jaws of death, but if he would honor his priesthood he would return home to his wife in safety." This proved to be a great comfort to VeNona later on.

Several of the glider pilots were married and living off base. Only a few had cars and even for those with cars gas was hard to get, but fortunately there was a good bus service that the pilots used. Charles and VeNona saw everything in the area that they had the time and inclination to visit. They even toured Mammoth Cave with two other military couples.

When they arrived at the entrance to the cave they were told that it would be quite cold inside and that they should dress warmly. The men had some extra army shirts and pants that they gave their wives to put on so that they wouldn't freeze. A colonel from a tank outfit at Fort Knox spotted the wives wearing odds and ends of military dress and launched into a tirade about their misusing officers' clothing. The couples listened politely as he spoke and then burst into nervous laughter after he left. Despite the colonel's disapproval the wives went ahead and entered the cave with their borrowed military layers.

Chapter 17
A Fool's Game

By now the glider pilots were further into their training and becoming skilled flyers. Some guys started to get cocky and to play games and do tricks in the air. The pilots would often play follow the leader. Sometimes there would be as many as 140 light planes flying in formation following the leader. Occasionally a pilot would come along who would put his wing under another plane's and turn a bit and try and tip that plane off course. They would get close enough to overlap another plane's wing. "Bye-bye," and they flipped the plane out of formation. Then the pilot out of formation was supposed to do it to the next guy and play follow the leader in that way. There were pilots doing all sorts of crazy things. Several people got killed because of stunts like that. These were dangerous games.

One night Charles was scheduled for a flight but had to cancel because of a toothache. The next day he learned that the pilot who substituted for him was killed when the two planes on either side of him sandwiched him in and tried to tip him off course. Two of the planes went down and two pilots were lost because they were just messing around. It came as a real shock. They had a lot of funny little accidents, but most were not of this nature or seriousness.

Charles was assigned to "take landings" on another evening. They'd have ten landings and three hours of flying time with no specific destination. Often nurses would be on board for these trips. On this occasion Charles got tired of flying in endless circles following the other planes in his group and thought that he'd set out on his own. He watched the guy in front of him and when he changed directions Charles turned off the other way and kept heading straight in that direction. He saw a light far off in the distance and decided to just follow that—all the while half dozing, half awake. Finally after he'd traveled a ways it occurred to him that it wasn't a plane he was following but the planet Venus! He wondered "What the heck am I doing," and said to himself, "I ain't goin' to Venus!" He quickly circled around and made tracks back to the base. When he landed there was some poor guy waiting who was with the next flight. He said "You're over-time, what happened?"

"Oh, I got tired of going round and round so I took a little journey."

"Is that right, where?"

"I just flew down the trail a little ways and back." A sheepish Charles then looked up in the sky and saw that his whole flight group was just coming in. They'd all followed him! The whole flight group had been on the road to Venus!

Another thing that the glider pilots got in trouble for was flying under a railroad bridge over the Ohio River just outside of Louisville. It was a high bridge about fifty to sixty feet out over the water. They'd fly over and then take the planes in formation playing follow the leader, threading the needle under the bridge. Some civilians seeing the planes at play, complained, and the commander soon put a stop to that. They put a big sign out on the field saying that anyone flying under that bridge would be court-martialed.

Chapter 18
Soldiers and Dogs

In September 1943 permanent squadrons were formed and the glider pilots were transferred to different fields to report. Charles was assigned to the 87th Troop Carrier Squadron of the 438th Troop Carrier Group stationed at Camp Mackall in Southern Pines, North Carolina. Major David Daniels was the commanding officer for the squadron and Colonel Donaldson was the commanding officer for the entire troop carrier group. The 438th Troop Carrier Group consisted of four squadrons: the 87th, 88th, 89th, and the 90th.

The area where Charles was stationed in North Carolina was a hub of air force activity; there were several big fields within thirty miles of each other. There were three paratrooper bases each less than twenty miles apart and close to 100,000 soldiers in the vicinity. Laurinburg (population 12,000) was the largest town in the area. Every little town and hamlet was chock full of GIs.

Soldiers would receive two days leave in order to not have so many in the immediate vicinity, yet the towns were flooded with soldiers. Enlisted men were only allowed one pass every two weeks. Officers were exempt and when they were not on duty could go and do pretty much whatever they wanted to do. There was not much to do there. The glider pilots did a lot of flying.

At Camp Mackall the glider pilots received their final combat training before going overseas. They flew fully loaded gliders with airborne troops nearly every day and practiced many different flight procedures. They had to land a glider in a lake and swim out and land amongst the pines using small pines to soften the landing. They also had more extensive rifle range, bayonet, grenade, Tommy gun, explosives, antitank grenade, and bazooka training, alongside the paratroopers.

Because they were officers they were allowed to live off base, but that wasn't necessarily the best arrangement. All Charles and VeNona could find to call home in Southern Pines was a single room at a resort. Their room had a single bed and a communal bathroom at the end of the hall.

After a month at Mackall Charles was transferred to neighboring Maxton Air Force Base in Laurinburg. VeNona searched diligently for a better place to live. Once she heard about a vacancy in Laurinburg she flew out the door to rent it. There was a room in the home of a woman with two small sons whose husband was a Seabee on overseas duty. She was hesitant to rent to strangers, especially northerners, but luckily she didn't have anything against westerners (they must have been neutral) so she decided to give Charles and VeNona a chance. By and by she figured that they were even respectable enough to introduce to her neighbors.

Harry Jordan, the money man of the town, lived across the street from them. He owned a bottling plant and several peanut farms. He had purchased the last '42 Buick available, and without a doubt had the nicest car in town. He was a good man and liked to do things for the people of his community. Late on Christmas Eve he drove to all the stores buying gifts for needy children, and then delivered the toys and goodies to the little folk. He loved playing Santa Claus to the children. He stopped at one home and when he came out with a big, bright smile of holiday cheer his expression soon turned to shock. His car was gone! Why he couldn't believe it; hadn't he parked it right in front?

Harry thought that someone was playing a mean trick on him, but when a couple of days passed and his car hadn't materialized it seemed more like it had been stolen. He had the police searching for it, but wondered if the thief hadn't abandoned it on one of the many country roads spiraling out from Laurinburg. He asked Charles if he wouldn't mind keeping an eye out for it while he was flying. Charles rounded up several of his buddies, assigned everyone different districts and took up Piper Cubs and blanketed the area for fifty miles in each direction. They scoured every inch, and found several abandoned cars, but not Harry's. Harry was very appreciative, but Charles felt badly that he couldn't do more for him.

About ten months later when Charles was overseas he heard that the police had located Harry's car in Washington D.C. Some crazy GI had stolen it and gone AWOL. He had torn it all to pieces and dumped it. Harry wrote that it was fortunate that it was insured because it wasn't even worth carting home.

It was no wonder that some people in the south didn't like soldiers. Most were good to the soldiers, but there were signs on lawns saying things like "Soldiers and Dogs Keep Off!" The area was so saturated with soldiers, and with low characters about like the guy who stole Harry's car, it was understandable that there should be people who felt negatively towards the men in uniform.

Chapter 19
War Games

While at Maxton Charles had several unforgettable flights. Flights were often long, four and six-hour endurance trials with landings. Much of the Southeast was blacked out at night because of fears of a German invasion, so it could be difficult to find landmarks on the long night flights. One night Charles and his buddy Best had been on a three-hour flight and were just coming back to base. Much of the country was blacked out, but they could see a few twinkling lights on the ground.

Suddenly Best said "there's the tee (the base signal light, three lanterns that let the pilot know which way the wind was blowing)" and reached for the tow release.

Charles said "Wait a minute I don't think that's it."

Best said "There's three lights right there—you see?" and started again for the release.

Charles firmly grabbed his arm and said "No, not yet," that he didn't think so. Best didn't argue.

Together they decided to be sure before they pulled the release. They agreed that if that had been the spot the tow plane would take them around again for another try. Their group continued flying in a straight path without turning for about another ten miles. Finally there was the field. Best asked "Well, what in the world was I looking at?" Charles said they must have seen the town's clothing factory and that the lights had not been sufficiently covered. Best said that if Charles hadn't stopped him they would have smashed right into it. Best said gratefully, "I'm glad that you told me no. I would have landed on those lights in the clothing factory."

Another time Charles was flying at night without a copilot on a double tow on a scheduled six-hour flight over Louisiana and Georgia. They were about two hours out when they were blanketed in a thick fog. Charles knew from the instruments that the formation had to have broken up because they were flying in every direction, not following any particular heading. When the fog seemed at its thickest all that could be seen ahead was about thirty feet of tow line, and from the angle it made across the windshield Charles could only guess as to his position.

Charles flew this way for about two more hours, not really seeming to get anywhere. He figured that the pilot was waiting for the fog to clear before returning to the field. Then suddenly his air speed plummeted from the usual 140-150 mph to 95 mph and then it further dropped to 85 for awhile. Charles thought the tow line had broken as he'd felt some strong jerks when he cut a turn short, and he had lost the buffeting sensation a glider experiences when flying just above the plane's prop wash. Within seconds he decided that rather than risk a blind landing into a Georgia swamp (part of their trip was over the Okeyphenokey swamp) that he'd ride his parachute down and take his chances. He was going to bail.

With the reduced speed Charles was flying at a much lower altitude than he should have been. He expeditiously unfastened his safety belt and had just turned to slide the parachute straps over his shoulders when wham, the glider jerked and nearly threw him out of his seat. Quickly realizing that he must still be on tow Charles found the prop wash and moved back into position. Not really understanding what was happening he determined to wait it out on tow. Airspeed stayed constant at only 95 mph and altitude continued to rest at a low flying 2,500 feet.

Finally after what seemed ages the fog began to disperse and for a moment or two Charles could see the exhaust flare of the tow plane's engines, a mighty welcome sight. Then through a hole in the clouds he got a glimpse of the field, an even more welcome sight. As he readied to cut loose Charles saw Best, who was on the short tow line just below him, cut loose. Best must not have known Charles was there because he made his turn contrary to practice, in the wrong direction, right in front of Charles's glider. Charles immediately peeled back on the wheel in a desperate attempt to avoid a midair crash; Best just cleared him by inches. Charles wearily circled the field again with the tow plane and cut off and landed.

When Charles strode into Operations Best turned as white as a sheet. Wonderingly he asked how Charles had gotten there. He'd just reported that Charles had cut off one and a half hours before over the Georgia swamp. When he discovered that Charles had still been on tow he turned a shade whiter and asked how they'd missed colliding. He could hardly believe they could have avoided a crash.

The C-47 tow plane pilot, Captain Anderson, came in a few minutes later. When Charles and Best confronted him saying "What the devil where you doing flying at ninety-five miles per hour," he explained that he'd lost an engine about three hours ago but had given the other engine full pressure throttle and was able to keep them both going at 95 mph, but nothing more. He'd been flying on one engine, and when the second glider, Charles's glider, cut loose he released the rope and came around to land. He cut his throttle to land, and then as if things hadn't been bad enough, the one good engine that had worked so valiantly to pull them all through froze completely. He was forced to land dead-stick just like a glider.

They all came very close to going down that night. Somehow miles away alone in their small upstairs apartment VeNona sensed their peril. When she retired to bed the night was clear as a bell, but at eleven she woke suddenly with a chill and looked out to see a thick fog. She had an overwhelming impression that something was wrong and could not rest. She stayed up praying and waiting until two o' clock when Charles returned home. She was mightily relieved to see him.

The fog hit pretty hard in North Carolina and could make flying difficult. All of the glider pilots had some harrowing experiences; they either had trouble with the fog or other conditions. Another time Charles was up at night over a blackout area; he picked his field to land in (they were to land in a zone away from the base) and cut loose. When he landed he was barreling swiftly across the field on his wheels when some guy yelled "Hey, there's a big stump ahead!" When Charles saw it he jammed the nose forward and dug the skids into the ground and the glider screeched and groaned and tore two paths of dirt with the skids and finally ground to a stop five feet from a huge tree trunk. If he'd have hit the stump it would have cleared the glider right out. Even under the very best of conditions landing a glider was risky; it was impossible for the pilot to always know he was going into.

One time the base was staging a mock battle out on three-day maneuvers. The glider pilots were to fly their men, a combat outfit of airborne infantry, into the staging area where they were to disembark and run off to capture a hill or some other landmark. Charles had about five men in his glider. His job was to land first in the field close by a fence so that he'd be out of the way and the other gliders would have room to land. Then he was to jump out and unload a jeep he was carrying and drive around and check to see if everyone had landed safely.

He had a veri pistol to fire if anything went wrong. The veri pistol was a big signal pistol that could be loaded with a charge to fire a colored rocket. If an ambulance was needed

Charles fired red. If they needed anything else or were lost they fired white. If no rockets were fired it meant everything was okay.

Upon landing Charles jumped in the jeep and chased around to each glider. There were no problems to report. When the gliders landed the men unloaded and set off to meet their objectives—take their hill or field, whatever they were questing for. It was to be three days of bivouacking and playing soldier. After Charles checked out the last glider he helped a friend named Terrell look over the gliders and decide if they were still flyable and whether they could get them out. That was Terrell's job. Once they were through with that the two of them were basically done with their duties.

The troops had dispersed and everyone was running around fighting battles. Charles and Terrell had a blue flag flying on top of their jeep for the blue army. The blue army was fighting the red army. The referees were flying white flags on their jeeps. Charles buzzed around a bit but couldn't find his unit. He backtracked and went down several different side roads, but still didn't find it. They were in a large section of land with lots of timber and logging roads. They couldn't find any blue area.

Terrell said to Charles "I'd just as soon not sleep out in the wild. Let's go get us a motel and sleep there." Charles convinced said "Why not?" Terrell then pulled off the blue flag and said "Let's get rid of this blue flag and put a white one up." They took a white flag and tied it on in place of the blue flag and drove on down the road. Charles didn't know when he'd been saluted so much, with that white flag flying. It was really quite gratifying to him and Terrell. They'd hear the call "The referees are comin'" and then the men would be on their best behavior saluting and all the rest. Charles and Terrell just drove around and watched the war.

Finally Terrell said "I'm getting hungry. Let's go find us a hot dog stand or something." They drove into a little nearby town and had a bite to eat. Then they checked into a motel for the night. Slept like babes in beds in rooms with hot and cold running water. They were in the motel with all the other regular referees with white flags on their jeeps, and made themselves one of them. They were one of the boys, the inspectors, the referees.

The next morning refreshed they chased around observing the units and jaunting all over the place. The third day Terrell said "I'm getting tired of this. I can't find my army. Let's go home." So they returned to base and left the jeep in the motor pool and went on their way. They were alone in the barracks all that day before their army came home. Nobody missed them.

On the glider pilots' final combat training flight they were to make a night landing onto an unfamiliar field with a full component of airborne troops. Charles selected his landing spot from photos of the field and noted that the field was very short and had ditches and fences on both ends. McVey was his co-pilot. They decided to drop the wheels at take off and land on the skids so that they wouldn't roll on the landing. They flew about two hours that night to the landing zone. The field had just been plowed and was very soft. They carried a jeep and five airborne, as much as the glider could hold. The airborne were scared to death and visibly quaking. This was their first night flight.

When Charles landed he tried so hard to make sure that they didn't go too far and hit the ditch or the fence that he set the glider down a little too hard. The glider nosed into the soft ground and broke the skids right off and then the nose tore into the earth and they came to a sudden jolting stop with about a foot of dirt embedded in the nose compartment. The men had to scrape some of the dirt out before the jeep had enough power to raise the nose so that it was free. However, despite these imperfections they landed directly on target with no injuries so it was considered a good landing. As a result of their performance in the North Carolina maneuvers, Charles's squadron was chosen to lead the coming invasion of Europe.

Chapter 20
Bon Voyage

It was one of the most depressing days of Charles's life when he got orders to ship out overseas and had to say good-bye to VeNona. They had such a good time together even though it wasn't under the best of circumstances. Being married to VeNona seemed to fill his life with joy and purpose. Charles's every thought from then on was to get things over so that he could go home to VeNona.

Charles was shipped first to Fort Wayne, Indiana, but really didn't spend any time there. He was only there long enough to be issued overseas gear and to get the required shots. Then he went on to White Plains, New York, and was stationed just outside of the city at Camp Shanks in Orangeburg, New York. VeNona was routed home to Idaho from North Carolina, but had to go first to Washington D.C. to Pittsburgh to Fort Wayne and then Chicago where she had to buy another ticket. She could only buy a ticket to as far as Chicago from North Carolina. She liked to say that she rode side by side to Fort Wayne with Charles (the one leg of the journey they had in common), only on different trains.

Her passage was not as comfortable as Charles's. In order

to ride on the train she had to be accompanied by a soldier and at each stop she had to change trains. She would try to find the youngest, most scared looking soldier and tell him that she was on her way home, and that her husband was going overseas and would he please accompany her on the train? As soon as she got on the train she'd watch to see what direction he was going and hurry off in the opposite direction.

In Chicago she had to travel across the city from the Southern Pacific station to the Union Pacific station and she had to get help because of all her luggage. This was very unnerving for a simple, little country girl from Idaho. At the Union Pacific station she was afraid that she wouldn't get a ticket to Cheyenne, Wyoming (her next stop on the road to Idaho), but saw a man try to cash in his ticket for the Pullman car to Cheyenne and bought it. It was for a sleeping berth! She was able to sleep in a Pullman car on her way to Cheyenne. She could hardly believe her good fortune and was very thankful to finally have this much needed chance to rest.

From Cheyenne to Montpelier VeNona rode coach standing up all the way. There weren't enough seats for everyone. The train was packed full mostly with women trying to get home. Some even had children, and it was a very rough trip for these families. VeNona, normally clean-scrubbed and fastidious about her dress, felt so filthy, dirty and exhausted that she could have died by the time she arrived home.

Charles was in New York for about three weeks before going overseas. He and his pilot buddies went to Radio City Music Hall, the Empire State Building, about four or five Broadway shows and saw the Brooklyn Bridge, the Holland Tunnel and many other popular New York City attractions. Servicemen could get tickets for Broadway shows for about a dollar. They asked about getting tickets for "Oklahoma." It had only been playing in New York for about a month. "Oklahoma" was booked solid for four years. They didn't see "Oklahoma."

Soon it came time for Charles to cross the Atlantic Ocean and travel to Europe. The pilots of the C-47's (the tow planes) in the 87th squadron, and their crews flew their planes over. Some had pretty harrowing experiences. They only had enough fuel to make the trip, not a drop extra, and a few of them came close to not making it, but fortunately, in the end they all arrived safely. The rest of the squadron traveled by boat. Charles sailed on the U.S.S. Columbie, a French passenger liner that had been commandeered with an all French crew. They were at the head of a convoy in the command ship.

There were about 300 men from Charles's squadron on the boat. The French crew made the room assignments, and in France flight officers are real hot shots, the equivalent of about a colonel in the U.S. Air Force. The *crème de la crème* of the French military elite were flight officers. Because flight officers were head honchos in France the glider pilots bunked with the majors and were assigned the best rooms on the top deck with two, three and four to a room with a shower in the room. There was even one glider pilot who had his own private state room. When an American colonel objected and demanded that the private room be given to him the French ship captain denied his request with an emphatic "*Non!*" Ship assignments could not be changed. The ship captain then added slyly that the pilot could invite the colonel to dine with him if he wished. Besides occupying the top deck and having the best rooms, glider pilots dined with the captain.

Anyone below a major had to eat in the mess hall. The glider pilots thought that the French system was just the best. They could go anywhere that they wanted on the ship, but the rest of the men were restricted to certain areas and for the most part stayed in their quarters. The captains and lieutenants were one level below at one side of the ship with eight to a room, and the non-combatants and sergeants and above, on the other end of the ship. Then down in the ship's hold were the rest of the enlisted men. Those poor guys, nobody knew how they stood it. They were in sling bunks five deep and only twenty-four inches apart, crammed like sardines into a can. Friends would go down to visit and could hardly stand it, because of the smell. They were all seasick.

Because there was mostly only salt water to clean with while on the ship, showering could be an unpleasant experience. The men had special soap to lather up with but the salt water could really make one itch. For those in the state rooms with soft water this was not a problem. The colonel who didn't get what he wanted as far as possession of the glider pilot's private room was placated by the pilot's generously offering him the use of his shower. It was enough of a privilege to use a soft water shower that the colonel no longer felt slighted.

Anyway, there were the glider pilots dining with the captain and sleeping in the finest quarters. With such comfortable accommodations Charles wasn't ever really seasick, he just got a little queasy now and then. At the first meal served at the captain's table a high class French waiter took the flight officers' orders from an extensive menu. The choices seemed, at least to the glider pilots, to be amazing after eating base chow for months.

Charles ordered and then the waiter said in broken English, "And what to drink?"

"Water."

The waiter looked perturbed and said "No, what kind of wine?"

"None, thank you, just water."

The waiter gave Charles a scathing look and said "Zhat's okay to wash your feet and flush ze toilet, but who's ever heard of drinking water instead of ze wine?" He then strutted haughtily away to a chorus of laughter erupting from the table. He obviously had great disdain for Charles's culinary tastes.

Charles's squadron was eleven days in convoy crossing the North Atlantic. It was so cold on deck that the men could only bear to be outside in their heaviest coats for a half hour or so or they'd chill clear through. Their clothing just wasn't that warm. On deck Charles saw several icebergs and spotted a few whales spouting, but other than that saw nothing but the blue-gray sky and the ocean with ships on the horizon in most every direction.

A thrill went through all when land was first sighted, but it seemed like it took another eight hours to finally make it to the shores of Glasgow, Scotland. Upon landing the glider pilots were immediately shuffled onto a waiting troop train and shipped to Langer Field in Nottingham, England. They arrived in Nottingham at about five o'clock in the afternoon. They were given two blankets and two biscuits (half mattresses) and assigned bunks in Quanset huts. They got settled and had chow at 7:30 p.m.

Charles then went up to the officers club about a block away from the Quanset. The radio was playing and Lord Haw Haw came on the air from Germany. Lord Haw Haw was a propaganda guy just like Tokyo Rose. His real name was William Joyce and he was an American ex-patriot who had lived for several years in Britain and had then moved on to Germany. He began each radio program by saying "Germany calling, Germany calling."

Lord Haw Haw commenced this broadcast by welcoming the 438th Troop Carrier Group to the U.K. and said that he hoped that they had enjoyed the crossing on the U.S.S. Columbie and congratulated Colonel Donaldson for getting the group settled in Nottingham. He said that he had kept them in mind since they left New York and had not bothered them, but that they should expect the Luftwaffe to pay a call. He said to beware because they'd get them tonight. Rattled, the men in the officers club shuffled apprehensively to their beds. The power planes had not arrived yet so it was just those who had made the ocean crossing by boat that were bedded down in Nottingham that night.

The bombing started at 11:00 p.m. and the glider pilots spent the rest of the night in the air raid shelter. The Heinkel bombers, Nazi light bombers, came and according to Charles, "bombed the hell out of Nottingham. They tore the field up good, but didn't hit the living quarters." The glider pilots had thought that Nottingham would be their permanent base, but it didn't turn out to be. The next morning they returned their blankets and their biscuits and entrained for a trip south to Newbury, England.

Chapter 21
What's the Password?

Greenham Common was the name of Charles's field in Newbury. It was on a beautiful, green foothill overlooking the town of Newbury, about five or six miles away. Greenham Common was one of three or four fields in the UK that had the longest runways. These extra long runways were designed for gliders and crippled planes returning from their missions so shot up that they couldn't land at their own fields. The longer runways gave them more room for error. Charles saw crippled bombers and fighters land fairly regularly all the time he was at Greenham Common.

Around thirty-five years after WWII, Greenham Common became one of two cruise missile sites in England. Huge anti-nuclear protests were staged at Greenham Common and again this field captured the world's attention. By 1990 the missiles were carted away and a couple of years later the field was closed.

In 1944 Nissen huts dotted the countryside near Greenham Common. The place was crowded with them. The Nissen huts were tin, oval shaped buildings with doors and windows on each end. They weren't very large and had big potbellied tent stoves to provide the men with some heat. They'd give them a bucket of coal or pressed coal chips for fuel, and that was their ration for the day. They'd throw the coal in the stove, make a little fire, and it would warm them up pretty well. If a man stoked the fire too much the stove would turn cherry red and then they'd have to open the doors and windows to cool everybody off.

On the drive out of Newbury one would first see the 87th squadron and then the 89th, and then on the other side of the field was the 88th and the 90th. The four squadrons of the 438th Troop Carrier Group were placed together. Then beyond that and just to the north of the field there was an immense staging area where the gliders were shipped in crates. Then there were other squadrons after other squadrons. The area was inundated with GIs and equipment.

Before D-Day Charles would take walks around the camp when he had a moment to himself. There were staging areas to explore on every little country road and in every little town and hamlet. So much stuff was packed in and piled around and covered with tarps that two lanes of traffic, two truck widths, barely fit on the roads. There was an unbelievable amount of heaping supplies stashed in preparation for D-Day, boxes and crates all over.

After D-Day when the glider pilots returned to England and were free to take a stroll (eight days after the invasion), they were shocked to see that everything in the staging areas was gone. The land was picked clean. There was no trace of the massive build up of materials that had been there. They'd shipped and trucked and pushed everything over to France. There was an enormous effort in terms of manpower and machinery to move the war front eastward away from England.

Prior to D-Day the staging area just to the north of the 87th squadron was huge and sprawling with eight foot wide, fifteen to twenty-foot-long crates, stacked all over filled with gliders waiting to be assembled. Once they were assembled the gliders were scattered out to different squadrons and different fields.

Only a few gliders were ready to fly when Charles arrived at Greenham Common. They were all American gliders, and it was about three or four days before the glider pilots had any flights in them. The pilots started flying as soon as they could but all the C-47's had to be thoroughly checked after their transatlantic flights so it took some time.

After the mechanics finished checking his plane, one of the C-47 pilots, a Lieutenant Zimmerman, asked Charles if he wanted to fly co-pilot with him and see some of the country. He said that he just wanted to go up and look the area over. Everybody was taking flights to get an idea of the lay of the land. They'd go flying he said, land in one of the towns, maybe get a bite to eat and be back before five. That was the plan. Charles said "Sure, I'll go up with yah," and they took off for Liverpool.

It was a smooth, uneventful flight until they were almost to Liverpool and the fog began to roll in. They landed and refueled and intended to take off immediately and return to base, but the tower advised them to wait until the fog cleared because there were some bombers returning from their missions and the fog was very thick. They waited for about an hour and a half thinking that maybe they were going to have to spend the night in Liverpool but finally were cleared for take-off.

With Charles as navigator they flew back to Newbury as quickly as they could. Charles had the field in sight at exactly six in the evening. They called the tower and the code number and word for the day were requested. They gave it to base control, but because it was slightly after 6:00 p.m. the code for the day had changed. Their code was for the day before. They were denied clearance to land. They couldn't provide the new code because they didn't know it. They'd just been given a code for the day with no further instructions.

Charles and the lieutenant hadn't been at Greenham

Common long enough to be familiar with the British system. The tower wouldn't clear them to land. They were stuck in a holding pattern above the base. Then the tower began flashing a red light at the plane. Even the uninformed Charles and the lieutenant knew enough to know that wasn't a good thing. Instinct told them to dodge that light. Later they learned for certain that if the tower is flashing a red light at a plane that plane is about to be fired on. The smart pilot would run for cover.

These strict security measures were imposed to protect the bases and airports from German attacks. The C-47 circled the field and kept calling base control, but they stubbornly refused to answer. It soon got dark and in England when it's dark it gets really dark all of a sudden, pitch black and not a bit of light to be seen. Charles and the lieutenant could hardly see the horizon, and kept circling, wracking their brains trying to think of something to say or do to get someone to respond. Finally they flew near London hoping to find friendlier air control (about sixty miles away). There spotlights were again flashed on the C-47 and recognizing an all too imminent danger they had to abruptly stop themselves from heading straight into the barrage balloons (balloons up on cables 1,000 to 2,000 feet high—planes flying into those cables would have their wings sliced off. Planes couldn't fly over London at that time). They did a 180 and started calling "Darkie, Darkie," the only help signal they knew, over the radio. No one answered, but each time they called more spotlights were flashed at them. They were afraid that security over London would try to shoot them down, so they'd turn away from the lights and take evasive action. They were frantically darting and dodging everywhere. It was driving them crazy. Everyplace they called "Darkie" from they'd shoot another light up. This went on for about half an hour with Charles and the lieutenant becoming completely lost fleeing the spotlights.

In the process they were trying all sorts of different frequencies on the radio and finally heard a voice with

American music playing in the background. It was a man
with an American accent (and boy were they glad to hear it)
who gave them a heading to fly and told them to hold that
course for twenty minutes. He said he had them on radar and
would give them landing instructions. They flew according to
his directions for about five minutes before they saw a British
Spitfire streak past them. The Spitfire positioned itself right
in front of them and turned on its wing and landing lights
and dropped its wheels and motioned with its wings for them
to follow. Charles and the lieutenant thought they'd better
follow; they really did not know what else to do. They went after
the Spitfire and copied its 130 degree turn. They followed the
Spitfire for about twenty minutes with him probably going as
slow as he could and the C-47 speeding on as fast as it could at
around 140 to 150 miles per hour. They were led to a runway,
and lined up straight behind the Spitfire. The runway could
only be seen from directly in front of it, fifty yards to the side
either way it was invisible. It was color coded, one third was
lit in green, another third in yellow and one third red. Once
the Spitfire pilot could tell that they had spotted the runway
he flew off from about 200 feet of altitude. They landed and
some British jeeps drove up to meet them.

"Where you blokes goin'?" they were asked.

"Where were you chasin' us?" they responded. The Brits told
them to tie their plane up and they'd take them to operations.
They secured the plane and went into operations.

They had landed at a British air base on the southern coast
of England. The British authorities asked what they were
doing flying all over the country and where they were headed.
Charles and the lieutenant explained their situation and how
they couldn't land at their home base. The Brits scolded them
for not having learned the British system in flight school so
that they would have known what to do. They said that they
had been tracking the plane for two hours all over the sky and
had heard the Germans giving a heading that would have led

Charles and his friend to Brest, France. It was then once they were headed to France, that the British authorities decided that they needed to get the plane down somehow. "But," Charles and the lieutenant protested, "We were following an American voice." "Oh, that was the Germans," they said. The Germans had honed in on them. Charles asked what they, the British, would have done if they hadn't followed the Spitfire and they said without hesitation, that they would have shot them down rather than let them land that plane, that new Dakota, as the British called the C-47, for the Germans.

Safe on the ground at last Charles and the lieutenant called their CO. He told them to wait until morning to fly home. They were assigned bunks and bedded down for the night. The next day when they returned to base and reported to their CO he said that what had happened to them could have happened to anyone. He said that the British had their own system for handling such situations and that all of the American pilots needed to learn it before they flew. All planes were grounded for the next two days while everyone attended flight school and learned the British system.

If a pilot was acquainted with the British system it was next to impossible to get lost. When they shined the spotlight (other than the red one) on a plane, it was a signal to follow and then another would pick up the plane and guide until the plane reached three lights forming a cone, a direction for the plane to circle the airport and find the runway. The British also had a radio guidance system that could assist planes caught in the fog. These instruments were not on the gliders though so they really weren't much help to the glider pilots for the most part.

It wasn't too long after Charles had arrived in England that the British began to exercise almost total control over their home skies. The German air force would fly over and try and muscle through but maybe one plane out of ten would make it. The German "buzz bombs" were one of the only threats to safety on British soil. The "buzz bomb" properly known as the V-1 bomb, was a pilot-less bomb with a jet engine carrying 1,000 pounds of fire power, and was introduced just after D-Day. The Germans would fire them out over the channel and set the controls for a certain distance. As programmed the engine would quit and the bomb would glide down and blow up on target. These bombs wrecked a lot of havoc after D-Day especially in London. It was a horrifying sight to see the "buzz bombs" raining down on the city.

The British really didn't know how to defend against them at first, but once they'd gotten over the initial shock and set to thinking about how to best defend themselves, they came up with some different ideas that worked. They had used the barrage balloons to effectively defend against piloted bombers. They strung balloons up all over the city. If a plane came over and hit a balloon cable the cable would tear the wings off the plane and the plane would fall like a stone to the ground.

In order to defend against the "buzz bombs" they took all of the weapons off the British Spitfire, the guns and the heavy armaments, and made a real speed plane out of the Spitfire. It was fast enough that at about 390 to 400 mph it could go chasing after the "buzz bombs" and fly under their wings and tip them off course causing them to explode in the channel. They'd chase the "buzz bombs" until they came within five miles of the coast. If they got past the Spitfires then the bombs were left to the antiaircraft batteries set to take them out. Soon very few of the "buzz bombs" got through but there were still enough to stir everything and everyone up.

Later the Germans experimented with the V-2 Bomb which because it was an even more advanced weapon than the V-1, posed an even greater threat. The V-2s flew at a higher altitude, and flew so high and traveled so fast that they couldn't be seen or heard. The British had no defense against them. The only thing seen in the sky with a V-2 Bomber was a bunch of ice where it hit the atmosphere, and besides the explosion on impact there would be no other signs of its presence. When they were detonated there would be ice and condensation collected around the site. Fortunately the Germans didn't have too many V-2 Bombers.

Chapter 22
Steve's Bike

When the glider pilots of the 87th squadron were first shipped to Greenham Common for a couple of days there were no gliders to fly and no duties to perform. The pilots walked around the base and saw the sights. Charles would sometimes go for walks with his friend Terrell who was a bit of a character. Terrell smoked like a chimney and would often smoke in his bed at night. He was terrified however that he might fall asleep with his cigarette aflame and start his bed on fire. He made Charles promise to take his cigarettes at night and lock them up in Charles's footlocker. The first night Charles confiscated his cigarettes Terrell woke him in the wee hours of the night and said with some urgency "Give me a cigarette." Charles demanded to know whether he was really awake and knew what he was doing. He said that yes, he was, so Charles produced a cigarette and he immediately set to puffing contently on it. Next thing Charles knew Terrell's blanket was on fire and he and his startled barracks buddies had to jump up and extinguish it. Terrell slept through it all. That was the end of Terrell's having cigarettes in bed. Charles locked his cigarettes in his footlocker every night after that.

But that wasn't the end of Terrell's nighttime disturbances. In the middle of one night Charles and his barracks buddies were jolted violently awake by someone yelling, "Duck, I'm going to shoot!" Two shots were then fired into the roof with a .45. Fearing for their lives it took a few minutes for the shell-shocked men in the barracks to come out from under the covers and realize what had happened. Standing above them was a sleepwalking Terrell with his smoking gun. From then on at night Terrell's gun was tucked in the locked trunk along with his cigarettes.

One day in their wanderings around the camp Terrell and Charles found some large cisterns that were about ten feet deep and fifteen feet in diameter filled with water to help in fighting fires or other emergencies. Each cistern had about a two foot high parapet and a little fence on top of it to keep animals from falling into the water. They'd run the trucks over to the cisterns, throw a pump in, fill the truck up, and move on. So they had a ready supply of water. They looked down two or three of these cisterns just fooling around, and saw what looked like a brand new blue Royal Air Force bike stuck deep in one of them. It was about a twenty-eight inch three-speed bicycle with a gear shift. The back wheel was all bent out of shape but otherwise it was a nice bicycle.

Charles told Terrell "I'd like to take that bike home and fix it up."

Terrell said "Ah, no they'll just take it away from you. It's a British bike."

But Charles persisted, "I'm going to take it anyway just for fun." They searched around for something to fish it out of the cistern with and found an old piece of concrete reinforcing rod and a hook. They attached the hook to the rod, reached down into the bottom of the well, hooked the bicycle and raised it up and out of the cistern. Charles kicked the bike on to its side, jumped up on the wheel and straightened it out a little bit so he could roll it back to their Nissen hut.

The guys back at the huts all said "What are you going to do with that bicycle? As soon as you fix it up the limeys will come and take it." Still Charles wanted to try and fix the bicycle and if the British decided they wanted it once it was repaired well, then that would be okay. He tore the bent wheel off the bike and took the bike apart. He cleaned it inside and out and was pleased to see that it hadn't rusted inside. It must not have been in the cistern for very long. Charles went through the gear box and everything; except for the wheel the bike was in good condition. He got a hammer and beat the wheel back into shape on a piece of board found in the yard. It wasn't perfectly straight but one couldn't tell that it had been bent either so he figured it looked pretty good.

Charles went to Updike, the maintenance supervisor for the squadron, and asked him if he had any bicycle spokes Charles could have. "Oh, yes," he said, "I've got some brand new spokes. How many do you need?" He gave Charles about twenty new bicycle spokes. Charles took them back to the barracks and restrung the wheel. He got a little slot with a hacksaw down at the shop that he used to tighten the spokes. Then he could see he needed a new tube. The tire was okay but the tube was broken. When he asked Updike about a new tube he said "Oh yeah, I've got a tube; give you a whole wheel if you want it." Charles said "No, I'll straighten this one here. I don't want a whole new one."

Updike was an American Indian and one of the strongest and stoutest men that Charles had ever seen. He could lift the front end of a jeep off of the ground like it was nothing special and take a three-hundred-pound engine off of a C-47 and heft it from one rack to another. He'd pick a man up by his shirt collar, out in front of him there, and lift him up and down like he was a yo-yo. He'd been a professional football player before he joined the service, the Pittsburgh Steelers, Charles thought, was his team. He was definitely all man and fortunately for the men around him something of a gentle giant. He said "If there is anything I can help you out with let me know." Charles said "Well, I am gonna paint it red so I'll need some paint." Without hesitation Updike fetched a half pint of red paint and a little brush and said "Paint it with this." Charles took the paint and the brush back to the barracks. He finished his repairs and painted the bike red. With its shiny new coat of paint it really looked sharp and ran well too.

Everybody in the squadron knew that Charles had fixed the bike up. They called it "Steve's bike," after Charles Stephens' nickname. Charles would park it outside the Nissen hut and it would disappear sometimes for a week or two. Somebody would ride it someplace and then somebody else would ride it back. Most of the time it stayed around the barracks; the rest of the time it was off on a jaunt to operations or some other building. Somehow it always found its way home like a lost puppy.

The squadron had a little thirteen or fourteen-year-old limey newspaper boy. He'd load up his old newspaper satchel with as many papers as he could carry and lug that heavy satchel around each day. He was making a living by delivering newspapers. His Dad was crippled and infirm and he had a little brother or sister at home. His mother took in any kind of work that she could get; laundry or whatever else she could do to bring in some income. They had an awful time.

There was another American Indian in their group as well as Updike, a full-bloodied Iroquois named Metoxen. He'd go on the warpath with the little limey kid. "OOOOOH," he'd howl, "Me heap big Indian! Me scalp 'em limeys," and such. He got the poor kid so scared that he wouldn't take the paper to him. The boy didn't dare approach him. The newspaper boy wasn't the only one who was afraid of Metoxen; when Metoxen went into his war dance and acted like he would kill everyone even the CO went a running.

Later when Charles was picked to go with the advance squadron to set up camp in Reims, France, Charles offered the bike to the newspaper boy. Charles asked "Would you like a bicycle to deliver those papers with?

"Oh, I can't afford a bicycle."

Charles said "Well, could you use this one?"

"Yes, but I can't afford to buy it. One of these days I'll get me one."

Charles said "Have this one if you want." He gave the boy the bike about ten days before going overseas. From then until he went to France the boy delivered his paper bright and early every morning. He'd say to Charles pleadingly, "Would you go and see if Metoxen is drunk? I can take some papers into the barracks and sell them if he's not drunk." (The boy didn't know that Metoxen wasn't really drunk; he only pretended to be to put on a show and get everyone worked up.) He was quite a boy; the only thing that seemed to faze him was the mighty Metoxen.

Many of the British people had a tough time of it during the war. When the American soldiers went to London and rode on the "tubes," the British subway system, (one could dig a post hole almost anyplace in England and find water; the tubes were big pipes with subway cars under the water) they found that families had moved in underground and made their homes along the walls of the subway. There was probably about ten feet of space between the walls and the subway cars, but instead of a ten-foot walkway, the space was narrowed to about four feet. Families that had been bombed out and had no where else to go had set up canvas tarps all along the sides of the tube and had sectioned off their little parcels for living quarters.

The tube provided cheap and easy transportation for GIs in London and was the preferred method of transportation. A person could travel anyplace in London on the tube much faster than by driving a car. As long as one had a map and could see where he wanted to go the tube worked very well. It was only a shilling or two with the GI discount.

When walking in London at night because the city was blacked out people had to feel their way along until they could find a sidewalk, and then they'd be well-advised to

stay on the path. It was slow going making one's way around.
Edward R. Murrow, chief European correspondent for CBS,
in one of his radio broadcasts described the darkened figures
of people passing in London as being "like ghosts shod with
steel shoes."[15] During the day Charles saw an area in London,
by train or bus, where for two miles there was nothing higher
than a Selfridge Store (one of the biggest department stores
in London) left standing. All the rest was rubble, piles and
piles of it for as far as the eye could see.

Chapter 23
Not all Gliders Are the Same

At first when the gliders came in the 87th squadron had all CG-4A, American gliders to fly, but one day another squadron swooped down onto the field and took about 80 percent of those gliders. The next day the British flew in their Horsa gliders, "Boom, Boom, Boom." Nobody in Charles's group had flown or even seen these gliders before. Nobody even knew if they could fly except they'd seen the British fly them in empty. They were the largest gliders that they used. The Horsa gliders could carry thirty men or a jeep and trailer and nine men.

The British had another glider bigger than the Horsa called the Hamilcar. It was 110 feet wide and sixty-nine feet long. No American glider pilots were required to fly the elephantine Hamilcar and they were glad of it. Flying the Hamilcar was like dishing the Germans up a big, fat, juicy target. Because it sat up high if the pilots left the wheels on for landing instead of landing on the skids, they had to jump out upon landing and let the air out of the tires and the oil out of the land gear struts in order to lower the glider so that it could be unloaded. This could be a nightmarish task when landing under fire, which was how most landings were. The Hamilcar could carry a weapons carrier with a howitzer tied behind it, or a British three-man tank, or two armored scout cars or forty combat equipped men. They'd free the howitzer to shoot at tanks at crossroads and then use the carrier to run back and get ammunition.

They did the same thing with the jeeps flown in on Horsas, running back and forth getting ammunition. They'd put a dozen bazookas or so in a weapons carrier to carry over and maybe stick twenty bazooka rounds under the carrier in cartons of four stacked all over the place. They'd fill the gliders with as much stuff as they could without making them too heavy. The Horsa gliders were about twice as large as the American CG-4A gliders and bigger than B-17 Bombers. The glider pilots of the 87th squadron were told to familiarize themselves with the Horsa gliders and to learn to fly them fast, as they were to be their invasion gliders.

Hitler designed some even larger gliders than the British, the Me 321 Gigants, for the proposed invasion of England, Operation Sea Lion. These gliders could have each transported an incredible 200 combat equipped troops.

Even though they weren't the biggest gliders, the American glider pilots viewed the Horsas as gigantic monstrosities. They were made completely of plywood even to the steering wheel with a doorway that was six feet off the ground. The British and the American gliders both had barebones cockpits. The windows were plastic and they had a simple dashboard like that of an airplane or an automobile with an altimeter to show how high the glider was flying, a bank and turn indicator to tell how much the wings were tilting, and a compass. Running along the sides of the gliders were wooden benches with seat belts for the paratroopers. There were two "pilot control wheels" or steering wheels, one for the pilot and one for the copilot. Pulling back on the steering wheel would make the glider rise and pushing forward on it would make the glider descend. The Horsa gliders had tricycle landing gear; the wheels couldn't be dropped as on the CG-4A, so the pilot had to be prepared to roll a bit. But they did have something that the American gliders didn't have to compensate. The Horsas had air brakes. They were equipped with an air tank that was filled just before take off with about one hundred and twenty pounds of air. The brakes operated by using air pressure to slow and stop the glider. The left and right brakes could only be used one at a time otherwise the glider might go into a spin. Pushing the right rudder caused the right brake to be applied. If the pilot hit the brake pedal itself the left brake would be applied. Glider crew used the brakes to steer in the air and at take off as well as to land. The gliders had spoilers or flaps that also operated by air pressure rather than by using a handle to manually manipulate them. The spoilers could be used to cut airfoil. They were about four feet wide and eight feet long and could be lowered about sixty degrees. When lowered the glider literally dropped out of the air at about a seventy degree angle without increasing airspeed.

The Horsas landed a little faster and flew a little faster than the American gliders. At forty-five mph a pilot could land an American glider, but with the British glider he'd have to have sixty to sixty-five mph or else the glider because it was moving too slowly, would bounce down, falling instead of gliding. Because the Horsas were so big the tow planes could only pull one at a time unlike the CG-4As that were towed two at a time; one on one side with a short tow and one on the other with a long tow so they wouldn't collide. The short tow would be the first to cut off, and then the glider on the long tow would follow.

Some guys didn't like flying the British gliders, but Charles didn't mind them. His commanding officer called the Horsa their D-Day weapon. He said that he didn't know when they'd be using them, everything was hush, hush, but that they had to learn to use them. They practiced landings and cross-country flights in formation with the Horsas. The Horsa was fairly easy to fly when empty. They even took empty Horsas up at night in formation.

Once a man had been flying awhile he got so that he could identify an airplane by the sounds that it made. German bombers and fighters made a different sound than their British counterparts and an entirely different sound than American fighters. One night the glider pilots of the 87th squadron rose up in the sky and heard the roar of engines; different sounding engines than those of the Allies. The pilots were unfamiliar with this noise at this point in their training; they just knew that it sounded strange to them. Fortunately on this particular night the glider pilots had rigged up a homemade communication system so that they could be in contact with the tow planes. They had taken wires and looped them along the nylon tow ropes connecting the gliders to the tow planes. These wires were attached to the tow planes' intercoms. Often this attempt to jerry-rig a communication system didn't work. If the wire wasn't looped just right it would drag on the ground at take-off and detach, or sometimes when the tow rope was stretched in flight the wire disengaged. But success was more likely with a Horsa than a CG-4A. Horsa tow ropes were a little bigger and more stable. The tow planes signaled with their lights if nothing else worked. They'd blink three or four times and repeat until they were sure that their signals were received. Later two-way radios were installed. But this night the improvised intercom system was working. Charles heard on the intercom, "The noise that you are hearing is German bombers." The pilots were instructed to break formation, scatter and try to land. The entire area was blacked out. Nothing could be seen in the sky or on the ground. The only way to see the lights on a plane was to be directly behind it. The lights on the planes were hidden from side view or from above or below. Sometimes a plane's prop wash could be seen from just below the plane. The flare of exhaust coming off the engines could also be seen on a clear night—if it was cloudy there wasn't much chance of seeing even that. Anyway, the 87th didn't want to be one big flying target for the enemy, especially an invisible enemy so they quickly broke formation and dispersed to land at the base.

One morning the paratroopers in the 17th airborne division needed a practice flight so the Horsas were loaded and all in formation for take-off with the 87th's CO first in line in his C-47 towing Best. Charles was the next glider in line behind his tow pilot, the operation's officer, Major Harwell. The CO decided they'd better try the first loaded glider alone rather than launch the whole formation at once, since they'd never tried flying the Horsa gliders loaded, and this proved to be a very good decision. He said he'd take Best off and then have him go around the field and land on the other runway. If there was no trouble then all of the gliders were to take off and land.

The CO pulled down the runway and when the glider was to leave the ground the nose came up and the tail went down, but it didn't lift off. By then the C-47 was in the air and three-fourths of the runway was gone and the glider still wouldn't rise into the air so Best cut loose. He rolled off the far end of the runway before he could get the glider stopped. The CO was up in the air flying with the tow rope snapping around some of the trees at the end of the runway, jerking the little trees this way and that. The CO landed and all the pilots conferenced together to figure out what had gone wrong. Best said that he was doing 140 mph when he cut loose but the glider just wouldn't fly. No one knew what was wrong.

Finally the CO said maybe it's just a bad glider, let's try another. Charles was next in line. Major Harwell said, "Hey, Steve, now if you can't get off the ground, cut loose and don't you make me go pulling trees out of the way!" He wanted to make sure that Charles understood that he would not cut him loose, but that once Charles could see that he wasn't going to be airborne he needed to do the job. Charles started down the runway and his glider began to act the same as Best's but for some reason he didn't completely understand he automatically grabbed the nose trim wheel and rolled it all the way forward. That was just the opposite of what they usually did in the Waco CG-4As, but it seemed to do the trick as the glider immediately jumped into the air. Charles and the major circled the field triumphantly and Charles landed and was towed back into formation.

All the pilots were called together again, and the CO asked Charles if he had done anything differently. Charles told him what he did and the CO said "Best, try that, and if it works for you after we've cleared the runway then the rest of the formation follow suit." It worked and from there on out there was no trouble getting the formation into the air. The next day there was a painted sign in every glider: "When fully loaded take off with nose wheel trim in full forward position."

Chapter 24
Stalag 87

The men of the 87th squadron knew that they were preparing for a big offensive, but that's about all they knew. Everyone was concerned and asking questions. When they weren't flying they had nothing to do but prepare, and be on hand, but for what they didn't know. There were no combat missions, no supplies to move. They were expecting something to happen, and would be ready when they were ordered to go. They didn't know who or what they were going to take or anything about it. "Just be ready," they were told.

They had a lot of time it seemed then, and yet it really wasn't very much. They were ordered to do odd things like have pictures taken of themselves in civilian clothes. These were supposedly for use with the French underground in case the men got lost or separated from their groups. Charles and his friends had some mug shots taken and attached silly nicknames like "Wizard" Williams (he was the only other fellow from Idaho in Charles's squadron and they were pals), "Meathead" Walters (that guy loved his name and really played it up), "Shorty" Allen, "Stinky" Wheelock (he had a little foot problem) and Charles's, "Chuck" Stephens, were a few of the names. As a group they were dubbed "Daniels's Raiders" after one of their commanding officers, Major David E. Daniels.

About two weeks before D-Day they were fenced into their barrack's compound. There was a barbed wire entanglement fence and an armed guard. They were marched to meals and to the showers in groups and not allowed to talk to anyone on the way, nor was anyone permitted near them or their area. There were no passes and there was no mail allowed in or out. For a joke someone placed the sign, "Stalag Luft 87" on the gate.

There were many briefings and sessions spent scanning pictures of the coast of France. Each soldier was only informed of their small part in the plan, but not the date or the scope of their actions. The men didn't even call it D-Day until after the mission. There was a glass-covered table set up at normal height with a stand so that the pilots could climb up and look over the top of the table and see the ground in France with a magnifying glass. It looked like the ground would from an altitude of 600 feet which was the altitude that they would be flying in on D-Day. Every little landmark was mapped out for the particular areas. The pilots used photo maps to pick individual landing sites. They met at Operations everyday and went through their routes and two or three alternative routes.

Commanding officers did their best to prepare and inform of possible obstacles, but still there were some that the men were not ready for. The German general Rommel, charged with stopping an Allied assault, along with littering the beaches with mines, booby-traps and gun emplacements also flooded fields further inland and installed "Rommelspargel," Rommel's asparagus as it was called, to make a safe landing nearly impossible for gliders. The asparagus consisted of tall poles (steel rails from railroad tracks were sometimes used) planted in the ground at about 75 to 100 feet intervals. The asparagus could rip a fragile glider to shreds as it landed, but if that wasn't enough to kill everyone on board often the asparagus was wired and set with mines that would assure the glidermen's demise.[16]

The small, postage-size fields in the bocage country, characteristic of Normandy, most not more than several hundred feet in length, encompassed about with thick hedgerows made up of stout bushes, rocks and trees, also posed a significant threat to the gliders. There simply wasn't enough room to land safely, what with the hedges and such. Often the Germans used these hedges to their advantage infesting them with machine gun nests so that they could shoot the unwitting glidermen at their ease as they tried to land and disembark.[17]

When D-Day strategy and plans were being discussed there were those amongst the highest military circles that thought that conditions were such that an American airborne assault should not even be attempted. They predicted 50 percent casualties for the paratroopers and up to 70 percent casualty rates for the men in the gliders. Leigh Mallory, the air commander in chief for the Allies, thought that the obstacles the American airborne would face were just too great and tried repeatedly even until the eleventh hour to stop "the futile slaughter of two fine divisions," as he put it.[18] In the end Eisenhower, trusting in the advice of his field commander General Omar Bradley, decided that though the risk of terrible losses was great, that airborne involvement was necessary to the success of the overall operation, and therefore worth the risk. Bradley refused to even consider attempting the attack on Utah beach without airborne support. Of course, the glider pilots weren't consulted about all of this, but they knew all the same that it was very risky business, and that it would demand the best that they had to give.

Charles was to fly with his squadron to Ste.-Mere-Eglise, a small French perfume town. There would be Allied paratroopers and gliders coming in all over the area. Ste.-Mere-Eglise was six or seven miles back from the coast, and at the crossroads of many of the routes to the beach. It was at an important intersection. The beach was solid with German gun emplacements pointed out over the channel and with other fortifications. The Allied objective at those crossroads was to see that no German reinforcements reached the beach.

There were German tanks and artillery scattered all over the crossroads, but as it turned out the bulk of Hitler's reinforcements never made it to the beach. Hitler, the American soldiers were later told, was expecting the Allies to attack up by Calais, north of where the Allies hit the beaches, across from the cliffs of Dover. All the battles up to that time had been pretty much in that area. The Diepp raid that the British dreamed up had been just north of there.

Charles's objective was to deliver doctors and hospital gear to the area. He carried a jeep and a trailer loaded with hospital supplies (blood plasma, stretchers, surgical kits, drugs and rations of all sorts) and seven men, nine men total counting himself and his co-pilot. The Horsa gliders in the 87th squadron carried loads that varied from thirty fully equipped airborne men to two jeeps or one jeep and a trailer fully loaded. Each glider was loaded to a maximum of 6,900 pounds. Only Charles and his co-pilot carried guns on the glider because the other men were part of a medical team. Medics did not carry guns. Glider pilots were armed to the teeth. Pilots were issued an M-1 rifle and bayonet, a trench rifle, ninety-six rounds of ammunition, and all the hand grenades they wanted to carry. Pilots also had Mae West life preservers, parachutes and a Flak suit. The parachutes were used mainly as cushions to sit the pilots up high enough in the front seats of the Horsas. No one intended on using them since they would be the only ones on the gliders, and flying low in heavily loaded gliders, they weren't generally of any use. A safe landing was really the only way out.

Pilots had escape kits that contained sixty dollars of French money and other things that they might need. There was a silk map of the French landing area and committed to memory were some possible escape routes that had been communicated to them. In addition they had entrenching tools (a pick and shovel), a gas mask, three days' rations, three or four vials of morphine, a couple of cubes of sweet chocolate, a piece of piano wire and an encapsulated pill to be taken only as a last resort containing cyanide. Charles also carried two extra pairs of socks and a change of underwear. The socks saved his feet from a lot of punishment.

Charles was to fly in at 600 feet down a country road past the school house that would be used for the commanding officer's headquarters. Then he was to fly across a little alley and land as close as he could to a field where the hospital would be set up, across from headquarters. Charles was assigned the fifth glider in his group. The first four gliders carried men and materials for the headquarters.

The gliders were loaded with great care and attention so that the pilots knew exactly where everything was. The gliders and tow planes, all of them, were painted before the D-Day mission. There were stripes on the wings, stripes on the bodies and stripes on the tail sections, white and black stripes. All of the planes that went over on D-Day were painted secretly within two or three days prior to D-Day. The first time Charles saw the stripes was when he reported to his glider on June 6th. They put the invasion stripes, as they called them, on so that Allied planes could be readily identified. The new coat of paint was the first of many surprises encountered by the pilots on D-Day.

Chapter 25
Ike Cheers the Men on; the Normandy Invasion Begins

The 87th squadron was supposed to be the number one squadron. For that reason, its power planes led the show on D-Day (Charles and his friends weren't convinced that this was entirely a good thing). The CO, Colonel Donaldson, had the lead plane, the Belle of Birmingham, the first plane to drop troops into France. The Belle is shown in many of the pictures of D-Day. Major David E. Daniels gave the signal for the first paratrooper to bail out over the Normandy Peninsula. Paratroopers were the first to take off in the planes. They were dropped into France at about four in the morning and then the tow planes returned to Britain and hooked onto the gliders and took them across.

Eisenhower was on the field the morning of June 6th talking to the paratroopers and the pilots as they boarded their planes, and Charles got to see him up close as he was helping lift the heavily laden troops into their planes. Some of the guys were loaded so heavy that they couldn't crawl up the ladders of the planes by themselves—so Charles helped give them a boost or carried materials for them. It did Charles and the other men good to see Eisenhower there. He was helping them, telling them what a good show they'd have to make to stem the "high tide of the Nazis" and telling them what their chances were, and saying now is the time. He said if they didn't go now they wouldn't be able to go for another six months, twelve months or eighteen months, nobody knew when they'd have the opportunity again. It was a must that they do it. He didn't like the situation, but it was a must or call it all off, and if they called it off the Germans would make advances. Eisenhower felt it was enough of an imperative that they must go now and take the risk. He wished everyone good luck and went down the line talking to the guys and shaking hands and slapping them on the backs. Then he drove off and the men loaded.

It was still dark in the early morning but there were enough lights from trucks and spotlights that the men could see what they were doing. After the first flight left, the glider pilots stood ready at their gliders. They waited for the tow planes to return after dropping the paratroopers. The pilots had been buoyed and encouraged by Eisenhower's visit but there was still apprehension. The men tried hard to keep their minds busy and on the task at hand rather than dwell on the dangers.

Once the paratroopers were dropped they were under orders not to shoot unless they knew for certain that they were in danger from enemy troops and had no other way of defending themselves. They were to kill with knives, bare hands, whatever they could use to get the job done quietly. They didn't want them shooting each other in the dark or alerting the Germans that there were Allied soldiers in the area.

The Paratroopers had "a cricket" like kids used to get in popcorn boxes. They'd say "halt" and two clicks of a cricket would mean a person was okay, he was friend not foe, and he could move on without further challenge. If the paratroopers didn't hear that click then they knew the intruders were Germans and out popped the knives first and then if need be the guns, but only as a last resort. All the paratroopers had those crickets.

Charles's squadron returned minus the paratroopers with no casualties, but reported seeing plenty of gunfire. Only one plane came back with a bullet hole in it. A pilot said a paratrooper he was carrying accidentally popped his parachute in the plane and at the time to jump, rather than wait and be separated from his buddies, the paratrooper grabbed the silk in his arms and jumped out of the plane.

The gliders got off the ground about an hour after daylight. Usually the gliders popped right up into the air before the tow planes ever left the ground but Charles's glider was so weighty that it would not leave the ground until after the tow plane was well into the air. One of his friend's loads was so heavy this fellow feared that the hook and cable on the tow plane would snap and come crashing through the nose of his glider. Sometimes this did happen and was extremely dangerous. His glider wasn't airborne until it was on a road beyond the airstrip.

By this time everyone on the base knew the invasion was under way and all turned out to see the men off. It was not unusual to have a crowd watch take-offs and landings, as they often did for training missions, but there was not the usual silliness and wisecracking. On every face was a look of genuine concern—almost as if to say, "I wonder if I'll ever see them again."

The skies over England were overcast and smeared with the trails of all the planes that had flown through. Charles and his group circled the base several times fighting prop wash all the way until they got into formation. They assembled their formation and headed across the channel; four planes and gliders wing tip to wing tip to form an element and one thousand feet between elements. They were finally on their way. Sweat broke out all over Charles and his co-pilot's faces as they were at the controls fighting rough and choppy air from the base to the coast. They were plenty warm. When they reached the coast of England and saw the end of the land sliding by beneath, Charles could feel a lump in his throat and thoughts racing through his mind. "Will I ever see these shores again?" he wondered. He could tell by looking at his co-pilot that he was having the same thoughts, but they didn't speak of them.

They flew about six or seven miles to the east when they left England and then turned south to St.-Mere-Eglise. The flight over the channel for the most part was very smooth. Overhead they were constantly seeing and hearing formation after formation of fighters and medium bombers, P-51's, P-47's, P-38's, A-50's and B-26's, combing the skies as their fighter protection. This gave them a strong sense of security.

As they neared the French coast Charles and his co-pilot put on flak suits and ordered the airborne to buckle themselves into their seats. They were to have gone in at 600 feet of elevation but were loaded so heavy going across the channel that they barely cleared the masts on some of the ships. A few gliders hit the water and had to cut loose. They stretched and strained to avoid the ships and to stay airborne.

When Charles crossed the beach he was flying at only 250 feet of altitude. There were landing craft all up and down the coast and some boats just leaving the ships. They could see the fiery flash of the guns on Allied battleships and the bursts from German guns firing back at them. With all the noise and the sights of battle so close Charles wondered if their own guns wouldn't shoot them down. There was a wave on the beach and dead bodies strewn along everyplace. As they passed over the German inner-defenses they could see numerous shell craters. Then instantly they were no longer merely onlookers but unwilling participants in the struggle; the glider took fire. The Germans turned everything loose on them. There was the constant, unnerving sound of machine gun bullets plunking through the glider. The blast and flash of artillery and mortar fire was a dance below. Many airborne men were hit in flight and just slumped over in their seats, but none of the men in Charles's glider suffered this fate.

It was with relief that Charles left the coast and flew inland about eight miles to the drop zone in Ste.-Mere-Eglise. He was supposed to make a 270 degree turn to the left to get to his designated field. He recognized all of the landmarks seen on the map: the school, the other buildings and the field where he was to land, but he didn't have enough altitude to make it to the field. The flight leader ahead instead of landing in the field as briefed, landed in an entirely different field lined with sixty foot trees and of a length of approximately 600 feet. Everyone in his flight followed his lead.

Later it was learned that the designated landing zone had been mined. Other squadrons in the group landed there and suffered heavy casualties. Not only were the fields mined but they were also infested with German guns. Many men were machine gunned as soon as they set foot out of their gliders. One man lay as if dead in a buddy's blood, and watched German soldiers approach his glider and machine gun two of his wounded men who had managed to crawl out of the glider. If it wasn't for their low altitude that made landing in the drop zone impossible and a quick thinking flight leader Charles and his group also might have flown into this trap.

Charles did a 180 and was at tree top level over the landing zone. In the less than a minute he had to focus on the newly chosen landing spot he could see that it appeared to be a small pond or a flooded area. He thought he would just be able to reach it. There were not so many trees there as in some other places, but trees enough on either side of the pond to wreck a glider.

Charles told his co-pilot, McVey, that he was going to have to brush the trees to clear. When Charles cleared he instructed McVey to immediately apply the flaps and help Charles push the stick to hold the nose down and dive the glider onto the water in hopes that it would stop before they hit the trees on the other side of the pond. McVey did exactly as instructed. They dropped, hit the water and scooted to the other end of the field about fifty feet away and just a short distance from the trees. It was as slow and easy a landing as they could make it. The sixth glider behind did the same thing and landed close by in the pond. They were about a mile and a fourth or a half from the original drop zone, but everyone was okay and the load intact.

The Germans were peppering them with machine gun fire as they hit the water, and some of the floorboards ripped out of the glider and gave them all a little bath. The Germans continued to fire like crazy as Charles ran to the doorway with McVey and pushed the door open. They were floating in about seven feet of water. Charles shouted for everyone to jump out and swim for the ditch at the end of the pond, and then hug its bottom. They all did except for one shorter fellow, an airborne who was just above five feet who stood stalk still in the doorway with a full pack strapped to his back and said pleadingly "Sir, I can't swim." Charles replied hastily "Now's the time to learn!" and gave him a shove out the door. He didn't come up so Charles jumped in and grabbed him. With both of them struggling and Charles pulling him up occasionally for air they managed to make it to the shore and crawl to the ditch. Fortunately they didn't have to go too far before their heads were above water.

They were joined in the ditch by others until there were about sixteen to seventeen men gathered. Every time they'd try to make a move a machine gun across the next field would open up and cut the bank of the ditch. They didn't have any weapons that they could use to fight the Germans from a distance, but they would "pop, pop" a few shots at the Germans with their rifles just to keep them from advancing. They figured most of their shots didn't even make it across the pond, but some of them must have hit pretty close because the Germans did occasionally duck inside their nest and stay there after shots were fired. Then when the glider force tried to make a move for the glider again the Germans would cut loose with the machine gun. The Germans couldn't harm the men as long as they remained in the ditch, but they riddled

the glider with holes. It had the look of Swiss cheese. The
glidermen were kept pinned down in the ditch for most of
the day. Late that afternoon things quieted down as more
paratroopers came into the area. They watched thankfully as
the Germans backed away carrying their machine gun with
them.

Charles and McVey waded into the water to unload the
glider. Before take-off Charles had wrapped the four bolts
that hold the tail section of the Horsa glider with Prima
cord. He blew the tail section bolts and cut the control cables
with wire cutters and swung the tail section away. Next they
lowered the ramps on the glider and pushed the trailer and
the jeep out into the water. Completely submerged, they pulled
them with a rope up out of the water and onto the shore.
The jeep then sat drying for about an hour while they got
things organized. They'd water proofed everything. They just
had to tear the masking tape off of the exhaust, the oil, the
carburetor, anything that would take water inside the engine.
Tore that off and the engine was perfectly dry. There were
several gliders in the pond and the men from these gliders
were doing the same things. They started the engines and
they ran fine. For security there were paratroopers gathered
around making sure that the enemy didn't blow the glider
pilots to pieces while they were unloading.

A doctor, a lieutenant colonel, was the ranking officer and
Charles showed him on the map where they had landed in
relation to where the command post and the hospital were
supposed to be. He asked if he could keep Charles's map
and Charles gave it to him. He then looked right at Charles
and said that he thought we needed to have some guns on
the front of the jeep in case they ran into anything. Charles
jumped on the fender and sat up front on the hood of the
jeep with his rifle and one of his buddies on the other side.

It was just turning to dusk as the glider force started to
roll down the road, a convoy of five jeeps and a little over
two hundred men following behind—most of which were

unarmed medics. They advanced in cautious silence unsure of what they might find ahead. After they had gone about three miles they sighted an armored GI truck setting up a roadblock. Was that truck ever a welcome sight! They heaved a collective sigh of relief and felt secure for about the first time since landing. The truck drivers gave them directions to the command post and they continued their journey.

They hadn't gone very far before they came to a stone wall with a five-foot-high hedge over the top. Someone yelled "Halt, Krauts, Krauts" and Charles looked over the hedge and saw two German helmets. The driver slammed on the brakes and Charles slid off the jeep and hit the side of the road. Many of the men dove off the road onto their bellies. Before Charles even knew what he was doing he instinctively grabbed a hand grenade and was ready to pitch it. There was the staccato sound of rifle belts clicking. All of a sudden Charles heard a shout from somewhere, "Hold it. Hold it, he wants to give up," and saw a rifle with a white flag waving back and forth. Then a German soldier stepped into an opening in the hedge with his hands on his head and said "Comrade." A group of forty-two German soldiers came from behind the hedge and laid their weapons and helmets in a pile at the Americans' feet. They each had a rifle or pistol and three or four of the large concussion type potato masher grenades. They had enough guns and grenades that they could have easily wiped out the medical unit. Had the German soldiers known how poorly armed they were it is doubtful that they would have surrendered. Later Charles learned from experience that sometimes when they were outnumbered or outgunned the Germans would raise the white flag, but that the true Nazis would not stop fighting until they'd fired all of their ammunition and had their backs against the wall.

One of the paratroopers spoke German and translated. He said that the German soldiers wanted to be taken prisoner. The Lieutenant Colonel asked Charles and three other glider pilots, including McVey, to hold the Germans there until the column got down the road and out of sight, and then to take them to a stockade, but he didn't know where they'd find one. That would be the glider pilots' job. The rest of the men needed to leave to set up the hospital. Charles and the other glider pilots stood with fixed bayonets and watched the column fade into the distance.

One of the prisoners spoke fluent English. He said "We are Polish. We had the choice either to go to a concentration camp or wear a German uniform and help out on the Western front. We chose this over going to a concentration camp. Most of these are Polish and they want to give up and be taken prisoner by the Americans. There are a few Germans here. I can point them out." One of the Germans said "We give up. We give up too." This particular German unit was made up of Czechs, and White Russians as well as Poles with only enough German soldiers to control them.

When they were ready to move the Polish soldier offered to help keep the men in order. He called "Achtung," and snapped them to attention and told them in German to put their hands on their heads. Charles said that wouldn't be necessary even though the Pole said he thought it made them look more like prisoners of war. Then he persisted, "If you want to I'll see that they stay in line." Charles said no, that they were all right. They were already in formation. Charles said to the Polish soldier "You understand one thing don't you; if we're challenged by the Germans you're all dead." He said "Yah, yah, we take our chances there. Germans do that too." Orders were when transporting prisoners to shoot all of them when challenged by the enemy. The thinking was that if the Americans didn't kill the prisoners when under fire the prisoners would turn on them—so the first thing to do was to shoot the prisoners.

After a short wait to allow the column ahead to put some distance between them, they began marching down the road. Charles was a bit uneasy about the route since he didn't have the map anymore and couldn't really plot the journey. They had to rely on the German/Polish/Czech/White Russian soldiers for directions more than he was comfortable with doing. They could have been leading the procession to Berlin for all they knew. But as it turned out they were no trouble at all. They may have been wearing the German uniform but their hearts were not into being German soldiers. They led them right in the direction of the command post in Ste.-Mere-Eglise.

They walked about a mile before they were hailed by an American MP who yelled "Halt, who goes there," and demanded the password. Charles gave it to him and the MP instructed him to advance and be recognized. At close proximity it was obvious that the shaky, young MP was just as scared and nervous as Charles. Charles explained who he was and that he had some prisoners, and the MP stammered incredulously "You take all those?" "No, they gave up." The MP made a call from a telephone at his post, and then said that because they were short-handed Charles and his men needed to take the prisoners down to the schoolhouse where there was a little field where they were keeping the prisoners. Charles and his group headed towards the schoolhouse/command post and were met there by some other MPs who took command of the prisoners.

In Ste.-Mere-Eglise Charles saw that the medics he had flown in had immediately gone to work at the hospital treating the wounded. They were still going strong without so much as a breather forty hours later when the glider pilots were ordered to be evacuated. There was firing going on all around the town, but for the present none seemed too close.

There was a captain, an aide to Brigadier General Donald F. Pratt who was in command at Ste.-Mere-Eglise. The commanding officer, General Pratt, the deputy commander of the 101st airborne, was killed in the invasion. He was the first general to die in the European campaign. He'd come in on a glider with Mike Murphy as his pilot. Mike was a head honcho in the glider program, a stunt pilot who was one of the men leading the push for the glider program. Mike was seriously wounded in the crash as well. The glider pilots were later informed that the crash occurred because armor plate had been attached under sections of the glider to protect the men and it was so heavy that it weighted the glider down. When the glider cut off from the tow plane it stalled in mid air and plunged down. So Charles heard. Sometimes it was hard to tell truth from fiction, because the men heard lots of scuttlebutt, but that's what they said happened, and it seemed to ring true.

Chapter 26
Some Things You Don't Forget

Ste.-Mere-Eglise was the first town to fall to the Allies during the Normandy invasion. Charles's Idaho friend G.L. Williams's assignment was to set up the command post there. The Germans were still in Ste.-Mere-Eglise when he arrived. Once the Germans evacuated G.L. had the precarious assignment of helping to rescue a poor paratrooper who was stuck on the town church's steeple. A soldier never knew what he might be called on to do. Charles and his group of glider pilots reported in at the command post and were told not to stray too far, that they were to be evacuated back to England just as soon as they could get them out. They might be needed soon for another air drop.

G.L also had to make a water landing. All the guys he saw land in the water with him, but one, made nice, controlled landings; sliding in as far to the end of the pond as they could so as to be out of the way of other in-coming gliders. G.L. saw Rufus Frost, a guy from Virginia, barrel in like he was being chased by the devil. He had his tricycle landing gear on and one of his wheels must have hit a hole because the glider abruptly kicked back and Rufus came flying out of the Plexiglas nose still strapped into his seat, clutching the control wheel in his hands. G.L. said that when Rufus flew by him *sans* the glider his eyes were huge. G.L. and the men with him couldn't help it, they all burst out laughing to see such a sight, but they weren't laughing for long. Rufus rolled end over end as he hit the water and when they finally retrieved him he had some serious slash marks all over his face from where he struck the water. Miraculously, except for the cuts, he and his cargo were all okay.

This wasn't the only scrape G.L. had with Rufus. While he was at Laurinburg-Maxton Army Air base Rufus, who was immensely proud of his southern heritage, invited several of the guys to visit his hometown, Galax, Virginia. G.L. went along in the front seat of Rufus's big, old Chrysler. They got to some railroad tracks and Rufus waited until a train passed and then hit the gas hard. It wasn't until he got on the tracks that he noticed that there was another train rapidly approaching from the other direction. Rufus froze, the car died and there they were stuck on the tracks without a moment to lose and all screaming at the top of their lungs for Rufus to do something. Before he could even think G.L. smashed his foot down on the starter on the floor (that's how it was in old cars) and the car leapt forward just missing the speeding train. What G.L. hadn't realized was that Rufus's foot had been on the starter and in powerfully jamming his foot down to escape the train he'd broken Rufus's foot. Anyway, G.L. had some good Rufus Frost stories.

It was near the command post and the hospital in Ste.-Mere-Eglise that Charles first witnessed some of the real horrors of war. They were in the heart of the main battle lines created by the paratrooper drops. The paratroopers were the ones who really took a beating. Every live paratrooper Charles saw would have been a frightening sight on any other day with their faces blackened and their clothing threadbare from crawling and covered in blood from their heads to their toes. On this day they were just another part of the whole macabre scene. Dead bodies both German and American, were laying every few feet apart, and in some places were two and three deep. The charred remains of paratroopers killed by flame throwers hung in some of the trees. German snipers were still active and Charles constantly heard bullets fly over his head and lick up the dirt at his feet, and saw men suddenly slump over and fall to the ground.

Charles saw men wounded beyond recognition stand and walk unaided to the first-aid station. One paratrooper in particular showed what real guts are. He was shot through the throat and in the leg by a machine gun, and still got up and tried to go on. He said "I'd better get back," and stumbled up onto his feet. When Charles offered to help him he said "No, I can make it alone. You go on." He applied his first-aid bandage to his throat, and hobbled on his one good leg using his rifle butt for support, and made his way to a Red Cross jeep.

Charles was angered to see some of the medical men shot up and killed with their Red Cross blazons plainly visible on their arms. Allied medics did not carry guns, but all of the Nazi medics that Charles saw in Normandy did even though American soldiers were instructed not to shoot them having been told they would not be armed.

French guerrillas and patriots joined in the fighting at Ste.-Mere-Eglise. They used their trucks, horses, carts, and even wheelbarrows to help evacuate the wounded. The few civilians Charles saw seemed very glad to see the American soldiers. Enterprising French women were out in the fields gathering parachute silk into large bags and carrying them to their homes. Bodies of some of the gleaning women who had been killed by German snipers were left scattered about in the fields.

Charles and his group ran into some other glider pilots they knew by the command post and dug a foxhole and spent the night there. An enemy plane came over and strafed them but there were no hits. The shooting, however, kept drawing closer until everyone became extremely antsy from staying in the exposed foxhole (they were right out in the open). Charles and a few other men finally moved to a patch of trees near an intersection in the road. At least from there they could see trouble approaching.

It wasn't long before they spied a small German tank about two hundred yards away crossing the road. A young airborne with a bazooka and a carrying case with shells ran up and said "Let's get him sir!" Thinking he was a bazooka man that needed some help Charles said sure and jumped up and took the case out of his hand and raced after him about a block and a half and then dove under a hedgerow for cover. The tank was still some distance away traveling very slowly with its turret swiveling from side to side.

Everybody around was ducking for cover. Charles figured the airborne fellow would do the same, but instead he stood there and handed Charles the bazooka and said "Take him, sir!" Charles said "What do you mean, take him? I'm not a bazooka man!" "Neither am I sir. I'm just a carrier and my sergeant got killed this morning." Charles all too keenly realized that the whole time they were talking the tank was rolling inexorably down the road. Charles made the young soldier take cover, grabbed the bazooka, shoved it through the hedgerow, took a shell out and pushed it in the bazooka and wired it up so it was ready to go. Then the bazooka carrier tapped Charles on the shoulder and said "Take him! Take him!" Charles ignored the fellow as best he could and hawk-eyed watched that tank crawling closer and rotating its turret. When the tank was maybe forty yards away Charles put the sight on the front wheel of the tank and fired. "Bam," he hit the tank on the left front wheel, breaking the track and spinning the tank in a circle. For a second Charles thought they were goners. The gun was swinging wildly. Charles crouched as low as he could in the hedgerow. About that time the hatch swung open and two Germans climbed out with their arms up. Paratroopers swarmed around them and took them prisoner.

The little bazooka carrier was ecstatic. "Good shot, sir," he kept saying. Charles handed the bazooka back to him and told him to find another bazooka man, and to get the hell out of there. "I can't find my outfit," the carrier said. Charles declared "I think that's them right over there." The men he could see were wearing the same blue braid around their caps that the carrier was. Some had caps and some had helmets. Charles couldn't be happier to help him find his unit. If he'd known that he was going be shooting the bazooka there was no way he would have ever hooked up with the little carrier. Charles thought that he just needed an ammo carrier.

No one wanted to be labeled a coward, but it wasn't a good idea to go looking for trouble either. Once people thought someone was a coward word got around. G.L. felt strongly that one of his fellow soldiers was a coward because of an experience he had with him. This particular soldier was driving a jeep with G.L. and Metoxen from the landing zone to the command post. When some Germans were spotted he floor-boarded the jeep and G.L. and Metoxen were accidentally knocked off onto the road. He didn't so much as glance back but raced forward leaving his friends there with the Germans to fend for themselves. G.L. and Metoxen thought for a moment that their days on this earth had come to an abrupt end; incredibly however, the Germans wanted to surrender.

G.L. probably had more trouble controlling Metoxen than the docile prisoners. Metoxen, always playing the part of the fierce Indian brave, wouldn't lead but instead took the rear in delivering the prisoners to the command post saying "Indian never show back to the enemy." The only real trouble the German soldiers gave G.L. and Mextoxen was that they were hungry and they had to scrounge up some food for them. Happily they found a bunch of K rations that had been paradropped in and fed them. G.L. and Metoxin never felt quite the same way about the soldier that abandoned them.

The glider pilots were asked to help out with the prisoners

until they were shipped back to England for flight duty. The Allies had taken so many prisoners that they had to keep shuffling them around in order to find places big enough to accommodate them and not compromise Allied safety. There was a warehouse about a half mile from the command post that Charles marched prisoners to with fifteen to twenty in a group. He made this trip four or five times a day taking more prisoners to the warehouse. There was a large group of glider pilots helping and no big hurry to make the transfers. The pilots paid no attention to the trail, it was all just routine. There was a GI laying on the trail shot; Charles and the others stepped over him and really didn't notice much about him. There were dead bodies lying all over, German and American.

On the fiftieth anniversary of D-Day Charles was watching a television special about the invasion and a British news correspondent came on who said that he went in with the 82nd airborne to St.-Mere-Eglise. He stated that he saw some of the combat and what the guys went through, and then he said that he wanted to show some pictures that had never been released before to the public.

He showed a picture and said "This is a GI that was killed on D-Day and fell on a trail just outside of St.-Mere-Eglise. For the six days that I was there he lay on the trail because there weren't enough men assigned to grave detail to attend to him." He then showed a picture of what the man looked like after six days. He had turned black and had bloated all over the place with flies swarming around him. That was the very same guy that Charles had stepped over many times as he walked down the trail to the warehouse with the prisoners! Same guy, same place. Charles sat in shock overwhelmed by the awful feelings that rushed over him. He didn't want to see or hear about it anymore. Fifty years hadn't erased anything. At the time the men thought there were so many bodies, what was one more? The horror of it all hit him again after watching that program. There were too many scenes like that. It was just one of a dozen. Charles cried to think again about stepping over the dead American soldier.

Chapter 27
Patton's Bounties

Come D-Day plus three, all glider pilots were ordered to report to the beach master for a boat ride back across the channel. They headed back to the beach in small groups of five or six and were sniped at most of the way. They tried to stay on the sides of the roads as much as they could unless they could see some of their own soldiers along the way. A column came by and at its head was "Old Blood and Guts," General Patton himself. He was wearing his trademark shiny, shellacked helmet and had his pearl handled pistols in holsters on each side of him, standing proudly in his jeep as though he could have cared less about being fired at. When he passed the glider pilots he gave them a salute and said "Good show men!"

When Charles and his group of glider pilots reached the beach, the beach master praised them and said that their flight over drew the Germans' fire enough that it allowed the American boys to get a foothold on the beach. He said that the first wave had been repelled and that they'd lost 95 percent of those men, but that the second wave had just hit the beach when the gliders flew over and drew German fire.

The Germans he said focused on hitting the gliders and this allowed the second wave to get a foothold. The beach master asserted that they would never have made it had the gliders not drawn the enemy fire. Charles wasn't sure if this was true, but he knew that they had attracted enemy fire, of that much he was certain. He hoped that it was true, that their crossing had helped the men on the beaches.

They were told it would be about an hour before they would have landing craft ready to transport the pilots. Captured Germans were being marched onto boats and the pilots were asked to help guard 200 prisoners that were being transported to England. When the boat arrived for them the tide was just coming in. They had to march their German prisoners through four or five feet of water to get to the landing barge. As the prisoners waded through deepening water they began to yell and turn around and protest (probably afraid of drowning and reciting their prisoners' rights). Charles was at the back of the column heartily wishing that he could speak German, but instead had to employ a universal language and prodded a couple of them in the butts with his bayonet to get them back on course. They sat in the man-made harbor that night trading three-hour shifts down in the hold of the ship guarding prisoners.

While Charles was on guard German planes strafed them and dropped mines. Mine sweepers had to come and clear the channel the next day before they could set sail. Charles saw three mine sweepers hit mines and sink. Two of the sweepers were about a half mile away and they couldn't really see much but the explosion. The third was only about a hundred yards away and Charles was watching when it hit the mine. It was a horrifying sight. The blast raised the whole back end of the ship out of the water, buckling it in the middle. In about two minutes the entire ship had sunk with its crew of eighty-one men. Only three of the men could be rescued. The concussion had ripped their clothes off and broken the skin on different parts of their bodies as well as bursting their eardrums.

There was still plenty of action going on around them. The Nevada never stopped shelling the coast for a minute and two cruisers alongside of her were doing the same. The fighter umbrella remained overhead flying through the flak bursts. Two P-51's flying wing to wing flew into the flak and one took fire and headed for the sea. The pilot bailed and safely parachuted into the water where he was picked up in a life boat from a barge. His flaming plane hit the water just 400 yards from Charles's ship. The other P-51 circled around them until the downed pilot was on the life boat. The plane then buzzed the rescue ship and flew back towards the Peninsula. The men on the boat kept their eyes on the plane until it was out of sight. It never rose above tree-top level. Charles was sure that the pilot went to pay a call on the flak installation that shot down his buddy.

Charles talked to a lot of paratroopers and they told him some pretty nasty stories about the Germans and their methods of warfare. One captured a German captain who spoke perfect English, as many of the German soldiers did. When the paratrooper asked the captain why the Germans didn't take prisoners and instead killed surrendering Americans outright the captain said, "They don't talk." The paratrooper incensed by this remark seized the captain in a rage saying "You won't either," and strangled him with his bare hands. Charles saw the captain's papers as shown to him by the paratrooper and from the pictures he looked like a fine, civilized man. Scenes and stories like this were things that Charles could never forget.

The boat with the glider pilots crossed the channel and docked in London with several other boats filled with soldiers. Charles hadn't thought too much of England up until then, but once he set his gaze upon the Queen's country he couldn't take his eyes off it until his feet were firmly planted on British soil. Men had been known to kiss the ground when returning from a voyage and Charles knew just how they felt. Every guy with him seemed to feel the same way.

The German prisoners were handed over to the authorities and from there the glider pilots were immediately loaded into trucks and taken to Paddington station and given a high priority pass. They were told that because they might be needed immediately for resupply missions that they should get to their bases as quickly as possible. At the station more and more glider pilots kept joining them. The station was packed because buzz bombs were hitting London and there was a mass evacuation of the city. British MPs literally threw people off the trains to get the pilots on, and when the trains pulled out of the station people grabbed handle rods, or jumped up on the train door steps, and clung to whatever they could to ride the train and get out of London. It was a desperate situation.

Charles had never been welcomed as warmly as he was when they arrived at the base. Every man was pulling for them and if they'd had the instruments they would have assembled a brass band. All of the glider pilots in the 87th squadron returned safely. The CO told them that he had only expected to see half of them again. Maybe it was just plain luck, but Charles preferred to think that the good Lord was riding with each and every one of them all the way.

Once the pilots had eaten the flight surgeon gave them a pill to help them settle down and rest. In the meantime the gliders were loaded (American CG-4A's this time instead of Horsa gliders) with men and material from the 17th airborne division. The pilots had flown in the 82nd and the 101st airborne on the first trip. Glider pilots were on ready alert, but were never given the command to take off. After three days on alert it was decided that another drop would not be necessary, and the gliders were unloaded.

Later all of the glider pilots in the Normandy invasion received an Air Medal. A citation with the medal states: "The magnificent spirit and enthusiasm displayed by these officers, combined with skill, courage and devotion to duty is reflected in their brilliant operation of unarmed gliders of light construction at minimum altitudes and air speeds, in unfavorable weather conditions, over water, and in the face of vigorous enemy opposition, with no possibility of employing evasive action, and in their successful negotiation of hazardous landings in hostile territory, to spearhead the Allied invasion of the continent. Their respective duty assignments were performed in such an admirable manner as to produce exceptional results in the greatest and most successful airborne operation in the history of world aviation."[19]

The glider pilots had a mixture of Horsa and CG-4A gliders from then on, and the squadron was strengthened by the addition of new glider pilots. The pilots had practice flights whenever they could and often enough to keep the 17th airborne on ready alert, but tow planes were not always available. C-47s were being used for parabundle drops, mainly to Patton's advancing armored divisions. They dropped a lot of material to Patton: fuel, supplies and ammunition, as he was racing across France. They'd fly across the channel, drop the supplies at a certain designated coordinate and return. Often they would land in Paris or Brussels en route and bring wounded soldiers to England for treatment. The C-47s were flying day and night and the pilots would get dead tired after pulling their typical fourteen hour days. The glider pilots tried to help out (when they didn't have training flights) and flew co-pilot on some of their missions. All of the glider pilots took a turn aiding the tow plane pilots that pulled them.

They also served as Officer of the Day in town for the over-worked power pilots. Flight officers were not obligated to pull guard duty as Officer of the Day. They could if they wanted to, but they couldn't be ordered to do it. But they'd put on an armband and strap on a .45 and go into town and watch the theatre and the dance halls at night for their buddies. Charles served such duty more than once.

Charles was sent to Reims in northeastern France as a C-47 co-pilot on a mission for Patton. They were supposed to land about ten miles north of Reims ahead of Patton's troops, but Patton had been delayed somehow in taking Reims. In flight they were instructed to land and unload at the Reims airfield rather than drop the bundles ahead of the troops. This generally wasn't the case with Patton. He often moved so quickly that the coordinates that he gave for air drops would be in back of his lines by the time supplies arrived. He'd set up in a ring of tanks that were all nearly out of gas and ammunition and shoot at the enemy until Allied planes dropped parabundles into the center of the tank circle. Before the planes could get out of sight some of the tanks were refueled, and they were on the move again. They were incredibly fast and efficient at gathering up bundles and refueling.

In Reims they were told that the airport had been bombed but that they thought it was serviceable. They were advised to buzz the runway first to make sure it was functional and that they could land safely there; that it wasn't muddy or chock full of potholes or the like. The field looked fine so they landed and unloaded. On the ground there were big six-wheeler trucks waiting to scoop up the supplies and move with them.

They had unloaded and were about to take off and go back to England when here came General Patton motoring in standing blade straight in a weapons carrier with his helmet, pearl handled pistols, and three yellow stars shining like new pennies. He pulled onto a ramp in front of them and shouted "Hold those planes and gather around men!" So they shut off the engines and walked over closer to him. He continued "I want the 438th group, 87th squadron to know how much I appreciate what they have done in dropping these supplies all the way across France. You've done a fine job! (every other word here was a cuss word) We've taken this GD city. Now it's declared an open city, but before we declared it an open city these GD Krauts (called 'em every name there was) had given us Reims, but before they did and had declared it an open city, we had captured the winery." He wanted to make it clear that the winery product was not considered Allied or

French but conquered contraband. It was a French winery but the Germans had occupied it for three or four years and it had been German run. So he'd personally seen to it that these spoils of war were confiscated. He had about six large GI trucks packed with champagne and cognac, and told the pilots to take it back to England and to "Pitch a bitch on General Patton!" The pilots opened a couple of cases and each of them had Patton sign a bottle as a souvenir, and then loaded all they dared carry onto the airplanes and headed for England.

When they got over London one of the pilots, a guy named Barney, raised them over the intercom and said that he had engine trouble and needed to land at the London airport. He said to tell the CO about his situation and that he would contact him and be in later. So Barney landed in London. The rest of the pilots, including four other planes, flew back to the base and unloaded their cargo of spirits, champagne and cognac.

They told the CO what happened and he said "Yah, I knew Barney was in some trouble. I know all about that." Charles didn't know whether Barney had contacted him or not, but the CO wasn't surprised. They told him about their cargo and he said that they should pass the booty out to all of the squadron, but that it would have to be done with discretion because they were on duty. They could be called into action at any time. There were to be no drunken brawls. The pilots decided to give the men some in the chow line, two quarts of champagne and one quart of cognac each, so that they'd all get to enjoy Patton's gratuities. Despite their best efforts the men became a bit tipsy and there wasn't much flying the next day. Since Charles didn't drink he kept two of the bottles that Patton had autographed and written his thanks on as souvenirs. He stored them in his footlocker.

His footlocker contained many things that were precious to him. There was a shoe box full of pictures that Charles especially treasured. Technically they weren't allowed to have cameras but his buddy Wheelock was a real camera buff and broke the rules and purchased a camera in London. They salvaged an old glider box, a huge twenty-foot glider crate, and made a photo lab out of it. They had a dark room where they developed their own pictures with supplies purchased at the base to make it all work. They had many pictures that Wheelock had taken in flight, a few that had even been taken in combat. The champagne bottles were the latest addition to the treasure trove.

Three days after their return to base Barney came straggling in minus his cargo. He said that the limey authorities had confiscated it, that he wasn't allowed any of it, but strangely enough he carried a flight bag stuffed full of pound notes. Shortly afterwards Barney bought a ranch just outside of Austin, Texas and a $45,000 home in Austin, and everyone was sure it wasn't from his army pay.

There was a regulation in England that a soldier could only send so much of his money home. They didn't want the American soldiers sending away all of their money and becoming broke or becoming wards of the British state. In order to get all of his bootleg money back to the states Barney went to all the enlisted men and everybody that he knew, and asked them to take 50 to 100 pounds and send it to his wife in Austin, Texas. He had dozens of people helping him out, and in this way got his money home without exceeding the limit. He would say "Here's a picture of my new home," and go around showing it to everyone, and it was a big, nice home. They all knew how he got it. Just about anything could be sold on the black market in London, and that's what the pilots figured Barney did with the champagne and cognac. They never said anything, but they knew.

Often PX rations were sold or traded. Soldiers were given up to two cartons of cigarettes, six candy bars, six cakes of soap, and two boxes of laundry soap per week, and these were all very desirable items. Nobody used that much over there, but everyone took their full ration allowance. There were a couple of guys that complained two cartons weren't enough cigarettes for them, and Charles took pity on them and let them have his until he discovered that they were taking the cigarettes to London and selling them for two pounds a carton, about eight dollars and six cents then. Charles kept his from then on, and had a footlocker full of soap, candy and cigarettes, besides a cardboard box about the same size as the footlocker under his bunk. He and his buddies traded these items for eggs, bread or anything someone had that they wanted. They found an English lady just off the base who was more than happy to do their laundry when they'd give her a box of soap in exchange. She took in laundry from the town, and said that was the only way she had been able to get soap for the last three years, and since she had soap she had more town business than she could get done.

Charles C. Stevens at age 21 in Louisville, Kentucky

Lovely VeNona at age 23 after marriage

A soldier borrows the bicycle Charles repaired

Pre D-Day mugshots of glider pilots

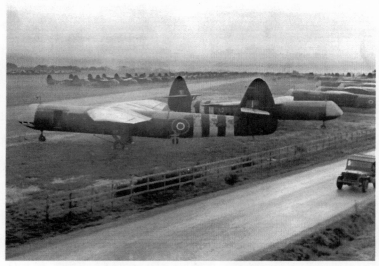

An array of gliders ready for action. Courtesy of the Silent
Wings Glider Museum in Lubbock, Texas

Charles in Britain relaxing before duty

Ten pilots after returning from D-Day. Clockwise from top left ("Chief" Metoxin, Robert Bastian, Frederick Allen, Pilot Beto, Charles Stephens, Arnold Best, Charles Carroll, Valey McNally, Charles Miller, Robert Arnold)

Loaded gliders in France prepared for airborne mission
across Rhine River. Courtesy of the Silent Wings Glider
Museum in Lubbock, Texas

Horsa glider on tow at take-off. Courtesy of the Silent Wings
Glider Museum in Lubbock, Texas

Chapter 28
Major Troubles

The glider pilots loved to visit London. All of the hotels had Turkish baths and when they could stay overnight they'd go to town just for the bath. They'd have a steam bath with a massage and a rub down, and oh, it did a body good. Attendants would wrap them in big heavy towels and they'd sweat like crazy until they started to overheat and then they'd hurry up and jump into the pool, and after that it was back to the steam bath. The baths were famous for knocking out colds. Every morning they'd bring them a breakfast of powdered eggs and a bit of bacon, and the pilots felt like they were really living! It was this kind of treatment that they liked going to London for.

Soldiers didn't get many opportunities for travel outside of the war zone. The only sights the pilots could see were pretty much those that they could spot from the air or from the roads on practice flights or in combat. But after D-Day when there was no immediate need for a resupply run the glider pilots were given three or four days leave. They scattered out all over to see different sights. A bunch of pilots got together and said "Let's go and see Edinburgh, Scotland," and Charles joined in. They climbed up a steep and slippery slope to Edinburgh Castle overlooking the city and in the distance the North Sea. Charles could hardly believe they made it. The hill was covered with glassy pebbles that made it nearly impossible to get one's footing. Shoes would slide right off those tiny stones and people would have to hang on to each other for dear life. Guides said that they'd take horses and carriages up there all the time and that they had no trouble leading the horses up to the top, but Charles could hardly imagine it. They said they even pulled their cannons up that way which was even more incredible. There was a beautiful view from the castle abutments with the cannons positioned all around to fire at opposing forces sighted approaching from land or sea. Charles enjoyed seeing the sights, but the time passed quickly and soon the glider pilots were back at work preparing for new missions.

While the American forces were advancing across the plains of France the 101st and the 82nd airborne divisions were gathered back to England, rested and supplemented with replacements from the states. All three airborne divisions were now in England and all stationed fairly near the troop carrier fields. It was clear that another airborne assault was in the works. The glider pilots were taking the airborne troops up regularly on training missions.

One day Charles was assigned to fly thirty men in a Horsa. They were airborne taking a four-hour flight so that they could collect their flight pay for the month which amounted to 50 percent of their regular pay. The ranking airborne was a major. He seemed to be a normal rough and tumble major. Being a major, he was pretty high up. He assigned the men seats and asked Charles if there were any further instructions that he should give the men because this was their first ride in an English Horsa glider and they really didn't know what to expect. Charles told them that all they needed to do was fasten their safety belts and let him do the flying. The flight was to be over northern England and of four hours duration.

The major strapped himself into the seat directly behind the copilot.

After they got into the air and in formation Charles reached back and opened the cockpit doors and motioned to the major to come up. He did, and was quite enthusiastic about being able to see everything that was ahead of them, the tow plane, and all the planes and gliders. Charles told him that if he was feeling at all insecure about being up there he could take a rope and tie himself to a post so that he wouldn't be falling out if something happened. "Oh, no," he said he wasn't concerned; he'd just stand there and hang on. He really seemed to be enjoying it, so Charles asked him if he'd like to fly the glider for a minute, and he said sure. Lee Wheelock, who was flying as co-pilot, got up and let him sit in his seat, and then Charles gave the major the controls. They were soon all over the sky and out of position so that didn't last too long and Charles quickly took them back. Then Charles gave him a short course in flying a glider and he remarked "Gee this wouldn't be too bad after you caught on to it." Then everybody wanted a turn sitting in the co-pilot's seat. Charles let all thirty of them have a quick turn in Wheelock's seat, but he kept his hands on the controls, only the major had a chance to try and fly the glider.

The major then wanted to stand in the aisle between the seats and chat a bit. He asked a steady stream of questions; where were they exactly, what did they just fly over, and lots of questions about the controls and the mechanics of piloting a glider. He seemed to be having a great time. When they got about twenty miles from the base Charles told him that they would soon be landing and that he should be going back to his seat and buckling up. He said that he'd like to stay standing there and just hold onto the seats while they landed if it was okay with Charles. Charles thought that he was being either awfully brave or somewhat reckless and said that it would be a lot safer for him strapped into his seat, but seeing his resolve said sure, if he wanted to; he was a major after all.

When the field came into view Charles pointed it out to him and told him the exact place they were going to land. Charles had chosen a spot at the far end of the field so that the rest of the formation would have room to land. The gliders did not all have to land on the runway. Wheelock asked what kind of an approach he was going to make and Charles said "Straight in with full flaps." Wheelock said "Ok." They were at 1,000 feet of elevation and the major kept asking weren't they going to cut off, and Charles kept answering that they would when they were close enough. The major said "Aren't we getting too close for it?" Charles answered "No, we're alright." They flew over the end of the runway and the major looked relieved and said "You're going around again, huh." Charles said "No," and when he got about halfway down the field away from the runway he told the co-pilot to cut loose and give him full flaps. As Wheelock did Charles pushed the stick full forward and the glider headed down at about a seventy degree angle to the ground. The major now horrified, bellowed "Pull it up! Pull it up! You're going to dive into the ground! You're out of control!" and turned to go back to his seat, but found himself frozen; he couldn't move with the glider at such a sharp angle. Charles said calmly "Just hang on!" And he did cling tightly to the side with only a few further protestations. When the glider was about fifty feet from the ground Charles pulled the nose up and made a perfect landing right on the spot that he had picked. It was all very routine.

The airborne and the major deplaned and Charles stayed in the glider for a bit and filled out the flight log. When he climbed out an enraged major grabbed him by the collar and called him every dirty, rotten name that he could think of, and was going to hit him, but was physically restrained by a couple of his men. He said that of all the dirty stinking tricks he ever saw that this took the cake. He said "I thought you were going to dive that thing into the ground and kill us all!" Charles told him that this was just a typical combat landing; that they were never in any trouble, and that in fact, he felt proud of the landing. His copilot, Wheelock, then backed him up and said that he thought that it was a good landing. The major snatched his hat off his head and threw it onto the ground swearing an oath to the effect that flight pay wasn't worth going through that, and that was his last glider ride ever. "They can have those damn matchboxes," he growled, "Never will I go through that again!" He was going to transfer to an infantry outfit. After he stomped off still muttering angrily to himself, Charles asked the guys who'd sat in the back how they felt about the ride, and they replied that they'd had the feeling that they were falling, but thought that he must have known what he was doing and didn't think much about it. Some guys like the major just weren't cut out to fly in gliders.

Chapter 29
Tragic Accidents and Loops

Charles saw some terrible accidents at Greenham Common. Every day they'd cease flying at about four o'clock so that the bombers returning from daylight missions over Europe would have free and uninhibited access to the extra long runways. Any of the airplanes whose hydraulics were shot out or that were crippled in some way would have trouble landing on a normal field so they were diverted to Greenham Common or to other fields like it. Sometimes even these runways weren't long enough to avoid accidents though. Right at the end of the runways there was a hill that dropped off and sloped to a wooded area. A lot of planes ended up crash landing in the woods below. The town of Newbury was only two miles down from the runway and if an airplane went off the end of the runway with any speed at all it could pancake near the town.

In the winter time the fog bank would settle in at Greenham Common. Upon rising in the morning the sky would be as clear as a bell. The bombers would take off and all that could be seen in the blue sky would be their vapor trails. Then within thirty minutes of their departure the sky would be completely obscured by dense cloud cover. Flying above the clouds they looked like one gigantic snow bank. The glider pilots would go up and practice gliding and landing on those snow banks. They'd make believe that it was a landing area. It was fascinating to see the thick, white clouds from above; the sky was crystal clear above the clouds.

On the ground there was very little visibility; sometimes it got so a person couldn't see the hand in front of his face. Planes that went down through the fog onto the runways couldn't always judge the ends. All kinds of accidents happened. Poor visibility along with mechanical problems, not to mention injured pilots, could make for disastrous consequences. Sometimes one wheel would lock and the others would be down and the plane would go into a spin and crash sideways tearing a wing or an engine off, and then there would be a burst of fire. They'd bring some guy in all bloodied and rush him to the hospital. The glider pilots would help once in awhile with the crash victims but usually the medics were able to handle everything.

One accident Charles surely wished that he could forget, but could not, happened when he was heading into Newbury with some buddies to go to the store. They were taking the bus into town and were waiting at the last stop before leaving the base. They took the bus often and it was usually fairly crowded when they boarded. On this particular day the bus was loaded with people; it was a foggy afternoon and rime ice covered the road. When there was fog and rime ice the roads would become like glass. They used to say about rime ice, "it's as slick as snot on a door knob."

They came to an intersection where they had to stop for planes that landed and taxied across the road to get to the marshalling area. The planes were scattered out in the area so that they were not all lined up as ready targets for the Germans. The bus cautiously approached this stop and so did not have any problems coming to a halt. It was just waiting for an approaching plane to cross the road before it started up again. A jeep coming from the other direction, the main

gate, was not so lucky. Charles and the other passengers on
the bus could see that the jeep and the plane were on a glide
path right at the highway intersection. And they could tell that
they saw each other. The pilot of the plane put his brake on
but the plane slipped and kept right on going. He was trying
desperately to avoid a crash. He locked one wheel and tried
to pull the plane in a circle to move away from the jeep but
the road was so slick that instead of circling the plane skidded
sideways and the prop ended up going right down the dead
center of the road. In the jeep too they were frantically trying
to stop. The driver was pushing on the brakes and sliding all
over the place. He had no control whatsoever on the stop. All
of them were screaming. They had a nurse up front with the
driver and two Red Cross girls in the back of the jeep. The
jeep slid right under the prop as the plane came around to
the center of the road and the prop sheared everything off.
The windshield was sliced off and the driver and the nurse
were left with only their hindquarters in the front seats and
in the back it was pretty much the same. Oh, it was horrible! It
looked like someone had taken a knife and cut across the top
of the jeep. There were parts of jeep and human remains all
over the road; an arm was lying here and another one there.
That's how bad it was. The plane had made mincemeat of
them. And the bus-riders just sat there and watched.

The pilot was out of the plane before it even stopped
rolling. He had shut off his engine but the windmilling prop
had carried the plane forward and he couldn't have avoided
that crash no matter how hard he'd tried. "Oh, my heavens,"
he cried "What have I done," like it was his fault. He was in
agony. They had to physically restrain him and give him a
shot to get him to the hospital he was so badly shaken.

Almost immediately after the accident an ambulance was
called from the tower and the medics arrived. The glider
pilots climbed out of the bus to see if they could help in any
way and the medics handed them pillowcases and asked if
they would help clean up the mess. They'd pick up a piece

of an arm or something like that. One of the parts Charles gathered was a piece of an arm with a wristwatch that was still going. "Oh hell," he thought "How do I do this?" And he picked that arm up and put it in the pillowcase. And a part of a woman's anatomy that was off to the side, he picked that up and put it in the pillowcase. They cleaned the mess up as best and respectfully as they could. Charles then went back to the bus and told the driver that he didn't think that he wanted to go to town anymore. He told him to go ahead and waved him on. Oh, Charles thought that was terrible! It made him sick to see that. It was one of the worst accidents that he'd seen.

Another time Charles was assigned a Horsa for a thirty man training flight. When he was inspecting the glider before take off his friend Best told Charles to come and take a look at something that he had spotted. They found some droplets of water from sweating all over the tail compartment and that the plywood had softened until one could dig in it with his fingernails. With a fingernail the wood fiber could be peeled off, it was so soft and mushy. Charles red-lined (reported the glider as being unsafe) the glider in the logbook and told the operations officer about the report and his concerns. The operations officer assigned Charles another glider and he and Best flew the thirty airborne on the training flight without incident.

The 436th Group was scheduled to fly the next day. Best and Charles wanted to watch them take off from the air so they checked out an L-4 plane (light airplane) and flew above the field while the glider fleet took off. As they were watching Charles saw to his surprise that the glider he had red-lined the day before was being lifted into the air for take off. He wondered what in the world they were doing with that glider. He and Best kept their eyes on the glider hardly knowing what to think. It was fine on take off but as it came around to the downwind leg to get into formation and gained a little speed they saw to their horror first small strips of plywood like ribbons flying loose, and then the whole tail section suddenly blew off, and the glider folded with the nose plummeting straight into the ground.

Charles and Best immediately landed, got a jeep and rushed to the crash site. By the time they got there they'd sealed the area off and wouldn't let them through. Both pilots and all thirty of the airborne troops were killed instantly. Charles's Idaho friend, G.L. Williams, also saw the crash from the air and said that he and his co-pilot initially thought that someone was "throwing garbage out" from the glider because they kept seeing debris falling from it and were astonished that someone would do such a thing, and then saw the glider release from tow and its tragic, ultimate end.

The crash was investigated and the logbook with Charles's entry was found and he was called in to operations. "You were assigned that glider the day before. Why didn't you fly it," they asked him.

"I red-lined it because I thought it was not airworthy," Charles said.

"What was wrong with it?" Charles told the authorities what he and Best had found and why he had red-lined the glider in the logbook and that he had reported it to operations and that they had pulled it off the line and assigned him another glider.

"And you flew that same mission the day before the crash?"

"Yes, with a different glider," Charles replied.

"Why didn't they honor your red-line then?" That question he couldn't answer.

"Well you did your part. We needed to know." That was the end of the inquiry as far as Charles was concerned.

Later Charles discovered underneath his notation in the logbook, another entry, "Have checked the tail section and can find nothing to indicate this glider not to be airworthy," this entry was signed by the glider pilot who had flown the glider on the day of the crash. Charles guessed that the sun had probably shone on the tail section and dried the moisture so that the wood couldn't be scraped off so easily. So they had said "Can't see anything wrong with it." To have looked at it a person wouldn't have known any different. Charles and Best just happened to see the water beaded up on the plywood.

When Charles read in *Silent Wings*, a publication for former World War II glider pilots, that on December 12th 1995, fifty years after the tragedy, surviving relatives and former comrades were meeting to dedicate a plaque to the memory of the two fallen glider pilots and the troopers they carried at Greenham Commons, it sent shock waves right through him once again. That was an awful day and for Charles the pain of it hadn't diminished that much.

Most of the time the work of the glider pilots was very serious, deadly serious, and there wasn't much room for error. But boys will be boys and they did do some horsing around even when they were training in England. To Charles's way of thinking it probably came naturally to the glider pilot to be something of a daredevil, otherwise why else would they do what they were doing? At least that was his excuse.

Charles and his good buddy and barracks mate, Terrell, were flying empty one day in a Horsa and decided to do the unheard of and loop a Horsa. Terrell said "You know I've looped everything that I've ever flown, I wonder if this sucker can loop." Charles said that if they had enough speed, he guessed it would. Charles was willing to try but said that he wanted more altitude so that if the glider didn't loop that they could get out of it safely.

They weren't so crazy that they didn't think they could make it; they wouldn't have tried it if that were the case. They thought they could loop that big, old glider. They called the pilot of their C-47 tow plane on the makeshift intercom and told him to take them to 10,000 feet because they wanted to loop the Horsa. There was an altitude restriction in the U.K. that stated that transports were not to fly above 5,000 feet. Only bombers and fighters could fly above 5,000 feet, nevertheless the tow pilot was game. He said "If you're damn fool crazy enough to try a loop I'll break regulations and take you up, but you'll have to promise me first that you will for sure do it. If after I break regulations and you don't there will be trouble." They promised to execute the loop and he took them up. After they reached 10,000 feet Terrell cut the glider loose from the tow plane and Charles put the glider into a dive to gain enough speed to carry them through the loop. The glider was red-lined at 195 mph airspeed and Charles exceeded that to 225 mph. That was as fast as he dared go, and then he pulled the wheel back hard into his lap and held it there. This is the way they looped a Piper Cub or a sailplane. The glider made it around okay, but as they were at the apex of the loop they nearly stopped cold; Charles's feet fell from the rudder pedals, and the wheel-chocks and the ladder that were on the floor in the glider and all of the seat cushions fell to the top of the glider with a terrible crash. For one short moment Charles wasn't sure if they were going to make it. It was a tremendous relief to move forward and down out of the momentary standstill and finally level out of the loop at 4,000 feet.

When they landed it was to the hoots and hollers of nearly everyone on the field. "Good goin' Steve," they were saying. They had quite a large appreciative audience. The tow pilot must have called the tower and said "Watch the air show; these fools are going to try and loop this thing!"

The celebration was extremely short-lived however, they were ordered to report to Major Daniels immediately. Charles said "Oh, now we've got it." Major Daniels hardly looked at them when they walked into his office. He stared fixedly at his desk, his papers or the wall, in a kind of nervous circuit. Charles and Terrell became mighty uneasy just watching him; he didn't have to say a word. When the major did speak his voice was stern as he launched into a lecture about all the rules that they had broken. Eventually though Charles imagined he could see the faintest trace of a smile that the major seemed to be struggling to hide. Finally the major couldn't contain himself any longer and gave a big smirk and said "Ah, hell, what's the use," and burst out laughing. "What on earth were you clowns trying to do? I never saw such a sloppy loop in all my life." They said "Well we'd looped everything that we've flown except this and we wanted to find out if it would loop." Major Daniels replied "Well, it's a hell of a thing to try, but I guess it will do if you want to call that a loop." Terrell then said "I've got one more ambition in my life." The major said "What's that?" "I want to loop a submarine!" The major gave a big guffaw and after a minute of tense silence he then said "What am I going to do about this?" Then he thought a minute more with that smile still on his face and started to laugh again in spite of himself and yelled in exasperation "Oh, get the hell out of here." Charles and Terrell didn't wait to be asked twice and hurried off out the door gasping big sighs of relief.

The next day a memo was issued to all of the glider pilots: "If anyone ever attempted to loop a Horsa glider it would be in flagrant violation of an order from the commanding officer and the offender would have his flying privileges revoked and would be court-martialed to the fullest extent!" As far as Charles knew he and Terrell were the only two pilots who had the experience of looping a Horsa glider.

Every glider pilot had stories but one of the most amazing glider stories that Charles ever heard was from an account in *Silent Wings*, the WWII glider magazine, about two gliders that cut off from their tow plane at the same time and somehow their tow ropes became entangled. They had been on double tow in a bad storm and were supposed to cut off and spread out, but their ropes had hooked together. The gliders followed each other around and landed with their ropes linked without the pilots knowing that they were connected. It wasn't until they got out of their gliders that they could see that their ropes were tied together. They had 600 feet of rope between them.

Those ropes could easily have gotten caught in the trees or brush or if they'd tried to land further apart who knows what would have happened. They were fortunate to be alive.

Chapter 30
Market-Garden and the New Co-Pilot

At the time of the invasion of southern France, two different large-scale air missions were planned: an invasion of southern France from Morocco and an invasion from eastern France in advance of Patton who was blazing a trail through France. All of the "older" more experienced glider pilots could choose which mission they wanted. Charles chose to fly ahead of Patton into eastern France. His squadron was split with half going to Morocco and half going to eastern France. His glider was loaded in England with airborne troops from the 101st ready to go in ahead of Patton, but Patton kept advancing so swiftly he'd overrun an area before they could even take off. Finally after ten days of waiting that mission was called off and they unloaded the gliders. The glider pilots from Charles's squadron that went to Africa for their mission from Morocco landed in southern France with very little opposition. It turned out to be more like a training exercise for them and they soon rejoined the group.

Next came the invasion of Holland, code named Market-Garden. It was a plan hatched by the British General Bernard Montgomery for a massive offensive that would, if its objectives were met, thrust the Allied troops into Germany and hopefully bring the war in Europe close to an end. Five bridges in Holland were to be captured and held so that Allied armored divisions could enter into the Ruhr Valley.

The 87th squadron took the 101st airborne into Eindhoven, Holland and was to capture the bridge there and the canal crossings from Eindhoven to Veghel. The 82nd airborne landed near Nimegan and was to seize the territory between Nimegan and Grave and the two bridges along that stretch. The British 1st airborne was dropped at Arnhem and was to take the bridge over the Lower Rhine River at Arnhem, the bridge that became famous as the ill-fated bridge chronicled in the motion picture "*The Bridge Too Far.*" The Polish Brigade parachuted down by Driel just south-west of Arnhem. The Allied airborne forces were scattered thinly along a 300-mile line. The British army was to drive "Hell bent" up the highway to the key crossings over the Rhine River bridges that airborne troops had secured.

It was the job of the airborne to try and keep the bridges intact and to cut off the enemy from a smooth retreat. They were to confuse and disorganize them so they wouldn't know which way to turn for an escape and to get reassembled. The British 2nd armored division was to make a mad dash to their aid in two days. The airborne were told that if everything went as planned and they could secure the area in two days then the British should be able to move forward, penetrating into the very heart of Germany. They wanted all this accomplished in October before the snow started to fall.

They didn't have enough glider pilots to staff the Market-Garden mission so the pilots were to fly without a co-pilot using the senior airborne man in the co-pilot's seat as back up if some additional muscle was needed to maneuver with or if anything happened to the pilot. Charles was assigned a medical unit in his glider, a jeep and five men. A doctor, a captain, was the senior man so Charles put him in the co-pilot's seat and started a lengthy discussion with him about what he should do in case Charles was killed or injured; how he could break off tow and land, the basics of flying a glider. Charles gave him very detailed explanations of what he should do and all the while the captain was nipping on a bottle and half-drunk. The first thing he did was to offer Charles his bottle. "Have a drink! Steady your nerves," he said. "No I don't drink," Charles responded. "Mind if I do?" was his question. "No it's your own business there," Charles said. All of his wonderful and informative instructions went in one ear and out the other. The captain said "Yah, yah nobody is going to shoot you." He paid no attention to Charles. He didn't say much but he had a long waxed, curled up mustache and every few minutes he'd twist it fondly and ask if Charles didn't want a nip on his bottle. Charles said no thank you, and soon they'd lifted off and the captain had finished his bottle. He lay down on the floor back under the jeep for awhile and then started in on his canteen which he'd also loaded.

Headquarters changed the route after take off. They were to fly further north than charted on the original route and this meant that they would be exposed to much more enemy fire in taking the new route, about forty-five minutes would be spent over enemy territory before reaching the drop zone. By the time they crossed the channel the captain was pretty well polluted. They were at 400 feet of altitude. As they flew over the beaches they could see German soldiers coming out of their pill-boxes and pointing their rifles up, and could see the puffs of smoke from their guns and hear the plinking sound of bullets ripping through the glider. This sobered the captain up right quick and he said desperately "Are they shooting at us?" Charles said "They're not playing games. Yah, they're shooting." Then with a heightened awareness of his situation the captain said "Wait a minute, what am I doing up here? What happens if you get hit? You weren't kidding when you said you could get killed, were you? What am I supposed to do?" Charles said exasperatedly "I've been telling you all the way across what you're supposed to do!" "Go through that again," he begged. Charles repeated his instructions telling him among other things to hit the release button to get off tow and to turn the glider to the left since Charles was on the short tow (the glider on the long tow would go to the right when releasing), and then to run the trim tab ahead and not to let the airspeed drop under forty-five mph and then to glide down and wait for the glider to land itself unless he had to turn to miss a tree or building. Charles said "There's 100 guys behind you in gliders and they'll run you over if you stay in the air so turn the glider out of the way." He tried to make it as simple as he could.

They were about ten miles inland when flack starting hitting them and planes and gliders started falling from formation. As they were flying over some of the major cities in the area they could hear what they called the "hack-hack guns" firing with a "pop." Flack from those guns hit Charles's left wing and tore a huge hole in it. It was about a four-foot hole. Immediately the glider dropped off and Charles could hardly hold it. The wing got so heavy that he was really struggling to hold it up to balance the glider. He adjusted the trim tabs to move out the tow to where the pull would give a little bit of extra lift, and Charles fought that glider until his arms and feet ached with the strain. Finally Charles said to the captain "I've got to have some help!" Charles told the captain to grab the wheel and to help him prop the wing up or to trade places with the biggest and strongest guy in the back and have him help, and have the rest of the guys in the back move everything to the right side of the glider. The captain didn't fail Charles. He said "You just tell me what you want me to do and I'll do it." Charles said "Hang on to the wheel here and hold it so the glider doesn't tip so I can rest a bit and take the other controls and try and get us through. Help me." "You bet I will," he said with conviction. This way they were able to stay in the air.

When they got within fifty miles or so of the drop zone Charles drew out the map. The firing had eased off a bit for the moment. Charles showed the men the area where they were supposed to land. Charles went through everything that they were going to need to do with the captain and the men in the back. He told the men "I can't make that, (the landing site where they were assigned to land). If I land up where I am supposed to near the command post, on the next field over to it where they're going to put the hospital, there are going to be gliders in the area and I'll wipe out our own troops." Charles knew that with the left wing damaged the way it was that he couldn't maneuver well enough to land in that field. He told the men that he'd have to land on the fringe of the drop zone so as to avoid colliding with other gliders. They weren't going to have a lot of control on the landing because he'd have to fly the glider into the group at an air speed of about 130 mph to 150 mph to keep the glider from going into a spin and crashing. "Whatever you have to do," they said.

Charles picked a landing spot on the outer edge of the drop-zone near some trees knowing they'd be under heavy fire, but also that they would not be as likely to wipe out other gliders or their own troops. That's where Charles knew that the Germans would be and he knew that they would be shooting at them, but taking their chances there would be better than risking killing their own troops.

One of the guys in the back said "How are we ever going to make that?" And then another said "Are the Germans going to be there?"

Charles said "Sure, the Germans will be there. They've infested this whole area. You fight your way from here to there."

"Well, I'm glad that you showed it to us. Now we know what to expect," said the captain.

From photos of the drop zone Charles knew that the fields were cross-laced with ditches so he also told the men that he was going to drop his wheels and land on the skids so they could get stopped faster. Charles told them that there were ditches that he could not possibly fly across and land between so that he was going to have to hit the ground on one side of the ditch and slow the glider a bit and then jerk it into the air to jump the ditch and then he would have to put on the skids and dig up the dirt to stop the glider before he got to the next ditch. Charles tried to tell them as best he could what to expect. It was going to be a rough landing he warned them.

"So buckle in tight."

"Okay, we're with you," they said. "We're holding on."

Charles told the men that when they landed not to try and run to the back of the glider to get through the door, but to exit through Charles's side window or tear through the sides of the glider if necessary with their trench knives and escape from the glider as fast as they possibly could and jump into a ditch for cover. Their survival depended on their getting out of the glider immediately. They'd have only seconds to escape, not minutes.

Then it was time to land. Charles said to the men "Here we are!" He cut loose and pulled the glider out of traffic and headed towards the field. Once they were in the right spot he dove the glider into the ground and dropped the wheels. He held his airspeed up to about 130 mph and came out of the dive and hit the ground and then quickly pulled the glider up again and jumped the first ditch. This slowed them up some and then Charles jammed the glider into the ground on the other side of the ditch filling the nose with dirt as he had done on the landing on maneuvers in North Carolina.

As they had gotten close to the ground machine guns started popping at them from every direction. They shot the glider full of holes. Upon landing Charles grabbed the struts above his head and swung over and burst out the side window almost before the glider came to a complete stop. All of the men followed right behind. They leaped into a ditch about twenty yards from the glider, and lay there while machine guns literally tore the fabric siding on the glider into shreds. Charles thought the Germans were going to blow it all to pieces the way that they were firing at it. They just kept their heads down and watched things going on as they could from the ditch.

Finally the firing quieted down and they could breathe a little more easily. Charles thought he saw some Germans leaving the area from where the firing had come and decided that it was time to unload the glider. He told the captain that he'd go back to the glider and try and get the jeep out. When Charles released the jeep the captain was to take a man and speed away in the jeep as fast as he could. Charles showed him on the map where the command post and the hospital were located and the best route to them. There was a set of gates that he'd have to pass through, a board gate and a wire gate. Charles didn't know if the gates would be open or closed. He said to the captain "Don't try to stop to open the gates. Just lower your head behind the windshield and crash through the board gate and do the same with the wire gate and hope that you'll break through. Do not stop. Floor board this thing. Go as fast as you can until you get to where the other gliders are landing." Charles told him that he'd take the other four men with him through the ditches and to the landing zone.

Charles crawled stealthily back to the glider and crept in through the holes in the sides. He then climbed into the jeep and started it up. He aggressively drove the jeep out through the back of the glider shell raising the nose of the glider as it went and showering himself with dirt from the formerly embedded nose. When the nose of the glider raised up another burst of gunfire hit the glider, but not the jeep. Charles parked the jeep alongside the ditch, ran out to the men and said "Go captain, go!" The captain and his man sped off in the jeep and Charles took the other four men with him. They came to a place where two ditches intersected as they were crossing the field and Charles could hear talking from one of the ditches and looked around and saw three or four German soldiers with their backs to them. Charles whispered to his men that he'd jump up and fire at the German soldiers to create a diversion while they ran up the other ditch and got away. He told them that they'd better hurry and run as fast as they could or he'd overrun them because he would be running like hell to get out of there. Charles stepped around the corner and turned his Tommy gun loose on the Germans and then ran like the devil and didn't stop to look back until they were in and around their own gliders and troops. Charles showed the four airborne where their unit was supposed to be and joined some other glider pilots at the command post. They were told to dig in and await further orders. Towards evening they were informed that they were all needed at the main bridge. The bridge was about a mile away so they all started walking towards it. They could see the remains of crashed planes and gliders all along the way. Dead bodies were everywhere. There were even bodies hanging in the trees, paratroopers dangling from their harnesses. All the while there was sporadic rifle fire so they were on their guard.

Chapter 31
Dutch Ingenuity

When they reached the bridge at Eindhoven they were given more ammunition and grenades and told to dig in because the Germans were determined to retake the bridge and establish a foothold there. They were told to expect to be fired upon from both the front and from the rear by Germans who had been cut off from their units on the other side of the bridge. Fighting went on all night. They were instructed to drop back once, and then to advance again. When daylight came the Allies still held the bridge, but it was reported that a tank had broken through their defenses and had gotten across the bridge. Charles was near the command post at the time this was reported, dug in his foxhole, and he saw and heard General Maxwell Taylor, the commanding officer of the 101st airborne, tell a sergeant to grab a bazooka and then the general himself jumped into a jeep and set out after the tank. He was going to get that tank! About fifteen minutes later the general was back. Witnesses said that the general personally got the tank. Charles always felt that "those guys weren't generals for nothing, they knew what they were doing."

G.L. Williams had an interesting experience with General Taylor. He went to sleep the night that he arrived in Holland and awoke to see General Maxwell Taylor of the 101st Screaming Eagles staring him right in the face up close and personal. Sometime in the night the general had joined them and had been sleeping right next to them on the ground. General Taylor regarded G.L. critically and said "Aren't you going to shave soldier?' G.L. wasn't in the best of moods after being awakened; he didn't say anything but in his head he was thinking, "We've got a battle going on and you're worried about whether I can pass inspection or not?" General Taylor then inquired about his socks—was he wearing wet socks? The general was adamant that the men change their socks so as to avoid trench foot. General Taylor was very tough and strict and G.L. who hadn't had one thought of shaving up until then got to it immediately using his metal helmet to put water in to help in the shaving process. Once he was presentable General Taylor then assigned him a duty; he and McVey were sent to assist in holding a bridge in the town of Son.

The airborne fought hard and held the area for five days before the British army started showing up, and instead of making a mad dash as they were told they would, one would have thought they were on a pleasure cruise or were guests arriving at a tea party. There was a German 88 gun that Charles could see in a patch of trees about a half mile away across the river, and every time a British Lorrie would pull around a curve in the road, that 88 gun would get it. After it hit about three Lorries and put them out of commission, it completely stopped the advancing column. A P-47 fighter plane was either called in or just happened to spot the German gun and made a low level pass over it and dropped a bomb and turned his guns on it and literally exploded the gun.

Charles and some other soldiers were alongside the river sitting behind a big log, and saw a German tank roll by on the other side of the river. One of the guys took a shot at it with his rifle, and the tank stopped and swiveled its turret around aiming the gun straight at them. There was a little brick building about 200 hundred yards directly behind them, and Charles guessed the Germans in the tank thought that was where the fire had come from because the next thing they knew the tank fired and the brick building was gone in a cloud of dust. Then the tank turned its turret and went on its way. The men didn't move an inch from behind the log until the tank was completely out of sight.

An air drop of badly needed supplies was scheduled to come in, but the Germans had infiltrated the drop zone during the night. That area was now infested with Germans. Securing the drop zone became the number one priority. Everyone was ordered to secure the drop zone so that they could get their supplies. All of the officers were assembled and the General told them "We must get this air drop or we are dead! Go through that field and clean it out of Germans. We are out of supplies. We are out of ammunition. We must not allow the air drop to fall into German hands or we are done for. We can't hold out." The American soldiers moved into the drop zone and around one thousand prisoners were taken that morning in clearing and securing the area. Charles and other glider pilots helped to count the prisoners and gather them into the stockade.

Then the word came down that they were to take no more prisoners; too many men were being tied up guarding and caring for the prisoners. One leader said "We cannot take any more prisoners. Don't take any more prisoners! Kill them because we can't feed them. We don't have supplies. We can't guard them. We don't have the personnel to guard them. No more prisoners."

The MPs came up and started moving the prisoners the glider pilots held from Stockade A to Stockade B. The glider pilots were assigned to guard the prisoners and count out those to be moved. They'd count out thirty men and turn them over to a paratrooper or to an MP to move them to the other stockade and then a predictable pattern began to emerge. The prisoners would be marched with their hands on their heads out into the forest into an isolated area and then they'd hear the "Brrrrr, Brrrrr," of a Tommy gun, and in a few minutes the paratrooper would come back with a frustrated look on his face and ask for thirty more men saying that the first thirty had made a break for it and he'd had to kill them all. So they'd give them twenty-five or thirty more men and off they'd go again this time going down a different trail. Once this had happened a few times all those German escape attempts began to sound suspicious. Later they discovered that there was no Stockade B. It was all a ruse.

When they got their orders to evacuate to Brussels, Belgium, there were only ten German officers and several hundred German soldiers that remained. That's where Charles states the 101st airborne got its reputation as the "Bloody Butcher Division." Afterwards Charles heard over the AFN radio (American Forces Network) that the Germans "would get even with the 101st for what they did to the German prisoners." Charles heard of all the atrocities the Germans did such as the Malmedy massacre in Belgium where nearly a hundred American prisoners of war were executed later during the Battle of the Bulge etc., but at the time none seemed to have been more brutal than what happened in Holland.

While they were waiting for supplies on one occasion when Charles and his group were guarding two dozen German soldiers a girl approached one of the prisoners crying and carrying on. She suddenly threw her arms around the prisoner weeping, and as she did they could see that she passed something to him. The troopers separated them, and spotted the package the girl had given the prisoner. A trooper grabbed it and as he did the girl ran away across a small canal bridge and down a trail along the canal. When the trooper opened the package he found a sandwich with a small caliber pistol between two slices of bread. He hit the prisoner with the butt of his rifle dropping him, and then ran for the girl. He jumped into the canal and came out on the other side just a step or two behind the girl. He was up to her in a flash and bayoneted her in the back knocking her to the ground, and then pulled the trigger of the gun. She was gone just that quickly. The German soldier didn't cry out or show any emotion for her. It was like it didn't matter to him that she had lost her life in attempting to save him. Like the German soldier, Charles felt that they all lost their sense of balance or understanding of what was important at times during the conflict.

Shortly after this incident Charles and some other glider pilots were watching some of the air fights as the planes flew over and they saw one of theirs being hit and catching fire. They knew the plane was going to crash and that it would clear them. Three or four parachutes suddenly popped out and the crew floated down into some trees just beyond the area the Allies had taken. The Germans were in that area. About a dozen pilots including Charles immediately said "Let's go help those guys out," and took off for where they thought they might have dropped. They ran sneaking along as quickly and quietly as they could hiding behind whatever they could find for cover so that they wouldn't be picked off before they reached the downed crew. They found the crew alright. They were dangling from the trees where they had been shot and their chutes set on fire. The flames were singeing their dead bodies.

Seeing those burning men hanging from the trees, sickened and enraged Charles and the other pilots. The feelings of brotherhood and hope that had led them to that spot turned to intense hatred and disgust. They wanted to shoot every German they could find. Just give them a tank and they'd go in there and take them all on. They walked back to their area hunting for Germans all the way. They were hoping that a German would stick his head out so that they could shoot him and they could have a fight. They were spoiling for a fight. Good judgment would have said hey, just get out of there, but they were beyond judgment. They didn't

find any Germans, and it was probably a good thing. They
had lost all sense; nothing mattered anymore but getting the
Germans. To Charles it was "a helluva of an awful feeling."
Charles hated to even reflect upon it.

When the air drop finally arrived about three days after
it was due, seeing the American soldiers all assembled, there
was a large group of Dutch people from a nearby town that
took courage and came out of hiding like rabbits from their
burrows, and began to be quite friendly towards the soldiers.
They were clustered all around. When the drop planes came
in, a huge formation of C-47s at about 600 feet, the people's
cautious but calm attitude changed to abject terror. They
immediately scattered to look for shelter. They feared there
were bombers coming after them and that they had been
caught out in the open.

As the parachutes came to the ground with their loads
the soldiers ran for them, and then grabbed the supplies and
discarded the chutes. Each parabundle weighed about 200
pounds and was about the size of a duffle bag. They'd just
kick those heavy bundles out the door. The chute was on a
static line so that when the parabundles dropped they would
break the lines and the chutes would pop out the door of
the plane and float the supplies right down to the ground. A
stream of them came floating down. The chutes were colored
according to their cargo: white for medical supplies, red for
ammunition, yellow for K-Rations, green for gas cans etc...

When the Dutch realized that they were in no danger
they silently emerged from their hiding places and observed
the American soldiers gathering in the supplies. Once the
Dutch discovered that the soldiers didn't care about the nylon
parachutes they started retrieving the bundles and cutting
the chutes free from the bundles before the soldiers could
get to them. Eventually they had to be restrained until the
contents of the bundles were identified. The soldiers would
pick up a bundle not knowing what was in it. They needed
to get to the bundles first then the people could take all the

chutes they wanted. When the Dutch understood the process things went better. The next day or so all the Dutch in the area were wearing brightly colored garments; green, yellow, red and white dresses and such, all made out of the discarded parachutes.

Chapter 32
A Gun that Doesn't Fire

By the time they were ordered back to Brussels (seven days after the Market-Garden invasion) for an airlift to London for another possible air drop, the British had pretty well advanced to Eindhoven. Brussels was about sixty miles away but it was the closest site where they could be flown out of to London. They were told to get there however they could, by truck, jeep whatever they could use to get them there the quickest. As it turned out they traveled by British Lorry. A captain that knew Charles assigned him to take charge of the first truck of German prisoners that was being shipped to a British compound near Brussels. They gave Charles an airborne to help with the prisoners—so had two guns, Charles's Tommy gun and the airborne's little carbine. Charles instructed the paratrooper that if the Germans challenged that between the two of them they were to see that none of the prisoners came out alive.

One of the prisoners was a German colonel that was all Nazi. Every other word out of his mouth was a curse upon them. He'd call them "filthy pigs" and those "bloody, damn Yankees" and everything else in the book. The colonel was

also speaking to his men in sharp tones in German. The little
Jewish paratrooper that was assigned to Charles could speak
German. He said to Charles "Sir, do you understand what he's
saying?" "No, not really," Charles replied. "I know he's cussing
and I don't like it." "He's telling them first chance they get to
jump you, stop the Tommy gun, and to stop this column." The
paratrooper then said "I'm going to shut him up if it's all right
with you." "No, you don't have to shut him up, I'll talk to him,"
Charles said. Charles knew the colonel spoke fluent English
so he said to him "Colonel, I don't understand German, but
I understand what you are telling your men. You are number
one to be killed if anything happens to this convoy. If we are
challenged, or if we are stopped for any reason by German
forces my orders are to kill every prisoner. You are first in my
sights. I will take the top of your head off if I hear another word
from you about trying to kill us or if anyone tries to jump me.
So you're in danger if you keep running off at the mouth."
Charles's orders were if they were stopped or challenged in
any way by the German forces to shoot all of the prisoners.
All of the American soldiers had these orders whenever they
held prisoners. Well, that didn't stop him from cursing up a
storm again. It was "those bloody Yankees" and "all you pigs
are alike" stuff once more. The paratrooper persisted, "Let
me talk to him. I understand what he's saying." Charles said
okay and the airborne walked over to the colonel and stuck
his carbine in his mouth and said "One more sound out of
you colonel and you're a dead man." The colonel sat back and
closed his mouth and they heard no more from him.

It was stormy and rainy in Brussels when they arrived so
no planes could land there. They turned their prisoners in to
MPs at a camp just outside of the city and Charles traded his
Tommy gun to the first American he saw, an American MP,
for his carbine. Charles thought the MP seemed very glad to
get a Tommy gun. They were billeted in the Cosmopolitan
(or Continental Hotel, Charles couldn't exactly remember),
the biggest and best hotel right in the heart of Brussels. The

British had bypassed the city, and the outskirts were still under siege by the Germans, but Brussels had been declared an open city. Neither the Allies nor the Germans could bomb it, just as Paris, Reims and some other places had been made open cities. Brussels had been under German occupation and they were the first American troops that the city's people had seen. The American soldiers all wore invasion patches with American flags sewn onto their left sleeves, so they were easy to identify. The people were thrilled to see Americans and wouldn't let them pay for anything. There were two soldiers to a room in the finest suites in the hotel where each room had a private maid to shine shoes, draw baths, or do whatever they wanted. The glider pilots could hardly believe how they were spoiled. Meals were even served in the rooms if they wanted. It was like a dream after being in combat.

After six days in the field the soldiers were as dirty as could be and looking pretty wild so they tried to do some cleaning up. Charles needed a haircut so he went down to the lobby. There was a barber there with about four men in line ahead of Charles. As soon as Charles walked into the shop the guy who was getting his haircut jumped out of the barber's chair and said "You're next." Charles said "Well, no I don't want to cut ahead of anyone." "No, no, no," they said, "Americans come, you're next." Much to Charles's chagrin they all insisted that he go first and wouldn't take no for an answer because he was an American soldier.

So he got in the chair to ask for a haircut and the barber lit a flame on a candle and took his comb and brushed Charles's hair "shhhhh," and singed his hair with the flame. The barber cut his hair with the flame of a candle! That was the first time Charles had seen or heard anything about such a thing. It was an excellent haircut, but the barber refused to take a cent for his work. He just wouldn't hear of it. "You are liberators," he said.

The soldiers were still a little uneasy in Brussels because there was some fighting and sniping going on so they took what guns they had wherever they went; Charles had the carbine and a .45 in his holster. That evening about six of the glider pilots decided that they'd go to a show. They stopped at the first theatre they could find. Carmen was playing on stage. They walked into the lobby and asked "Do you have any seats?" "Oh, yes of course we do." "How much is the show?" Once again the owners wouldn't take money for anything and insisted that the tickets were free. Then the usher asked where they'd like to sit, "Anyplace you like," he said. Charles's friend Wheelock could speak French and told the usher "anyplace near the front." The usher then replied "How about third row center?" Wheelock said okay. The usher left for a minute and returned saying "Follow me." He then opened the curtain into the theatre and switched on his flashlight to guide them.

As they started down the aisle to their seats the houselights flashed on in a blaze of light and the show which was already in progress completely stopped and everyone in the theatre rose as the orchestra played a stirring rendition of "The Star Spangled Banner." The pilots then saw to their shame that the usher had moved six people out of their seats to make room for them. Charles was never so embarrassed in all his life. They took those poor people's seats! Oh, he felt like a fool for knocking them out of their seats. If Charles could he would have crawled right under his seat and slunk out the back door.

After they played the Star Spangled Banner the houselights dimmed and the show finally commenced again and proceeded in French. Charles didn't understand a word of it but the music was beautiful. He always felt that they shouldn't have done that; accepted those seats. They didn't even really know what they were going into. They'd thought it was a picture show.

After the show it was time to retire to their luxurious hotel room; the room with a bath and a maid in the room attending. Anything that a person wanted was free. No money was accepted from Americans. Oh, they could scarcely believe it.

The next morning it was still stormy and the pilots were informed that there would be no planes coming in from England. Charles and Wheelock decided to take a stroll and see the sights of the city. There were British MPs around the hotel and the town, but just a block or two away from the hotel conditions were unsafe. There were snipers firing at the British. Charles and Wheelock had to dodge fire when they were shot at once on their walk.

They stopped in a little plaza and were looking at a large public monument with old statues and inscriptions when a man came running at full speed towards them shouting "Americans, Americans," and waving his hands wildly above his head. They didn't know whether he would attack them or was directing fire at them or what to think. Wheelock said "I don't like the looks of that guy. He might have a grenade. What the hell's goin' on here?" To the man he yelled "Halt or I'll shoot," and he drew his gun. "Halt or I'll shoot!" he warned even more loudly. "Oh Americans, Americans," the man repeated and just kept on coming. Charles pulled out his .45 pistol and aimed at him, but couldn't bring himself to fire for some reason. Something held him back. After they'd warned the man two or three times and he ignored them, Wheelock decided that they'd better shoot him. Wheelock was fumbling trying to get his .45 out but had it caught some way and was yelling at Charles "Shoot, shoot!" When Wheelock did get his gun out he couldn't seem to make it fire, "trrp, trrp," it would snap but his gun wouldn't fire. He pumped another shell in it but it still wouldn't fire so he kept on yelling at Charles. "Shoot him, shoot him!" Charles said "Doesn't look like he's got anything." "He's probably got a grenade waving his hands like that. Shoot him, shoot him," Wheelock hollered. Charles held his gun out on the flap, but by this time he could see the man clearly and held off because he could tell that he didn't have anything in his hands, and Charles didn't feel that they were in any kind of danger. Charles let him come up to them without challenging him.

When he reached them the man kept saying with great feeling, "Americans, Americans," and told them how glad he was to see them, and asked what part of America they were from. He said "Welcome, welcome," and "You are the first Americans that I've seen." They told him where they were from, Idaho and New Hampshire, and he asked if they knew where Salt Lake City, Utah was. Charles told him that he lived only 156 miles from it, and then he wanted to know if Charles had ever seen the Mormon Temple there. Charles said surprised "Yes, I've been in it." The man said excitedly "Are you Mormon?" And Charles answered yes, that he was. The man, overjoyed, threw his arms around Charles and gave him a big hug. Tears came into his eyes and he could hardly talk he was so choked with emotion. He said that it was his life's dream to go to the temple in Salt Lake City. Charles talked to him for about an hour about the church and then he invited Charles to visit their small branch (parish) outside of the city. It was about two miles outside of Brussels. He told Charles that he was the Elders Quorum President and begged Charles to come and speak to the quorum. This was against regulations and Charles didn't dare go; there was also too much sniping still going on. The man was asking him to enter occupied territory. Charles was sorry but no way could he do that. Charles thanked him for the invitation but had to decline. The man said "I will guarantee your safety. We'll bring the whole quorum, I'll guarantee your safety if you come to our ward. We'd like to show our appreciation to the Americans for our liberation," and so on. "I'm sorry," Charles just had to say; he couldn't go.

Charles kept thinking after this meeting, suppose he would have shot this guy? Normally he would have. Any other time a guy approaches a soldier under those circumstances refusing to stop, they would have been shot. Charles couldn't fully explain the feeling that came over him as he held the gun on the man and every reason told him to fire, but he couldn't, and sure was grateful that he didn't. Wheelock kept badgering him afterwards asking why he didn't shoot, and Charles had no answer to give him. Wheelock said "I would have killed that man." He kept asking Charles how he knew the man was a Mormon, and Charles told him that he didn't know. Charles only knew that he couldn't shoot.

Soon the weather cleared and they were flown to England to await other missions. Wheelock came up one day and said "Let's take a little stroll out in the toolies here and test my gun. I want to see what's wrong with my damn gun. I can't see anything wrong with it, but it wouldn't fire. It misfired twice. Let's go check and see if it's alright." "Okay," that was fine with Charles. He strapped on his .45 and Wheelock took his gun and they set off out in the boondocks beyond the base a bit. They threw a can up out there and Wheelock said "Let's see if I can hit that can." "Pow," the gun fired right off on the first shell and hit that can straight on.

"Well, I wonder why it didn't fire over there in Brussels," he puzzled. He tried it again for a second time. "Well, what in the devil is goin' on," he said "There's nothin' wrong with my gun so why didn't it fire? And why didn't you fire? That man could have blown us up if he'd had a grenade."

"If he'd had a grenade I would have shot him," Charles said.

"How did you know that he didn't have one?"

"I didn't know, but I just had no desire to shoot him." And it went on. It all seemed some great mystery to him.

Chapter 33
Nuts!

On December 16th of 1944 just before Christmas, the Germans counterattacked and swept through the French forests of Ardennes in an effort to push to the port of Antwerp, and cut off Allied supply lines. The Allies were caught off guard in the dead of winter at a time when they had pulled some of the front line fighting units back for a little R&R (rest and relaxation) and had plugged in new units on the front lines in a hold ground position, with the troops being scattered thinly. From the reports that the soldiers were getting in England the situation sounded bad for awhile as the Germans broke through the lines in different places. This German operation made history as "The Battle of the Bulge."

There had been pretty much a static line with the weather itself becoming an obstacle to the Allied forces, but the Germans continued to rally and to beef up their forces along the line massing tanks and supplies at critical points. Then with renewed strength the Germans hit the line like a battering ram, smashing their way through. The Allies were scrambling to fight to regain territory that was lost along the line and to break through to the German side. Some of the Allied units were surrounded and the call went out for an airborne offensive to provide relief for these units. The minute that the Allies had notice that the Germans had broken through the line the glider pilots were put on alert and told to be ready for an emergency airborne mission. So they started loading up the gliders.

Soon word came that the 101st at Bastogne was surrounded and might be totally wiped out. The Germans asked them if they wanted to surrender. Brigadier General Anthony McAuliffe's famous reply was the emphatic "Nuts!" Just imagine the headache that word gave the German translator. "Vhat itsch dist 'nuts'? Dhat means you say no?" The Germans couldn't decipher General McAuliffe's meaning and their attack was temporarily stalled until they could get further clarification. General McAuliffe and his men were not going to give up without a fight. They were going to try and hold out for as long as they possibly could with the hope that help would arrive soon.

Charles and his group were ordered on full alert for an airborne mission to take the 17th airborne division to St. Vith to relieve the 101st and to assist them in maintaining their hold on the key road system there and to stop the Germans in their powerful charge to muscle through the lines. The Allies still held the major crossroads there, but their grip was slipping.

St. Vith was a little village right next to Bastogne. There was less timber there than in the surrounding areas so it was thought that the gliders would have an easier time landing. The gliders were loaded, marshaled and ready on the 20th of December, but ended up sitting on the runway for three days waiting for the weather to clear. The engines on the tow planes were kept warmed up and the tow ropes were hooked to the gliders, all in readiness, just waiting for the skies over the drop-zone to clear.

Some of the units who had already moved into France

were close enough that if the weather broke even for an hour they could and did make the flight in, but none made it from England. In fact, the glider pilots flying in from different bases in France were a tremendous help to the soldiers in Bastogne. Gliders and parachute drops delivered 1,050 tons of supplies that allowed the Allied forces to maintain their tenuous hold in the area. Some of those gliders were transporting gasoline in dangerously large quantities.

Private Robert A. Flory, 506th Parachute Infantry Regiment, 101st airborne, states his feelings about the gliders and tow planes that came to their aid.

"We would not be able to repulse another attack. We were praying for an ammunition resupply; forget the food, just bring us some ammo. About 10:00 A.M. the fog began to lift, and we could hear the sound of distant aircraft. First came a wave of P-38 Lightnings going after those German tanks and artillery and antiaircraft positions. Then we could hear the distinctive sound of those beautiful C-47's. Looking to the west, we could see a skytrain of C-47's towing gliders through all kinds of German ground fire. The first serial of three planes was coming in at about 1,000 feet, but the lead plane was on fire. That C-47 pilot never wavered. We could tell that he was determined to tow that glider to the proper landing zone. At just the right moment the glider pilot released and, after a steep, diving bank to the left, that pilot brought that beautiful craft to a perfect landing right next to the gun pits of those 75mm pack howitzers. I have no idea how the glider pilot knew what we needed and where, but that glider was loaded with 75mm artillery shells. And that heroic C-47 pilot flew his plane to a crash landing in German territory. Later, another wave of C-47's flew over and dropped more supplies by

> parachute. Then more gliders came in carrying
> K rations, C rations, gasoline, and much-needed
> ammunition. Several planes were shot down and
> some gliders landed behind German lines. But with
> the simply extraordinary efforts of those tow pilots
> and glider pilots, we were able to start pounding the
> hell out of those Germans again."[20]

In preparation for their mission to Bastogne Charles and the other glider pilots took turns guarding their planes and gliders on the runway while others were eating or getting a four-hour rest period. On December 24 the pilots were told that there was a high possibility that German prisoners in the U.K. might try and escape from prison camps and the pilots were ordered to stay through the night in their gliders and to take turns sleeping and guarding the loads. There was a big compound just across the field with numerous German prisoners. If they had broken loose the first thing they would have done would have been to head for the airplanes and gliders. So Charles sat in a hulking British Horsa on Christmas Eve with a Tommy gun propped in his lap.

On Christmas day the situation in Bastogne was so desperate that it was decided that the gliders should fly to their aid despite the treacherous weather. They'd just have to risk it. They had barely gotten a few planes into the air when they were called back and told to land before the rest of the squadron got off the ground. Charles had just reached the channel when his tow plane received word that the mission was aborted. They were told to wait another day and see if they were needed because General Patton's 4th armored division had broken through to relieve the 101st. When the weather cleared their services were no longer needed and the mission was cancelled.

The C-47's were flying cargo missions quite frequently. The glider pilots were detailed to tear the glider shipping crates apart and to salvage the lumber from them. They had huge piles of good boards all over the place. The glider pilots were asked to take Officer of the Day duty in the nearby towns because there had been such a large transfer of commissioned officers to France that there weren't enough around in England to do this kind of duty. Charles agreed and was OD twice a week for two weeks at Newbury. He was given a .45-caliber pistol, a whistle, a jeep, a sergeant, and a carpool with a weapons carrier if needed. He was to patrol all the joints and the theatres and whatever public places the soldiers frequented. There were still four troop carrier air bases in the area though most were stationed across the channel: an American airborne division, a couple of British posts and a Negro Quartermaster outfit each within twenty miles of the town. There was a big dance hall and always plenty of girls to dance with but quite a bit of friction between the white and black soldiers, and between the American and British soldiers. The English girls would dance or date anyone and that made some people very unhappy. American and English soldiers didn't like white girls dating the black soldiers and there were many fights over it.

Charles went into the dance hall one night and heard a commotion coming from the men's restroom. He pushed on the door to go in, but it wouldn't budge. It was being held shut from inside. He pounded on the door and yelled "Open up!" A black soldier opened the door a crack and said "We got the situation under control white boy," and shut the door in Charles's face. Charles pulled out his .45 and banged it on the door and the soldier opened it again ready to tell Charles off, but when he saw the .45 and the armband he backed away and Charles was able to enter the room.

When Charles entered he saw three other black soldiers and one white GI that was really taking a working over. Charles lined them all up against the wall with their hands in the air without really knowing what he was going to do with them. The white guy was bruised up and had a bloody nose and looked like the devil, but said that he was okay. Charles asked him what had happened and they all started talking at once. It seemed that the white soldier had a date with a girl that night that one of the black soldiers had dated and the black soldier was afraid that he'd take her away from him. Charles asked where the girl was but they said that she had gone. By then, quite a crowd had gathered, and Charles's sergeant came into the building. Charles told him to take the black soldiers out to the weapons carrier. He pulled out his .45 and marched them out. Different groups around said that the white GI hadn't done anything wrong, that the black soldiers had caused it all and some other black soldiers confirmed the story so Charles let the white soldier go and told him to go back to his base and get cleaned up.

The sergeant and Charles drove to the Quartermaster base in the weapons carrier with the four black soldiers in the back. The black soldiers started talking to each other about what had happened and how they wished they hadn't gotten involved, and how if Charles took them to their Provost Marshal they would be restricted to base for the duration of their time in the U.K. Charles stopped the carrier about fifty yards from the gate and ordered them to fall out and stand at attention. While they stood bolt upright eyes looking nervously ahead Charles instructed them that he'd let them go. They wouldn't be restricted, but he'd be on duty for the next two weeks and he didn't want to see them in any kind of trouble again. They thanked him profusely and for that moment were four of the best acting fellows imaginable.

As they drove away the sergeant said, "You know sir, I thought there for awhile that you were going to take them in," and then he told Charles that not only would they be restricted to base, but that they'd get every dirty detail that came along, because the officers over them were white, and determined to maintain tight discipline at all cost. They were only allowed a minimum of passes anyway.

There was a lot of discrimination in the service at that time. In the South where Charles had been stationed, blacks still had to ride in the back of the buses, and were not allowed to eat in the white restaurants. Even the theatres had a section roped off marked "colored," where they had to sit.

Growing up in Montpelier Charles had never known or even seen any black people except maybe folks involved with the carnivals or circuses that came through town. He didn't recall there being any black families living or children attending school in the valley. And it was the same attending college at Utah State. The first time he ever took any notice of them was in the service. When he left Fort Douglas in Salt Lake on a train and was assigned to take charge of the men in his car; there was also a car load of black troops on the train. In Colorado when they disembarked from the train for a meal Charles marched his car to a restaurant at the station. The black car followed right behind until they reached the restaurant, and the black men were marched to the rear entrance for their meal. This was new to Charles and didn't seem right. Charles and other soldiers talked amongst themselves about the unequal treatment black soldiers were given.

Later Charles was shocked still more by the way in which the black soldiers were treated at the different army bases. In New Orleans at the base theatre there were two ticket booths. One was for whites and one was for blacks. Blacks had the seats on each side of the theatre down front for about the first ten or twelve rows marked with "Colored" signs. These signs could be moved from row to row depending on how many seats were needed for the whites.

When Charles received his first pass to go to town in New Orleans he got together with five other men and boarded the bus as a group. At first it wasn't very crowded but once they got closer to town the bus filled up. There was a "Colored" sign marking off four or five rows to the back of the bus. About halfway to town seven women boarded the bus and there were no available seats for them. All the seats in the white section were filled so Charles and his group rose and gave the ladies their seats. There was one woman still standing and in back of the "Colored" sign there were two empty seats, one behind the other.

A guy named Williams with Charles's group walked back and moved the "Colored" sign back one seat and asked the black soldier sitting in that row if he would move back a seat so that the lady could sit down. The black soldier looked up at him and said "White boy, I done paid for this seat and I gonna sit right here." Williams taken aback snarled "What did you say?" And the man said "Like I told you, I done paid for this seat, and I gonna sit right here." Williams reached into his pocket and took out a switch blade and pushed the button on the knife and a three-inch blade shot out and he jammed it against the guy's throat and said, "Nigger get up!" He did and the lady sat down.

Charles was shocked and dumbfounded; he had never seen anything like that before. When they got off the bus he asked Williams "What would you have done if that GI said again that he'd paid for that seat and he was going to sit right there?" Williams responded "I would have slit his throat from ear to ear and removed him from that seat." Williams was three or four years older than the rest of the soldiers in the group and said that he had worked on a rubber plantation on one of the islands. He'd been a foreman of a "nigger crew" as he put it and said he always wore a .45-caliber pistol on his hip, rode a horse and had a three-foot-long black snake whip that he used to control the crew. He was one mean, tough customer.

Charles felt during his time in the service that the black soldiers really had it rough and were treated unfairly. They often got the dirtiest details and missed out on some of the benefits that others enjoyed being soldiers. They proudly wore the same uniform that Charles did and represented the same country, but were not treated the same.

Chapter 34
The Orange Trade

In February 1945, Charles and Terrell received orders to move to Reims, France. Charles was to go as one of ten officers and fifty enlisted men in an advanced echelon to set up a base there. He was assigned to be the mess officer (of all things) and had two cooks and four other enlisted men in his detail. He was given a jeep and a driver at his disposal and was responsible for seeing that the mess was ready for operation, for drawing rations from the Quartermaster and for planning the meals in conjunction with the cooks. That was his official job but he was an impromptu jack of all trades helping in any way that he could to get the camp set up. Lumber and tents came from England by the plane load and everyone was busy building floors, pitching tents and getting everything ready for the troops that would soon be arriving.

The cooks handed Charles a list every morning of the items they needed to prepare the meals. Charles took the jeep to the Quartermaster's and picked up whatever was needed. He'd usually end up talking the Quartermaster out of giving him something that wasn't on the list, such as an extra dozen loaves of bread or three or four extra hams etc... They were always trying to give him more than he requested. One day they had some oranges so Charles ended up with four crates of oranges to take to the men.

That evening the cooks put an orange on everyone's plate. It wasn't often that they had so many oranges so everyone thought that it was a real treat. They only used about a crate and a half of oranges at dinner so Charles decided to put another orange on each plate for breakfast.

About eight at night Charles walked over to the mess tent and noticed that the two crates of oranges were gone, and so was the weapons carrier. He went looking for the cooks and found that one of them and a GI had taken the oranges and had gone to a small village down the road a few miles. Charles went back to his tent and talked Terrell into going on a ride with him. They put on their .45s and OD armbands and got into the jeep and took off down the road.

When they reached the village there was the weapons carrier parked in plain sight on the main road. They approached the building where the weapons carrier was parked and as they opened the building door out trooped the cook and his helper. Were they ever surprised to see Charles! The cook fumbled for words and finally said "I thought that the men would rather have champagne and wine so I traded the oranges for them." Then out marched a bevy of Frenchmen with six cases of champagne and wine. Charles said "Well, I guess that's a fair trade, but I'll take it back to the base." So Charles got into the weapons carrier with the cook and Terrell took the Pfc. with him in the jeep and they headed to the base.

On the way the cook said nervously, "Are you going to press charges against me?" Charles told him no, that he thought that he had made a good trade, but that he wanted it made clear that the champagne and wine would be passed out to the whole group. The next day for the evening meal they set six cases out for the men to each take a bottle of whatever they wanted. Major Harwell wanted to know how the devil

Charles had gotten champagne out of the Quartermaster and had a good laugh when he heard the story.

There was a lot of open space near the base. Charles wondered whether it had been agricultural land or not, but it was not in production at that time. They'd take walks through the fields and sometimes do some shooting practice. There was a huge valley that they avoided with big eight-foot wire fencing all along printed with the words "Forbidden Area: Mustard Gas from WWI," in every language imaginable. The locals told them that people had gone into the valley and never returned. The gas was thought to be still concentrated in the valley.

One Sunday Charles and Terrell took a couple of carbines and went out onto the plain. They were going to try and hunt jackrabbits. Charles knew they were in jackrabbit country. So far the only threat of invasion they'd had in Reims was from jackrabbits. Charles had been on guard duty one night and assigned to monitor all of the base guards when he'd first learned about the jackrabbit menace. Guards were posted all along the perimeter of the base with one man in a big 6X6 truck with a soft shell cab on it and two fifty-caliber machine guns. The guard there would sit for four hours posted in the truck and then the guards would change positions. That night about eleven or twelve o'clock Charles heard the machine gun ripping away "Brrrrrrr, rup, rup, brrrrrrr," and jumped into the jeep to check the guard post at the truck. He found the guard shooting away like crazy. "What's going on?" Charles demanded. The guard looked a bit sheepish and said, "It's these damn jackrabbits. They are overrunning me. Man, it's fun to shoot them!" Twin fifty-caliber machine guns shooting at jackrabbits with a searchlight!

So there were Charles and Terrell with their rifles slung across their shoulders looking for jackrabbits. They weren't alone on their quest; soon they noticed quite a number of country folk scattered throughout the area. They were taking nets and putting them over the rabbit holes. Then they'd take ferrets out of their pockets and put them down the holes. Pretty soon there would be a squeal and out would jump the rabbits right into their nets. They'd whack them on the heads and they'd have their dinners for that night.

When the people spotted the two American soldiers with their guns all activity ceased. They just stared at them with a look of terror in their eyes. Charles was sure they thought they'd shoot them. Neither Charles nor Terrell spoke any French so they kind of ho hummed around trying to appear as harmless and non-threatening as they could until finally one man made motions to them of what they were doing and Charles asked, "You're catching rabbits?"

"*Oui, oui, diner, diner.*"

Charles said "Okay, go ahead we'll just watch."

"You not stop us, not stop us?"

"No, no we just want to see what's going on." So they went ahead and put the nets down and caught a couple of rabbits and scooped them up in their nets.

Some of the rabbits would escape in areas where the nets didn't quite cover the hole. The rabbits would rush out of there with the ferrets chewing on their hind ends and the people would grab the ferrets and stuff them in their pockets and the rabbits would lope off and then at about twenty or thirty yards away turn to see if they were still being pursued and cast a taunting glance back. That's when Charles and Terrell decided to shoot the runaway rabbits. They went out and downed the first rabbit and instantly everyone stopped and became silent again. "Oh no," Charles knew they were thinking, "we've had it now." Charles and his buddy walked out into the field and got the rabbit and brought it back and offered it to them.

"Would you like this?"

"For me, for me?" they questioned.

"Yah, you can have it."

"You no want it, you no want?"

"No we don't."

"Oh, you shoot rabbits for us?"

"Yah, sure," and so it went. They put the ferrets down the holes and out would come the rabbits. The people would clear out of the way and the Americans would shoot the rabbits. They shot about a dozen jackrabbits for them that way. To their minds they had some good shooting. The French would whack the rabbits on the head and into their bags they'd go to be taken home for dinner. Those people had nothing. For Charles and Terrell it was sport, but for them it was life.

They saw a ranch house out on the plain and Charles thought that they should visit some time and see if they could trade some rations for eggs. When they were in England if there weren't any eggs in the mess hall they'd go to one of the nearby farms and trade for eggs or for bread. They'd boil the eggs and add a little vinegar and pickle them and eat them with a big piece of English bread, marinated mustard and with sardines or cheese or anything they had. They'd buy the huge loaves of English bread; it seemed like the bread must have weighed around five pounds; the bread was so heavy and soggy without any wrappings on it and they'd cut it in thick slices and toast it black on top of the potbellied stoves. Was that bread ever tasty with all of the stuff piled on it! Charles and his fellow *gourmands* so looked forward to eating their bread creations!

Charles took Wheelock with him to a farm house near Reims on an egg run. Wheelock spoke a little French Canadian and told Charles that he thought he could make himself understood. Their plan was just to see if they couldn't buy some eggs and pickle them and have a little snack. To trade Charles had an old pair of GI shoes that hurt his feet strung on shoelaces around his neck and they'd filled their pockets with candy bars, a couple of packs of cigarettes, a couple of bars of soap and they each had an orange in their pocket.

As they approached the house they could see several sets of eyes peering out from behind the curtains. Whenever they thought that the two Americans might see them they darted behind the curtains as quick as could be. They seemed to be frightened. Charles and Wheelock knocked on the door and a woman answered with a bushel of children clinging to her skirts. Wheelock tried to speak to her in French Canadian and it seemed to Charles that it was enough like European French that she understood. She spoke to them in French; "*Non*," she said she did not have any eggs to sell. Charles and Wheelock had seen quite a few chickens out back, but they said okay, she didn't have to sell. One of her children who was all eyes began peeking around the door and Charles took an orange out of his pocket and said "Would you like this?" The child just stared at his out-stretched hand, not knowing how to respond. The woman then said in perfect English, much better than Wheelock's French,

"She doesn't know what an orange is. She's never seen an orange."

Charles continued "Would you like to have this for her?"

"Oh, you don't know how much it would mean to have my children have something like that," she thrilled.

So then Wheelock said "I have one for you too. We have only the two of them, but you are welcome to them." Charles gave her an orange and she started to cry.

Charles said "Is your husband here?"

She answered "No, he is with the Germans on the Russian front. He had to go with the Germans. I am alone taking care of this place."

Charles said "Would you like this," and gave her some candy bars and some gum. "How about these cigarettes?"

"I don't smoke, but I know someone who would love to have them," she said. So Charles gave her the cigarettes. She turned to her children and rattled something off in French and they all scattered and Charles could hear the slamming of the back door.

They talked with her for a few more minutes and then gave her a bar of soap. At that she just broke down and bawled. "Oh," she moaned, "I haven't seen a bar of soap since the Germans occupied France. I would love to have a hot bath with a bar of soap." They gave her all the soap that they had and then asked if she knew anyone who could use Charles's old shoes. "Oh, *oui*," she said that she would love to have those shoes. Charles gave her the shoes and she sat and cried and cried while Charles and Wheelock looked on helplessly. She said "I couldn't believe that Yankee soldiers would give us something like this. The German soldiers would come and shoot us. They would come and take anything they wanted and they would shoot us. I was afraid that the American soldiers might do the same thing." She had been scared to death that way. They said "Oh, no, no," that they wouldn't harm her and her children. They were getting ready to leave and Charles said that he hoped that the children would enjoy the candy when there came a clatter and the children came rushing in with water buckets filled to the brim with eggs.

The woman said "We have plenty of eggs. We have chickens. We have plenty of eggs." Charles and Wheelock said "Then we'll trade you something for the eggs."

She said "*Non*, you don't need to trade."

Charles persisted and said "Well, then we'll pay you for them," and handed her four or five French bills.

She said "I couldn't take that much."

Charles said "Yah, you need it worse than I do. Take this." She was crying all the time now. "Oh thank you, thank you," she said. They took those eggs back to the base and boiled them and had pickled eggs for themselves and anybody else who wanted them. It was wonderful!

About a week later they said "Maybe she could use a little more help. Let's go and get us some more eggs." They started down the road and got within sight of the farm house and soon there came the kids on a dead run, "Yankees, Yankees!" They gave them candy bars and a banana that they had saved for them. Just like the orange they didn't know what the banana was. They had a couple of cans of Spam, some soap and laundry soap and some knick knacks that they'd brought along. "Would you like these," they asked. "Oh, you don't know how much! I appreciate that. I have some eggs for you." So they got another bucket of eggs to boil. The Mrs. was tickled pink by their visits, and those kids why they could hardly be contained, by golly they were friends for life.

Chapter 35
Deadly Fire

When it rained on the airfield at Reims, which was often that winter, the field turned to mud. The soldiers laid mesh landing strip down on the runways and when a plane rolled along it, it would ripple like waves on the ocean. When it was really muddy as it frequently was, the planes couldn't get off the mesh strip. The wheels would sink in and there they'd sit. The glider pilots only stayed at Reims for about three weeks after their planes and gliders arrived because they were unable to fly from the field. They were moved to Melun, France which was just twenty miles outside of Paris and had to share that base with another group.

Because of overcrowding and needs in different areas some of Charles's squadron members were reassigned. Some were sent back to England and flew with the British. Charles was assigned to fly with the 82nd troop carrier squadron and the 436th group for the Rhine River airborne crossing. His friend Wheelock was to fly as his co-pilot. They thought that this mission would be as one glider pilot put it, "a milk run," and that the Germans would all surrender with their arms up, but it turned out to be one of the most costly and dangerous missions of them all.

Charles carried a jeep and five airborne troops in his glider. The designated landing zone was about eight miles east of the Rhine near Wesel, Germany. En route shortly after they crossed the Rhine River in formation they were pounded by fierce gunfire. There were no other Allied planes in the immediate vicinity so Charles's squadron alone was taking all of the hits. There was another American stream of traffic heading for Wesel from a different direction and the British had a formation coming in from another direction. They were to converge at a common landing zone in Wesel.

Under a blistering enemy antiaircraft barrage Charles's tow plane was hit and both engines erupted into fire. The tow plane began losing altitude and gaining airspeed and turned off course about ten to fifteen degrees. Charles stayed on tow as long as he could because the firing was so intense at that moment. He didn't want to have to land right in the middle of it. Then the tow plane went into a dive and they knew they'd have to cut loose even though they were still four or five miles short of the drop zone. They didn't want to be drawn into the explosion and go down with the tow plane. Charles cut loose as did the other glider on tow and witnessed the awful sight of the tow plane plunging into the ground and exploding.

Charles spotted a field that he thought they could land in, a cow pasture or something, and made a turn to get out of the way of the aerial formation coming from behind. Just as he straightened the glider out a bullet hit him in the left hip and nearly knocked him out of his seat. Charles yelled to Wheelock "I'm hit!" Wheelock cried "I've got it," and had just taken the controls and straightened the glider out again when "Boom" a machine gun cut loose across the front of the nose canopy, over Charles's head and across the top of the jeep. Wheelock's helmet flew off and blood spurted from his head and he slumped forward and to the side of his seat. In a split second Charles knew he was gone and when he quickly glanced back to check the airborne men he could see that all five of the airborne had also been killed. They were still sitting buckled into their seats with their heads slumped down. There was no time to mourn. Charles operated by reflex now. He squirmed over and grabbed the controls again hitching his one good foot on the rudder pedals. He couldn't move his left foot at all. He pushed the wheel forward and dove at a nearby field that he picked in that instant. He knew he didn't have time for second thoughts. He leveled the glider out and landed about a hundred yards or so from a little grove of trees. The Germans never stopped firing and hitting the glider, all the way down.

Upon landing Charles lunged at the side window and forced himself through it and outside of the glider, half jumping, half falling, to get clear of the glider. He hopped on one leg towards a ditch that was about forty feet ahead and to the left of the glider. He had gone forward about ten feet and was near the end of the left wing when another shell hit him in the left shoulder and spun him down hard, flat on his back. He couldn't move. His arm felt shattered and devoid of feeling. All he could do was lie there. As he lay sprawled on the ground the firing into the glider continued and he could see an 88-caliber gun firing from the edge of a wood about 300 yards away. The other glider on tow landed about 100 yards behind Charles's. The pilot and co-pilot, Anderson and Lawly, came out with their hands on their heads and were taken prisoner by German soldiers and marched away in the other direction. Anderson and Lawly had an identical load to his, but none of the airborne soldiers came out of the glider. Charles assumed they were dead.

Several minutes later Charles was approached by a group of about ten or eleven Germans. They started shouting at him in German and one shoved his hand inside Charles's coat and took his .45 from his shoulder holster with his hand dripping with Charles's blood. He wiped Charles's blood off on his pants and put the gun in his pocket. All of his weapons were stripped from him including his knife and grenades. Another soldier who appeared very angry cocked his rifle and did some cursing and put the rifle up to Charles's head ready to fire, but "*Nein, nein, nein,*" he was told and the other men restrained him and pushed him out of the way. Several other soldiers were going through the glider. A soldier came out of the glider with a blanket and threw it over Charles. Another grabbed the GI cans of gas off of the jeep and sloshed gasoline all over the jeep, the inside of the glider, and on the wing, and then set it aflame. All of the men then ran back towards the 88 because they were being buzzed by Allied fighters.

Charles thought he'd burn up from the heat of the flaming glider. Several cases of bazooka shells and 30 and 50 caliber ammunition were in the glider and when it got hot the shells all started to ignite. Charles heard them whistling over his head. When the bazooka rounds exploded they flew out like 4th of July rockets. Charles was miserably hot and uncomfortable. He floated in and out of consciousness.

At some point during the day he heard and then saw a British Hawker Typhoon fighter circling overhead. The fighter pilot must have spotted the 88 gun because he made a pass at it and fired two rockets. They hit the ground about half way between Charles and the gun and didn't do anything. They were both duds. Then in the afternoon a P-47 flew over the gun and strafed it and then circled and came around by Charles. As the P-47 went by at treetop level he waved his wings and then threw his wheels up and at full power flew almost straight up and then off to the north. Charles thought well, he's gone, that's the last of him I'll see, and then suddenly the fighter turned and put the plane into an almost vertical dive over the gun emplacement. He released a bomb and pulled out just as the bomb burst in a huge explosion that rocked the earth. Charles felt as if he was being bounced into the air the air force was so great. The pilot must have used an extremely heavy bomb because everything just blew. There were parts and pieces of material flying everywhere; some of the debris even landing around Charles. Two Germans ran from close by the trees, and that was the last of the movement Charles saw from the gun emplacement. He was alone in relative quiet, and slipped away again into oblivion.

Chapter 36
Loved Ones Lost

Many years after the war Charles was again reminded of the Rhine River mission by a letter he read in *Silent Wings*. The letter read as follows and was accompanied with pictures of the soldier in question:

"Your name [*Silent Wings*] has been given to me as a possible source of information concerning the WWII death of my uncle, Flight Officer Levi F. Anderson Jr. He was a glider pilot assigned to the 82nd troop carrier squadron of the 436th troop carrier group. Flight Officer Levi Anderson Jr. was killed in action near Wesel, Germany on the 24th of March 1945. Although we were given a sketchy account of my uncle's death we have never been able to learn any of the particulars of the incident and the whereabouts of my uncle's grave was also unknown for some time. In an attempt to locate anyone who may have been in the glider with my uncle I am enclosing two pictures. One shows him alone and the second photo shows him with a group of glider

pilots or mechanics. I would appreciate the return
of the photos. In subsequent adjutant general's
correspondence on the 25th of October 1949, my
grandparents were notified that my uncle's body was
found and interred in a U.S. cemetery in Neuville,
Encondours, Belgium. They never received any
more details concerning his death. Any information
my uncle's squadron mates or your readers might
furnish would be greatly appreciated.

> Very Sincerely,
> Gary M. Anderson, S.M. Master Sergeant,
> U.S. Air Force Retired

Then there was an editor's note included with the letter
that stated:

"The war correspondence enclosed with the letter
indicates that Flight Officer Levi Anderson Jr.,
assigned serial number T60600, was a crew member
of a cargo glider participating in a glider mission
to the region of Wesel, Germany on the 24th of
March 1945. The glider was shot down and landed
in an open field near Wesel. They were fired upon
and everyone at once left the glider. Flight Officer
Anderson was struck while lying on the ground
during ten minutes of machine gun fire. An
eyewitness reported that he died almost instantly
of numerous wounds. If any of you can furnish any
additional information regarding this event please
advise Sergeant Anderson as soon as possible."

When Charles read the notice he immediately rose from
his chair and went to a chest where some of his wartime

memorabilia was stored. He opened a drawer and pulled out a pair of little wooden shoes that he'd brought with him from Holland after Market-Garden. He'd had all the members of his squadron present sign the shoes. Amongst the many individual signatures there was Levi F. Anderson's name on his shoes. He had been in Charles's squadron, the 87th troop carrier squadron of the 438th troop carrier group. Because their airfield in Reims had been so bogged down with mud the glider pilots of the 87th at Reims had been placed on detached service to other airborne bases scattered around Europe. They'd both been sent on temporary duty to Melun with the 82nd and 436th. It was then with this new squadron that they had been dispatched on the Wesel, Germany mission.

They'd shared the same tow plane; Charles was on the short tow and Anderson was on the long one, and they'd both cut loose and landed in the same field after the tow plane was hit. Now years later Charles knew the sad and devastating truth about what had happened to Anderson and Lawly. He had watched them being taken prisoner by the Germans as he lay wounded by the side of his glider. That was the last he had seen of them.

Sometimes it was better not to know what happened to squadron mates. It was so much easier not to ask questions and to assume that men, like Anderson and Lawly, were alright, that they had survived.

Still Charles was eager to help Sergeant Anderson any way that he could so he wrote to him and enclosed a picture of his squadron including Levi Anderson. In the group photo Charles stood holding the wooden shoes with Levi's signature. Charles explained that Levi was with the 87th troop carrier squadron on temporary assignment with the 82nd airborne and gave him all the information that he had about Levi including his having seen him exit his glider near Wesel. Sergeant Anderson in reply said that his family had never known much of anything about Levi's military service. They didn't know where or what he trained in until after his death. They hadn't even known that he was a glider pilot.

Several months later there was another article by Sergeant Anderson published in *Silent_Wings*. It read as follows:

> "I wrote with reservations not being familiar with this publication for information concerning my uncle, Flight Officer Levi Anderson Jr. I was not certain you would consider my request worthy of mention. Secondly I was not sure that any of his comrades would remember or be willing to go so far back in the past to bring back what might be painful memories and to share them with a complete stranger. I am more than happy to say that I was wrong on both counts. When you sent me the copy of *Silent_Wings* and I saw the article that you had written about my uncle, it raised a lump in my throat and caused the adrenaline to race through my body. I wasn't sure that I had done the right thing. Was I really ready to accept the information that I was asking for? Was this better forgotten? Although I had no memories of my uncle you have shared your remembrances with me. You have given me a little of what he was like, his character and how he died for his country, much more than I ever expected to find out. I can honestly say that his one remaining brother was extremely grateful to receive the information that I have been able to send him. It has meant so much to our entire family. I have enclosed copies of what I have received from those caring individuals who have so willingly shared their lives and memories with me."

Sergeant Anderson then proceeded to thank each person individually who had written to give him information about his uncle including the soldier who had sent a picture of Levi during training and a copy of his airborne graduation program and the priest who had sent a postcard from Holland telling him where Levi was buried and of the liberation museum there and of the honor that the men buried there deserved. Sergeant Anderson said that he could not thank these men enough and then in closing he said:

> "Finally Mr. Charles Stephens, how can I ever express to this man the great emotion he stirred within me: the joy, pride and sadness and loss. He had shared Levi's last flight with me and then surely the final moments leading to Levi's death. To know these facts meant a great deal to me personally and to my family. Mr. Stephens will forever have my sincere gratitude and thanks. Once again my sincerest thanks and appreciation to those who took the time and effort to introduce a present day airman, to an airman of the past."

Charles wept when he read Sergeant Anderson's message and has to this day to choke back tears whenever he thinks of it. He sorely wished that Levi had survived, but was at least glad that his family had some closure and knew more about the circumstances of his death. It felt good to be able to help and to use some of the painful memories that Charles struggled to forget for a useful purpose.

Chapter 37
Prisoner of War

Charles must have been unconscious for some time. He was overcome by the unremitting pain of his wounds and the heat of the burning glider. Just as it was getting dark two German soldiers walked up to the charred remains of the glider. When they saw Charles they came over to him, and talked to each other. One then set off at a run while the other stayed with Charles. As they approached Charles could see that they were no more than boys. They looked much too small to be wearing military uniforms. The young soldier that was with Charles tried to communicate with him, but it was no use. Charles couldn't understand him and didn't have the strength to try and make himself understood.

A few minutes later the other soldier returned with a wheelbarrow. Together the boy soldiers gently picked Charles up and one boy took off his jacket using it as a cushion for Charles's head, and put him into the wheelbarrow for one of the roughest rides of his life. Rolling along in that wheelbarrow he could feel every rock, rut and bump along the way. They crossed the field and mercifully got onto a road which was a little smoother and took the road to a farm house that was being used as an aid station. The boys unloaded Charles onto a litter cart and wheeled him over to the side of the building, and that was the last that he saw of those two young men.

Wounded German soldiers were coming in and out of the house, and some of them were sitting up on the front porch. The porch had once been screened in but all of the screens appeared to have been kicked out. After a few minutes passed some robust, uninjured German soldiers came out of the building and began looking at Charles, pointing and talking back and forth amongst themselves. "Boots, boots," one said as he stared and pointed at Charles's new pair of paratroop boots just broken in for the Wesel mission. They tugged off his boots and then they started helping themselves to the rest of his clothing. His socks were next. It didn't seem to bother them that his right sock was bloody from a nick on his foot. What was a little blood? The socks were under new ownership. The soldiers were having a gay old time, giggling and laughing as they stripped Charles clean. His coat, shirt, pants and underwear all went and then they really had a hoot looking at him lying there naked.

All that Charles had left was the little gold wedding band that VeNona had given him. One of the soldiers began tugging and pulling at it. He tried grabbing Charles's finger from various different angles, but the band was so tight that no matter what he did he couldn't get the ring to budge. He complained and threatened, until finally with a determined look on his face, he took out his trench knife and prepared to carve Charles's finger off. Just in the nick of time a couple of soldiers pushed him away. A little nurse who happened to be outside on the porch saw what was happening and flew over like a mother hen after her chicks. She slapped the offending soldier up the side of the head and yelled "*Nein, nein,*" and kicked him away. Then she hollered for two of the other soldiers to take Charles inside. He was wheeled inside the house and there she covered him with a half sheet somewhat preserving his shattered dignity.

In the aid station Charles was left practically alone in a far corner of the building's main room where it was fairly dark, but from which perspective Charles could see everything that was going on in the room. The doctor and the nurses were rushing from one patient to the next and sewing up wounds on some of the soldiers with no anesthetic. They were tearing up sheets or whatever they could find for bandages. There was a young girl about twelve years old who had a broken leg and a soldier and two nurses jerked and pulled the leg straight while she screamed pitifully. Then they put a cast on her leg, all without anything to kill the pain. Another little girl had a broken arm. The doctor used boards or shingles of some sort and wrapped her arm with rags in this crude brace. She screamed and screamed in misery and then finally fainted she hurt so badly. They had a little plaster of Paris that they daubed over the bandage and put her arm in a sling and laid her in a cot while her mother watched sobbing all the while.

By the time that they had treated all of the patients it was dark. Charles had lain there under the sheet for most of the day without being approached by anyone. Then a German doctor came to his cot and said in perfect English "You're American?" Charles responded in the affirmative and he went on to say, "Do you know where Northwestern University is?" Charles said "Yes, in Chicago." He said "That's where I received my medical training, but I'm German and you're my enemy. I have nothing to treat you with and I wouldn't if I could. We've got plenty of our own soldiers to take care of." He then looked at Charles's leg and his shoulder which was now a mass of fresh and dry clotted blood spilling down his side and all over the cart. He jammed a bandage about the size of a hand towel at Charles's shoulder and put his foot up against the gurney and gave Charles a shove that sent him scooting across the room where he bounced off the opposite wall. Here he was left, isolated again from the German patients and the medics. Any able-bodied individual who could help was soon occupied in closing the curtains, blacking out the lights, and preparing for the night. Charles just lay there alone and forgotten in the darkness.

Late at night a truck rumbled up to the house. Some of the soldiers were hastily removed and then only half-aware of what was transpiring Charles's litter was seized and he was thrown roughly onto the floor of the truck with a blanket tossed over him. As the truck wrenched to a start and heaved ponderously down what must have been a worn and rutted road judging from the jolts and bumps; Charles hurt so bad that he thought he would split in two—every nerve in his body seemed to be on fire. After a time mercifully the way became smoother and Charles surmised that they must have driven onto a highway or main road of some sort. A short time later he heard the familiar drone of Allied night fighters and felt a lurch as the truck swerved precipitously off to the side of the road. The truck nearly tipped over as the Allied fighter deliberately strafed them. This happened two or three times during the night as they traveled. Charles didn't know whether to cheer or cry at the straffing. He felt bitterly cold and was in such severe pain that he wasn't sure whether he would be able to bear much more anyway—either that or he'd bleed to death. His hip wasn't bleeding much but his shoulder was a constant source; blood from his shoulder soaked clear through the biscuit on his litter.

About noon the next day they drove into a town. Charles was hustled out of the truck and into a hotel that was serving as a makeshift hospital. They hoisted him up the stairs to the second floor and into a spacious dining room where he was unceremoniously deposited on one of the long, smooth, wooden tables. The remaining dining tables were set with the bodies of wounded and suffering German soldiers. There was a large plate glass window through which in happier days well-fed and contented restaurant patrons must have gazed pleasantly upon what was probably a picturesque little German village but which bright aperture today framed the streaks and flashes of Allied bombers and fighters as they flew over the town.

Instead of the merry sounds of laughter, polite conversation and the cheerful chiming of glasses, china and silverware in motion, there were the hushed tones of the doctors and nurses and the anguished cries of men in pain. In broken English a German doctor asked haltingly who Charles was, what outfit he was from, and the like. Charles told him that he could only give him his name, rank and serial number. Fortunately he accepted Charles's answer and didn't trouble him anymore. He handed Charles a roll of toilet paper for his wounds and took the blood soaked sheet that Charles was draped in leaving him with only the blanket. Unlike Allied medical staff this doctor carried a gun in his medicine bag, as did all of the German doctors and orderlies.

A huge picture of Hitler hung menacingly over the entrance to the room, and the soldiers in robotic fashion snapped to attention and saluted upon entering or leaving the room. Some even appeared to relish this repetitive exercise and added flourishes and dramatic flair that were uniquely individual. One spit and polish S.S. man made a particularly big show of it. He stepped importantly in front of the picture and stared chin thrust high, and chest uplifted in a patriotic swell at his Fuhrer. Once established there before the picture he clicked his heels together forcefully causing the room to ring with the sound of shrill staccato strikes and proudly yelled "*Zeig Heil*" at the top of his lungs and strode out of the room with the air of a man well pleased. Charles was left there in the dining room unmolested and unattended for the rest of that day and the next.

The following night Charles heard the whistle and sputter of a train pulling out, and knew from the sound that they must have been near railroad tracks. The train chugged and plugged and just as it had about cleared the hotel, Charles heard an Allied fighter make a pass at it, either a P-47 or a P-38, and saw the flash of fire from its guns. There was a huge explosion that shattered the dining room window and splattered shards of glass everywhere. There wasn't so much as another chug from the train. The fighter had scored a direct hit. The panic-stricken Germans rushed frantically to carry out their wounded on litters.

By morning Charles was the only one in the room. An orderly was the last to leave. In parting he roughly tore Charles's blanket from him and threw him another roll of toilet paper. Charles kept tearing small pads off the roll as best he could and applying them to his shoulder to try and staunch the bleeding. Whenever he tried to remove his wadded and soaked toilet paper dressings he felt like his flesh was being ripped to shreds; it was so bitterly painful. Between the intense discomfort he was experiencing from his wounds and the cold from the open window, Charles was in bad shape. There had been heat in the room when he was first placed there but now there was none.

No one came near him the next day. He saw and heard nothing. It had gotten to the point in his captivity where he no longer even cared to look out the window, and didn't have much interest in anything.

Then one morning a nurse and two orderlies with a litter came into the empty dining room. Strangely, the orderlies were no longer wearing their guns. Something was different. Their mood was somber and they worked in silence as they hefted Charles from the table onto a litter. The nurse was carrying a pajama top and a sheet. She wiped Charles's shoulder with a fresh pad of toilet paper, helped him into the top and draped the sheet over him. He was carried down to a crowded and noisy basement being used as an air raid shelter and tucked away in a corner of the room as isolated from the rest of them as they could manage. There were of course the same moans and groans of the wounded as upstairs in the dining room and there was the quiet conversation and scurry of the medical teams, but some people seemed paralyzed and several of the nurses were crying inconsolably and seemed almost hysterical. Even in his weakened, disoriented state Charles couldn't help but wonder what this was all about.

Charles was in the basement for about an hour when he saw wild-eyed nurses come sprinting through the swinging doors into the room and then heard a loud bang and saw the doors flung off their hinges, falling with a crash onto the floor. In walked the biggest, handsomest man he'd ever seen. He was a Scottish Captain and a full seven feet tall to Charles's eyes and built like old man football, all muscle and blood, and covered with blood and dirt from his head to his toes. "Where's the American?" he shouted. Charles rasped "Right here sir," as loudly as he could. The Captain was to him in a second and looked at him and said "My God man you need some attention!" Then he asked "Have they done this to you? Have they abused you in any way because if they have I'll turn this God-damn sten gun loose and kill every God-damn one of 'em!" Then he waved the gun around the room to show that he meant it. There were some scared Germans there, Charles could witness. Charles confided that they hadn't done anything for him, but that they hadn't abused him either.

The Captain then asked how long Charles had been there. Charles replied "What day is this? I don't really know what day it is. I only know that I was captured on the twenty-fourth of March." The Captain said "It's the first of April. And they have treated you like this?" Charles repeated "They haven't done anything. They just moved me down here this morning from a hotel room above, from the dining hall up above." Charles didn't want him to shoot anybody. The Captain let out a blast to the ceiling with his gun and swore again. Charles thought he was going to shoot the whole place up. He said "What in the hell has happened to you that you look this way?" Charles weakly said "Well, I've been here for seven days." The Captain said "Good hell, I'll kill every one of these Krauts!" "No, no," Charles remonstrated. The Captain paused and gave a scathing look around at the Germans to show that he meant business and then went on to explain that he was leading a reconnaissance patrol that was about twelve miles ahead of the front and that he had only ten men and one motorcycle, but that he would send the motorcycle back for an ambulance because Charles looked like he needed immediate care. He said that they didn't have any medication at all or that they would give it to Charles.

Then he asked if Charles wanted anything from that place to keep as a souvenir. Charles glanced around and all he could see was a picture of Hitler on the wall and some hotel postcards on a rack so he asked for the picture and a postcard. He thought he could maybe send a postcard to the family. The Captain brought the postcard over and it turned out to be a picture of the upstairs dining room, showing the tables on which Charles and the rest of the wounded had been bedded. Charles told the Captain that he was tired of seeing everyone salute Herr Goobler (Hitler) as they walked past his pictures and could he have the picture of him above the door? The Captain pulled out his trench knife and "slash, slash, slash," he ringed the picture of Hitler in the frame as easy as could be, and took it out and rolled it up and handed it to Charles.

Finally the Captain said to just hang on and that they'd get him out of there as fast as they could. He said that the town had surrendered and that Charles was in no more danger there. The Germans were flying a white flag from the hospital building so that Allied forces would not shell it, and he had told the Germans that he would return and that they'd better treat Charles well or they'd suffer for it. "I'll shoot them," he declared. "So they shouldn't be bothering you." He had to go on, but he assured Charles that the soldier on the motorcycle would soon return with an ambulance. Charles thanked him and he left, his firm steps pounding briskly across the floor. A little limey soldier, a pale reflection of his commanding officer, came in with his helmet under his arm and said that he'd taken a collection from the men for Charles and had a couple of sticks of gum, a few cigarettes, a piece of chocolate, and a few crackers from a K ration kit to offer him. He said that he wished he had more to give but that was all that they had.

Charles guessed that he should have been touched by their kindness but he hadn't eaten in so long and felt so terrible that none of the items seemed the least bit appealing to him. He didn't even want to think about eating. The soldier went on to say that he'd do anything, anything Charles wanted. Charles said no, that he was all right. The soldier said that he'd like to write a letter home for Charles to let his parents or his wife know that he had been liberated and that he was in good hands. Charles said that he couldn't write, that his finger was broken and sore as could be. He said that he would be pleased to have the little soldier write to VeNona. That letter became one of VeNona's prized possessions.

He wrote: "Recaptured your husband. He's in good hands. Love and kisses, X's and O's, X's and O's," and then he signed his name.

The letter took a long time to get to VeNona, in fact she didn't get it until after Charles was home. He beat it home, but it was very important to her. She still keeps it tucked away in a special place. The telegram saying that Charles was missing in action had been mistakenly delivered to VeNona's brother-in-law who took it to VeNona in Price, Utah where she was working. After he handed it to her she was shaken and immediately turned and went into her bedroom where she fell to her knees and prayed. As she prayed she heard President Jensen's voice saying "You will walk through the jaws of death, but I promise you that if you will honor your Priesthood you will return to your wife." From then on she knew that Charles would be alright. She had the most peaceful feeling come over her. She called Charles's folks and let them know that he was missing, but that she knew that he was safe. Charles's Mother and Dad were devastated. Mrs. Stephens misunderstood what VeNona said and thought she didn't care. Several neighbors had lost children and Charles's cousin who was a mining engineer in the Philippines was never heard from again after the Japanese invasion. Charles's brothers, LaGrande and Sterling, were also in the military in the Merchant Marines. They had lots of worries, and didn't dare hope Charles was still alive.

Chapter 38
Cooked Alive

Charles thought he'd have to wait for a few days for help, maybe three or four for an ambulance to come. He didn't anticipate anything happening in a hurry. He was used to waiting and reassured himself that he would have the mental capacity to do so. He expected that it would be like waiting for the British to come in Holland and maybe he could hang on for another week or so until they got around to it. He was surprised and so very grateful then when just half an hour or so later he heard a siren screaming and an ambulance came right to the hotel. Two British Medics bolted in with a litter and gently laid Charles on it and carried him straight to the ambulance. They said "This is going to be a tough ride with your injuries. We don't have any morphine to give you. The road is pocked all over with shell marks. We'll avoid them and give you the smoothest ride that we can, but tough it out as best as you can and we'll stop the first American ambulance that we see to get you a shot of morphine." Charles said "Okay, let's go." So away they went down the highway. They were right about the ride, it caused Charles to suffer excruciating pain, especially in his hip.

They had traveled about ten miles when they yelled "There's an American ambulance up ahead!" They turned on the siren and took off in the direction of the American ambulance. Upon reaching the American ambulance they stopped, the British said "Good luck sir," and Charles was transferred into the other ambulance and given a shot of morphine. He was soon riding high on the morphine. He felt so great it wasn't even funny. He couldn't feel any pain and actually enjoyed the rest of the ride across the Rhine River to a Ninth Army Field Hospital. He was pointing out the sights like an awestruck tourist and was as happy as could be. Just before they crossed back across the Rhine River Charles saw the pontoon bridge there and practically fell out of his litter straining to see it from every angle, "oohing and ahing," and exclaiming over and over "Oh boy, oh boy ain't that a pretty sight!" The medics had to tell him several times to lie down and relax, but "No," he would say, "I gotta see this!" They practically had to sit on him to keep him from moving. Charles had his picture of Hitler and his postcard and his first chance to really study the postcard which showed a picture of the dining room of the hotel, and the table where he had lain. It was labeled Splaun, Germany.

After they unloaded him at the Ninth Army Hospital, a triage hospital up at the front, a doctor looked him over and asked "How long has it been since you've eaten?" Charles told him that he really didn't know how long it had been that he had been taken prisoner on the twenty-fourth of March.

"Seven days?"

"Yah, I guess so."

"What have you had to eat?"

"Nothing."

"Are you hungry?"

"No, not particularly."

"Well, we'd like to examine your wounds, but you're in no condition to undertake an operation of any sort now. We've got to build you up before we can do anything. We'll put you

over here and take care of you, nurse you back to health—then
we'll operate and find you what's wrong with you." Two nurses
then scurried over and took command of Charles scrubbing
him from head to toe and front to back and cleaning up all
of his wounds. They hung a bottle of whole blood on one arm
and plasma on the other. That continued pumping until he
had received two bottles of whole blood and four of plasma.
They asked Charles if he was hungry and he told them that he
was a bit hungry, yes, and thirsty too now that he was thinking
about it. Charles said that he hadn't had anything to eat or
drink since take-off. "My heavens," the nurses said. They
brought a dish of broth and a glass of water and teased him
with them only giving a tablespoon of broth and a swallow of
water at a time. Then he'd have to wait for two minutes or so
before he could get any more. This was all right at first since
Charles really wasn't that hungry, but the more he ate the
hungrier he got. All of a sudden he was famished, and could
hardly bear to smell the broth.

Charles began to beg in Oliveresque type fashion after
each spoonful "Come on, can't you give me some more?"

"We have to wait a few minutes. Do you feel like having
more?"

"Yes, I do. How about a bowl full? Come on give me a bowl
full."

"In due time," they'd say, "In due time," and then they'd
just keep piddling. They kept asking Charles how he felt and
such. Charles said "Yes, I'm hungry. Let me have it!" Finally
Charles growled "Hey look either let me have it or get the hell
out of here. This has gone far enough. Don't be teasing me
with that food!" He was beginning to see the nurses as wicked
temptresses rather than careful healers. All the while they kept
saying that they just didn't want him to swell up or get sick or
vomit or anything. The nurses and the doctor were constantly
checking his stomach. "How does your stomach feel?" They'd
say. "Does it hurt here? Is it hard anyplace?" They were nearly
an hour feeding him the one bowl of broth and by then he

was feeling starved and quite bothered by the process. All the while he was being poked with I.V.'s it seemed, and they were pouring stuff into him through his veins. Here a poke, there a poke, everywhere a poke, poke. But they redeemed themselves when after he'd passed the broth test they let him have the ultimate reward, a sweet glass of juice.

"What kind of juice would you like?" they asked.

"Watermelon," Charles said.

"Oh, we don't have that. How about prune or orange juice?"

"Orange juice," Charles said emphatically. Practically gushing in his enthusiasm he told the nurses that was "the best damn orange juice" that he'd ever tasted!

By the next morning he was feeling better and they let him have some breakfast which too was wonderful. Charles kept asking when they were going to fix his leg and dig all of the shrapnel out and they kept saying as soon as he was ready. It wasn't too much time before they said that he was ready and they started prepping Charles for exploratory surgery. Charles asked what he should do with the treasures from his confinement; his picture of Hitler and his postcard, so that they'd be safe while they were operating. He wanted to make sure they knew that they were souvenirs he was interested in keeping and that they not be misplaced or thrown away. They were all that he had from his period of captivity. A nurse said "Don't worry about them. I'll see that they're okay. You just leave them right here."

That afternoon they gave him sodium-pentathol and instructed him to count to ten. Charles remembered getting to three and that was it. When he came to a nurse was sitting next to him beating him on the face. He was laying in a cast from under his arm pits to his toes in a spread eagle position nearly on top of a potbellied stove that was being used to dry the cast and which made him feel like a steak on the grill. He was mad as hell that this was happening to him. There was little nurse wiping the sweat off his brow and slapping him,

"Wake up Mr. Stephens, Wake up." From what he was told later he learned that he called that poor nurse every cuss word he could think of for cooking him and beating his face.

"Move me away from that damn stove! You're cookin' me!"

"We've got to dry this cast," she argued.

"The hell with the cast! Take it off here! I'm going to get out of this if I have to roll off this table onto the floor and break it! I'm going to get away from this stove!" Charles accused her of being a cannibal and who knows what other horrible things. He apologized to her afterwards after he'd realized what he'd done and she just laughed and said that she knew that he wasn't completely out of the anesthesia and said that anyway, she'd heard worse. She asked Charles where he'd learned to swear like that, and he said that he'd heard Patton speak. She responded "Oh, well that explains it."

When the doctor came in he said that he had set the broken leg but that he had to leave the bullet in Charles's hip. He said that it was lodged in the soft part of the bone at the neck of the trochanter of the femur and that it would cause more trouble to remove it than to just leave it there and let the tissue heal around it. If they tried to get the bullet out of Charles's hip at best if everything went well he would be a long time convalescing; at worst he could be a cripple for life. If they left the bullet in Charles would probably be walking again in six weeks. As far as his shoulder was concerned the bullet had gone through cleanly and out the back without hitting any major blood vessels or bone. The doctor said that wound should heal fine. He removed several pieces of shrapnel from Charles's back and legs and set his broken finger and removed a piece of shrapnel from the finger. Charles also had a shrapnel wound on his heel the doctor attended to that had barely missed the Achilles tendon. He'd just have a sore foot for awhile. "So lots of luck soldier," the doctor said as he sent Charles on. He knew that Charles would probably be moving on to an evacuation hospital soon.

Two orderlies carried Charles to a tent grumbling "You's a lot heavier than you looks!" Charles felt like he must have weighed around 300 pounds. Oh, his cast was uncomfortable. They stretched him out on a bunk, but it wasn't quite long enough so they put a small stool at the end to rest his legs on. After lying there for a few minutes unable to move Charles began to feel dizzy and short of breath. He could hardly breathe. Finally he called out for someone to help and a medic came over and said "We'd better get a doctor quick! I don't know what's going on." The doctor came and said "How are you feelin'?" Charles said, "I am light-headed and dizzy and am beginning to not see very well." The doctor said Charles wasn't resting at the proper angle. His head and feet needed to be propped up so that his blood could circulate.

After that they watched him closely. Soon he was feeling better, relatively speaking. It wasn't easy being immobile. He felt like a living mummy from one of the old horror picture shows. While he rested he was pumped with more blood and plasma and put on a regular diet. Charles still had his postcard from the restaurant in Germany but the picture of Hitler had mysteriously disappeared while he was in surgery. No one could find it.

Chapter 39
Agent Stephens

About five days after the surgery orderlies came through checking charts and marking tags as to where patients were to be sent next. A guy put a tag on Charles's toe. Charles said "What's that for?" He responded "That's your destination." "What do you mean?" He said "Your war is over soldier. That's a Z.I—you're going home." "What's a Z.I.?" Charles questioned. "That's zone of interior." Charles was told that because he had been a prisoner of war that he could have his pick of hospitals in the U.S.; that he would be air lifted to the states as soon as they knew where he wanted to go. The orderly said that Charles could travel to either coast, to anywhere in the north or south; Charles was to name the place and he could go there for as long as it took to convalesce.

Charles shocked the fellow by telling him, "No way! The hell my war is over! Take that tag off! I'm not going home til' I walk home!" Charles wasn't going home like an invalid. To his mind he was walking when he came to Europe and he'd walk when he went home. The orderly asked if he was serious and he said yes, that he was. Then he said "Well, where would you like to convalesce, England, France, Belgium?" Charles told him England and they put U.K. on his tag. He was emplaned to Paris and unloaded overnight at a hospital there, and then shipped on to Frome, England.

In Frome Charles did the same thing that he had done in the hospital at the front and in Paris; he lay motionless on a cot in his cast. The cast he was wearing had never been comfortable but the second day Charles was in Frome it became unbearable. 1st Lieutenant Bagsby was the nurse in charge of the hospital ward, and Charles talked to her about how insufferable the cast was:

"This is a terrible hard cast. I'm going to have them take this off."

She said "Well lots of luck, but I don't think that you're going to get them to do it. You've got a wounded femur bone and it is going to be six weeks healing, at least."

Charles said "No, it's not. It's coming off."

"Well, talk to the doctor."

There was a captain from a tank outfit over in the next bunk on a lower bed. He had been shot in the jaw and had his jaw wired shut so that he couldn't talk. He lay in his bed taking everything in. When the doctor came to see Charles he hadn't more than introduced himself before Charles said "Doctor I want to take this cast off."

"Not for six weeks."

"Oh yes, it can come off sooner. That leg healed in the seven days I was in the Germans' hands. It's in place. It's painful in this cast. I was resting pretty well before they put this cast on—so it's coming off! I'll cut it off if you don't!"

"Well, I'd just have to put another one right back on in its place, but maybe it would be more comfortable than this one is. This is an awfully heavy cast, a shipping cast is what they call it. But you are headed home."

"No, I'm not going home, not until I'm walking anyway." The doctor conceded a bit of ground to Charles and said "We'll take you down in the morning and I'll check it and see. I'll cut it off and if we can I'll put on a lighter cast and make it a little more comfortable. We'll do that." Charles asked him to wrap his leg and to please not put a cast on again. The doctor said that he'd look to see how the leg was healing after the cast was removed, and then decide.

When Charles awoke the next day as he was being wheeled from the operating room he was thrilled to discover that the cast was gone and in its place were elastic bandages. They were so much more comfortable! The doctor came in and said "You were right. Your hip is healing fine. It's in place. It has started to knit very well." He said that if Charles would promise to stay fairly still and not try to get out of bed or to move around too much and if he didn't develop any kind of pain or a crack in his hip or leg, he'd let him go without a cast for the next three weeks to see how it went. "Fair enough," Charles thought. So he lay still on his cot without a cast, praying for a swift recovery.

Charles was careful not to move any more than he had to and was slowly getting stronger. His shoulder had quit bleeding for the most part and was healing along with his shrapnel wounds, and his finger was healing in its soft cast. He just rested while his body did all the repair work. Without the body cast he could rest, and that felt good.

The tank captain who had been quietly observing Charles and all the goings on in the ward began to write Charles messages on a pad that he had. He wrote "Who are you that you can tell a doctor to take a cast off and how he does it? Is your Dad a general—in the Pentagon? Is he a senator? What pull have you got?" Charles said no to everything and insisted that he had no influence of any kind. "Oh," he wrote back giving Charles a doubtful look.

A few days later Charles thought "I want my watch." He had left his watch in a shop in Amiens to be cleaned before his last mission. He decided to write and to try and recover the watch. He didn't have any of his things at the hospital, none of his uniforms or personal clothing of any kind, but his first objective was to get his watch back. Charles wrote a letter

to Flight Officer Terrell or any other glider pilot on extended
duty or detached service from the 438th troop carrier group
in Amiens. Terrell was with Charles when he went into the
instrument shop to drop off his watch. Charles asked "Could
you please go to the instrument shop and get my watch out
and send it to me at this address?" Maybe he'd get his watch
back and maybe he wouldn't. He had no idea whether Terrell
would get his letter or whether Terrell had even survived.
Charles never did find out exactly who got the letter or hear
anything more about his friend Terrell. But somehow the
letter wound up in the hands of his commanding officer,
Colonel Johns. About four days after Charles sent the letter
Colonel Johns and a major who was Colonel John's copilot
came to the hospital carrying Charles's two footlockers, his
flight bag with his uniforms and personal effects, and his
watch. Colonel Johns was wearing the watch on his arm. A
pin could have been heard dropping when they entered the
room. Here was a colonel and a major bringing Charles his
flight bag and such! They didn't usually make house calls.

Colonel Johns had flown in from France because he
wanted to know what had happened to the tow plane and
its crew, and an intelligence officer and an adjutant of the
squadron who had been riding with them, and what had
happened to the other glider's crew and airborne troops, and
the rest of the men flying with Charles. Every one of those
men including Charles had been listed as missing in action
up until now. Charles could confirm the deaths of the C-47's
crew and all its passengers as he had witnessed it crashing
and exploding. And he could confirm the deaths of his co-
pilot, Lee Wheelock, and the five airborne he carried.

In addition, Charles told Colonel Johns about seeing
Anderson and Lawley being taken prisoner, but of not seeing
any other American soldiers exit the glider and of assuming
that the airborne were dead. Charles wished profoundly that
he had better news. Colonel John's purpose in coming was
to find out what had happened with the mission and to his

crews and cargos, but Charles thanked him for visiting, and told Colonel Johns that he appreciated his taking the time to bring him his things. Then after a short visit they were gone.

The tank captain began to scribble like crazy on his pad as soon as the colonel and the major were out the door.

"Who do you think you are fooling? What are you doing as a flight officer?"

Charles said "That's my rank."

He replied "Oh yah, I know, I've been in this army for fifteen years. I happen to know a little more about this army than you think I do. Nobody as a flight officer or a junior officer to a colonel has him bring his flight bag to him and a major as company with him there, without some authority from someplace. Now you say your Dad is not a general in the pentagon or a senator or something from Washington?"

"No," Charles said adamantly.

"I know now what you are. I know that you can't tell me. You can't tell me because you are sworn to secrecy. But you don't fool anybody. I know what's going on."

Charles protested, "No, you're wrong. I'm just a flight officer."

He said, "Have you ever been an enlisted man?"

"Why yes."

"That's what I thought. Take any rank that you want don't you?"

"No, I don't. I was a staff sergeant and I graduated as a flight officer."

"Yah, yah, yah, I understand now." That pretty well ended the conversation. For Charles it was like talking to a brick wall. The tank captain had made up his mind that Charles was some kind of big top secret agent. Yah, that was Charles. Bond, James Bond.

Chapter 40
Felix and Paris on a Dime

The head nurse in the medical unit, Lieutenant Bagsby, often talked about her wonderful fiancé, a captain and a doctor in the 101st airborne division. She had asked for duty in England so that she could be near him while he was stationed in England. Then he was sent into France and on to Holland and got wounded and was back in the states convalescing. She would complain about being stuck in England and say that she should have just stayed home. "We only had a couple of dates here in England," she would whine drearily. On and on she would talk about her Felix with the handle-bar mustache.

After a couple of days of hearing about Felix nonstop, someone asked her jokingly if she had a picture of her Felix. "Let's see this great Felix. Why don't you bring us a picture of this Felix that you miss so badly? Let's see if he is the 'He Man' that you say he is." So all the guys in the ward were teasing her about him and having a gay old time, and then one day she surprised them and brought in his picture. She drew a picture of Felix out of her wallet and passed it around. Everybody got to see it and of course now the teasing began again in a different vein; "Now you're over here and he's having fun with all of the girls in the hospital at home," they'd say tormenting her.

When the picture came to Charles he started. He couldn't believe his eyes. Charles said "Is this your fiancé?"

She said "Yes, Why?"

"You've got to be kidding me," Charles responded.

"Why, do you know him?"

Charles said "I don't really know him except that I got acquainted with him."

"When was that?" she said.

"He happened to be with the medical unit I took in on the Holland invasion."

Her Dr. Felix was the soused captain that Charles had taken in his glider in the Holland invasion. Charles told her all about the mission and how they only had enough pilots for a single pilot in each glider so that the older pilots were asked to go without a co-pilot and that the senior man in the airborne unit was then asked to act as the co-pilot. And that her Felix was Charles's senior man and that Charles had put him in the co-pilot's seat. "Help me in case of an emergency if I need some extra hands on the controls," Charles told him. "That's your Felix!"

"Really," she stammered.

"Yah, and I'll tell you something else about your Felix. He was drunk when we went into Holland."

"He was?" she questioned.

"Oh yah, when we came to load up there he was loaded himself."

Charles told Lieutenant Bagsby all about the flight including how he'd said to her Felix that he'd have to fly the glider if Charles was shot, and how he'd tried to instruct him. Felix was getting a little happier all the time; he was drinking his bottle and didn't seem the least bit interested in learning to fly the glider. The mission, Charles told Nurse Bagsby, was to hold Eindhoven with the 101st and the 82nd was to hold Nimegan and the British 1st and the Polish Brigade were to take Arnhem. The objective was to make breach heads across the Rhine River and to get a foothold into Germany before winter. They were to hold those breach heads while the British army charged pell mell up the highway to reinforce their positions. That was Montgomery's plan to end the war in the fall of '44.

Charles explained to the lieutenant how when they crossed the channel the glider drew fire and they heard bullets spitting through the glider, at which point Felix sobered up faster than any other man Charles had ever seen. He was all business and attention. "Well tell me again what I am supposed to do," Felix said. "Golly you could get shot!" It had finally dawned on him that they were in a dangerous situation and he needed to know what to do in case anything happened to Charles.

Charles recounted to Lieutenant Bagsby how he gave Felix a crash course in glider flight and how Felix helped to steady the glider when the wing was damaged. Charles told Nurse Bagsby the whole story, finishing with her Captain Felix speeding off with a man in a jeep towards the field hospital. The last Charles saw of him was a trail of dust he told her. She and most of the ward including the captain with the wired jaw listened with rapt attention.

Nurse Bagsby said that Felix got hit about two weeks after he landed in Eindhoven, Holland and was sent home to Virginia. He was just now beginning to be able to do some doctoring there at a military base in Virginia. Nurse Bagsby said that she was going to write home and tell Felix that she was Charles's nurse and tell him about what had happened to Charles. "He won't believe this," she said.

One morning she rushed into the ward just elated. "I heard from my Felix," she effused. "I've got to read you the letter he sent about you!" "Maybe I shouldn't listen to it," Charles said. But she said "No, I think you should." Charles listened as she read to him. "You take care of that man. He knew what he was doing. He explained every move that we were to make and how we were to make it, and where we were to go, like he'd been there dozens of times. The tank captain then interrupted, "I wonder why?" Then he looked directly at me and said "You don't fool anybody. I know why you can't tell me. You're sworn to secrecy." Nurse Bagsby ignored him and went on, "He knew exactly where to put us and what to do. We all made it through. All of us. Several days after we landed the Germans hit the hospital and I was wounded and evacuated back to Virginia." Then Felix continued to carry on about the way Charles had gotten them down after being hit and how he got them to the command post. Felix told her to see that Charles was given the very best of care—which she did. It seemed that there wasn't anything that she wouldn't do for Charles.

They'd have movies in the evenings sometimes in the hospital ward and one night during a movie Charles was talking to two of the night nurses. One of them said "You know I feel terrible. All my life, even as a little girl, I've wanted to see Paris. I volunteered for overseas duty hoping that I would be sent to France so that I could see Paris. Now the war is almost over and here I am stuck in England. I'll never get to see Paris. They'll evacuate me home." Both nurses told Charles how disappointed and depressed they were that they wouldn't get to visit Paris. Here they were in Europe, afraid that they weren't going to get to see Paris before the war ended and they were sent home. Charles asked them how long they could take off if they really wanted to see Paris. One of the nurses said "How much time would it take?" Charles replied "Well, it's just like any other big city. You see what you want of it." The nurse said "What chance have I ever got?" Charles said "If you want to go there badly enough I'll tell you how you can get there." They said they had this coming weekend off and a three-day pass that they could take when they wanted. Charles said "That's time enough. You can see all you want to see in five days." They laughed and said "I guess so," not really believing Charles. "You really want to go to Paris I'll tell you how to get there."

"Yah, I guess you can," they teased. The tank captain was listening to every word Charles could tell, but didn't say a thing.

Charles continued and told them to take the train from Frome to Newbury and then from there to take the bus to Greenham Common, his old field. They'd see a whole string of buses at the train station he told them, all headed to Newbury. They should take the first one leaving for Greenham Common. As they neared Greenham Common they'd go up a hill past the castle and then they'd stop at a gate. The MPs would board the bus and walk down the aisle and take a look at everybody. As long as the nurses were in uniform they probably wouldn't even ask to see their passes. Then they should just go through the gate and stay sitting on the bus until they saw the 87th troop carrier squadron marked on the right. That was Charles's squadron. They were to get off where it said 87th squadron and wait at the operations building, a big warehouse type building, until a C-47 with either a 3X or a 4U painted on the nose landed. The nurses should then tell the pilot of the C-47 that they knew Charles and that he'd told them that someone there would take them to Melun, France. "Tell the pilot that you want to go to Paris," Charles said.

"Oh I guess so," they said again disbelieving.

"Well, try it and see, if you really want to go to Paris." From Melun it was only a short bus trip to Paris, Charles told them. On the return trip they'd come back the same way; they'd take the bus from Paris to Melun, catch a 3X or 4U plane to Greenham Common, take a bus to Newbury and then a train to Frome. They could do it all in three days.

The nurses couldn't quite believe that it could be as easy as all that and went on and on making up excuses and so forth, but finally for lack of anything better to do they decided to give it a try. Charles didn't see them for several days and wondered if they had decided to make the trip. Later Charles heard that they took their three-day pass and set out on a train for Newbury all the while thinking that they must be crazy. At least they thought that they'd see a part of England that they'd never seen if they didn't make it to Paris. Sure enough after they took the train from Frome the buses were there in Newbury just as Charles had said and they boarded the bus for Greenham Common. So far so good they said to themselves. They saw the castle and the hill and the MPs boarded the bus at the gate, but they got through the check point fine. They rode the bus through Greenham Common and got off at the 87th just as a 3X plane was landing, and the nurses said to themselves, "Well, so far he's been right." They walked up to where two guys were sitting with their feet propped up on crates and asked "Is one of you guys a pilot?" One of the fellows answered "I am, why?" The nurses said "Do you know flight officer Stephens?"

"Steve, sure. He got killed on that last mission."

"No, he's in our hospital ward at Frome." They told the pilots that Charles had sent them. The pilots said "Steve told you to come? We thought he was dead. Well, for heavens sake."

"He told us to come down here and you'd take us to Paris."

"Why sure we'll help you," the pilots said. "We're just about loaded. If you want to go to Paris we'll take you." They gave the nurses two sets of coveralls and told them to step into the operations office and to slip the coveralls over their uniforms. They were going to have to ride in the cargo compartment of the airplane where it was a little dusty.

Next thing the nurses knew they were loaded onto a plane and off to Paris. They were really going to Paris! "What the devil is going on?" they were thinking. It seemed like a dream, but there they were in the air heading for the English coast and the channel. The pilots flew them to Melun and then told the nurses that if they could wait a bit while they changed their clothes that they would drive them into Paris instead of their having to take the bus. Charles had told the nurses to walk from operations in Melun to the guard post where they could catch a bus to Paris. Every twenty minutes there was a bus to Paris. The bus would be labeled "Paris" and they'd ride for about twenty miles until they reached the first stop, the USO, where they would get off. They could register at the USO and get rooms and then head off in any direction they wanted to see the city. Of course though when the pilots offered to escort the girls they were thrilled to not have to take the bus and jumped at their offer. The nurses waited for a half hour or so while the pilots quickly showered, changed their uniforms and then drove up in a jeep. The nurses ended up having a four-day tour of Paris in a captured German jeep. They saw more of the city than they'd ever dreamed of seeing. Then the pilots drove them back to Melun and flew them straight to Frome. The pilots told the nurses to say "Hello" to Charles and then went on their way.

Two very happy nurses danced into the hospital ward the following day. They were bubbling over to tell Charles how much fun they'd had in Paris.

"You made our war," they gushed.

"What do you mean?" Charles replied.

"Oh, we would never have believed it. We never believed that you could make it so easy. We had the best time! We went to Paris in a German jeep! Everything was just like you said. How did you know how to tell us where to go and who to go with to Paris?" They said that if word got out about their adventure that Charles would have every nurse in the hospital after him to find out how to get to Paris. At this the tank captain gave the nurses a sharp look and fired words at Charles again with his notebook.

"Now you tell me you're a flight officer? Have you ever been an enlisted man?"

"Yah."

"What?"

"I have been a staff sergeant and a private."

"What about the in-betweens?"

"I skipped those."

"That's what I thought. Why in the hell would you want to take the lowest officer's ranking? You could be a general."

"No," Charles insisted.

"What do you take me for, a damn fool! I know what you are now. Don't try to fool me anymore. Hell, I'd like to hear your whole story."

"No, I'm just a flight officer."

"Yah, I know you can't tell me. You're sworn to it. I understand that. I've got fifteen years of service and I know this man's army well enough."

"You don't know that," Charles protested. At this point he didn't know quite what to do with the fellow. There was no arguing with him. Worse than that, half the guys in the ward thought the same thing as him.

Chapter 41
The Placebo Effect

Charles was still in the hospital on V.E. Day. His first day walking with crutches his friends, the two traveling nurses, came rushing in saying that they wanted to take him to London to see the lights go on again in the city. They said "You made our war and now we're going to show you a good time!" The nurses said that they would take good care of him, but Charles was afraid to go. He said "No, I don't want to make that trip. I can't walk that well yet."

The nurses persisted saying "You won't have to walk, we'll take a wheelchair. We'll be your chaperones and you'll have no trouble at all. We want to repay you." Charles thanked them, but didn't dare go. "I've seen London dozens of times," he said. "Lights on, lights off, so what was a light bulb?" He knew that there would be big crowds and he didn't want to be jostled or pushed. He'd come so far that he couldn't bear the thought of suffering a set-back. Charles desperately wanted to get better and go home.

Then as if to change the subject, nightmare of nightmares, the captain started in on him again. "Ah, you don't fool me," he wrote. "How long have you been in the Inspector General

Service?" Charles said firmly "You've got me wrong." He scribbled, "No, I know you can't tell me. You're awfully young. Have you ever been a general?" Charles said incredulously, "Good heavens, no."

"What's the highest rank you've had?"

"Flight officer!"

"Ah, come on tell me at least that," and he kept at it needling Charles. He just wouldn't believe that Charles was just a lowly flight officer.

While Charles was at Frome they brought in some of the prisoners that had survived the death camps of Auschwitz and Dachau and others. Charles couldn't find words to describe the awful, emaciated condition of the people he saw. They were walking skeletons, skin and bones. He couldn't believe his eyes. The ghastly pictures that he saw after the war of the concentration camps and their prisoners were not one bit exaggerated. "Oh hell," Charles thought as his heart ached when he saw them. He was ready to get right out of his bed and go grab a gun and go back and shoot whoever did that to them. That was the most tragic thing that he'd ever seen. They couldn't stand or hardly walk and had to be helped to lie down or anything. They were terrible looking things; those poor people.

The average American soldier didn't realize the full extent of what was going on in the concentration camps. Charles was sure that had they known they would have searched the camps out anytime and anywhere they could have. All the GIs he knew felt that way. From what Charles heard they had an awful time controlling the GIs when they first went into the camps.

Near the close of the war another Allied glider mission was planned to send gliders and paratroopers to every prisoner of war camp under German control. The Allies had learned that Hitler had given an order to kill all of the prisoners of war. Miraculously Hitler never signed this order, but according to Doug Wilmer who was one of the glider pilots called up for this mission, two hundred more gliders were transferred from the states to Europe for the rescue of the prisoners of war.

Not long after he mastered the crutches Charles was walking fairly steady on his own two feet. The doctor came in one day and asked "Are you feeling all right? Try to walk for me and show me how you are doing." Charles walked for him then and showed off a little. "You're okay. Do you want to go home?" Home, of course, Charles wanted to go home, it sounded so good to him. "Yes," Charles said he was ready. "Do you want to go by boat or would you rather fly?" Charles said that he'd rather fly. The doctor said that he'd be flown to Prestwick, Scotland in a week or so for an air evacuation to the states. "Hooray!" he was ready this time.

There was a young man named Robinson, just a boy really, a corporal who had been wounded and had recovered pretty well and was acting as a ward boy who often came to visit Charles. He ran around doing errands and talking to everyone. He and Charles would joke around a lot together. One day, "Robby," as they called him, came in and said "How come you get to fly home and I gotta go by slow boat to China?" Charles replied teasingly "Well, I guess you just have to know how to treat people." The captain penned crossly "Yah, if they hadn't flown him he'd have ordered his own damn plane!" There was just no reasoning with him.

There was a new guy in the bed next to Charles and he'd had his elbow shot clear through. He must have been in a lot of pain because he'd moan and carry on something terrible. The doctors wanted to amputate his arm but he wouldn't allow it. He said "That arm is not coming off until it rots off. Don't you dare touch that arm!" Because he was in severe pain he was kept heavily medicated. Then after some time the doctors cut down on his pain medication. The other patients would get involved talking or doing some activity and he'd forget all about his pain it seemed, but once he was asked how he was feeling he'd start moaning and groaning all over again. "Oh, hell it's starting to hurt," he'd complain and carry on about how he wished the doctors would give him something to ease his suffering. Charles said to him "Why don't you ask the doctor to give you something for that pain?" Then he'd answer "Oh, I've talked to him and they don't give you anything that way. He tells me I've taken all the medication that I can have."

One day when Robby came by and the new guy was carrying on loudly and making a spectacle of himself, Charles said to Robby with a wink "Why don't we give him a pain pill?" Robby looked at Charles kind of funny and said "How do we do that?" Red Cross packs were passed out to the wounded regularly with big packs of M&M's in the large size. Charles pointed to one of the big red M&M's and said "We'll give him those." Charles said "Here take these and put him on a diet of pills and tell him that they come from the doctor." Robby said "Okay," with a mischievous smile.

Charles gave Robby all the M&M's that he had and Robby left the room. Soon after he returned and approached the soldier with the injured arm. Robby was carrying red pills in a little paper cup. He said "How's your pain? I talked to the doctor and he said that you can get all the medication that you want." The soldier said "Oh, good, good." Robby continued, "Do you want to take two right now?"

"Two?"

"Yah, the doctor said to give you two at a time."

"Oh, boy I like that!" Then Robby gave him two of the big M&M's. The guy gulped them down greedily. Charles could hardly imagine how he got those big M&M's down his throat.

Charles waited for about ten or fifteen minutes and then asked "How's your arm pain?" The soldier said sounding greatly relieved, "Oh, those pills help. It's not bad now. I can take it. I'm really glad that Robby asked the doctor about that." The captain with the wired jaw tried to laugh and couldn't. He wrote "cut that out you're making my jaw ache!"

Robby kept that soldier on a daily regimen of M&M's

for about a week. The guy's sister was a nurse from another hospital and every so often she'd drop in to see how her brother was getting along. One day in the course of the experimental chocolate pain treatment she came to see her brother. She asked him "How's your arm feeling?" He said "Since they gave me these new pain pills I don't have any pain. It's pretty well healed." Then he showed her his shriveled arm and how it was healing. Her brother went on to say, "When they started me on those two pain pills every two to three hours I began to feel lots better. I've done pretty good on that." She then asked "What pills are you taking?" He said "I don't know but they sure helped!"

Charles took the nurse aside and said conspiratorially "We put him on those pain pills; they're M&M's." She said, looking shocked, "You what?" "Yah, we fed him M&M's. It's all psychological with him." She said "Really?" Charles said, "Oh yah." Then she said angrily "Well, that's a damn dirty trick! I am going to talk to the doctor about that." Charles said "The doctor doesn't know anything about it. We just gave him a diet of M&M's and it worked to take away his pain." Then she thought a minute and said "Well, as long as it worked, I guess it didn't hurt him a bit either." Charles said "No, it didn't hurt him." Charles said to the guy "You still like those pills?" "Oh yah," the soldier said enthusiastically, "I couldn't get along without them." Charles said "Why don't you bite into one of those pills?" "No way," he said "I bit into a doctor's pill one time and it was nasty, the most bitter thing I have ever tasted in my life!" His sister laughed at that. Then he swallowed a couple of those huge M&M's down with a look of sheer contentment on his face. This went on until the day Charles left the hospital. He wasn't sure what Robby did after that.

Chapter 42
The Kindness of Strangers

Finally the long awaited day arrived for Charles to begin his journey home. He flew to Prestwick, Scotland with his footlockers, flight bag and everything else he owned for the first step in his air evacuation to the states. Charles was flown home as a litter patient, as a precaution, even though he could walk. After Prestwick the plane landed in Iceland to refuel and then on to Maine. They were supposed to have stopped in Newfoundland on the way but bad weather set in and they continued on to Maine to refuel. Then it was off to Mitchell Field in New York City. The plan was for Charles to rest for three days in New York before continuing the journey. Charles was told again that since he had been a prisoner of war he had special privileges and could choose a hospital any place in the states for his convalescence. Charles chose the one closest to home, Bushnell in Brigham City, Utah.

Charles figured that since it would probably be the last time in his life that he'd be in New York that he'd just as soon stay three days in a hotel in town than at the base hospital. He didn't want to just lie around in a hospital bed and miss seeing the city. He changed into his uniform, walked out of the hospital, caught a bus and then took the subway to Times Square. Charles hit the subway at rush hour. He thought that he'd be knocked off his feet and trampled before he could get out of his subway car and onto the street; he felt so weak. Charles thought that the swarming crowd off that subway would stomp him to death.

There was a large man on the subway who could see that Charles was struggling with great difficulty to move forward in the press and asked if he could give Charles a hand. "Soldier," he said "You look like you're having trouble. Could I be of any assistance?" Charles told him yes, that he would appreciate some help, if he could just get him out onto the street and to a hotel. The man said "Are you just coming back from overseas?" Charles said "Yes," that he was. The man put his hands on his hips and said "Just follow me," and bulldozed a path through the crowd like a linebacker saying "Sorry, sorry, sorry," as he knocked people right and left and delivered Charles safely to the Astor Hotel. Charles said that was mighty fine and thanked the man for his kindness and entered the hotel feeling much relieved.

Charles got a room and lay down for an hour or so exhausted. When he began to feel better he walked down to the restaurant. He was going to order a bite to eat, and go right back to bed. Charles still felt awfully weak, but hoped that a little food might strengthen him. He entered the coffee shop and sat alone in a booth.

There were six jibber-jabbering young ladies in the booth behind him speaking very loudly. Charles was trying hard not to listen but it was impossible to avoid hearing them. He wasn't going to have any peace. It seemed like all they could do was complain about this or that. Physically Charles was still feeling pretty miserable and when he heard one of the ladies say "Geez I'll be glad when this war is over so's I can have sugar in my coffee again," Charles had reached his breaking point. He'd heard enough. The hackles rose on his neck and he stood up and turned around facing the ladies.

He then proceeded to tell them what he thought of this war and no sugar in their coffee. He told them that if they wanted to see what this war was all about to take a look at some of the POWs that were coming out of the German prison camps and to see how much sugar they'd had in their coffee. It got so quiet then in that coffee shop that Charles guessed you could have heard the slightest whisper. Then Charles said angrily, and he wondered afterwards at saying such a thing, he wished that just one German bomber would come over and drop a bomb on New York so that they'd know what the war was really like.

At that point Charles's anger spent, he began to be embarrassed because of his outburst. He sat down weakly, feeling foolish. He could feel the blood pulsing through his veins and was sure that his face was flushed crimson. Up jumped the six ladies, out of the restaurant they strutted marching as fast as their legs could carry them with hardly a sidelong glance at Charles. They were all red-faced and humiliated. A man began to clap and said "Good for you soldier, good for you." All was silent then. It took a few minutes for the restaurant to return to normal. After that Charles quietly ate his dinner and retired to his room for what turned out to be a very sweet and restful night's sleep. He guessed that he needed to get that out of his system. He was kind of embarrassed for making a speech, but the ladies were talking such nonsense that he couldn't abide it. They just didn't understand.

The next morning Charles was refreshed and raring to go so he hailed a cab for a tour of the city. He told the driver that he had just come from overseas and would probably not have another opportunity to be in New York and asked if the driver would show him the famous New York sites. He said "Well sure," and inquired as to where Charles had already been. Charles told him that he had been to the Empire State Building and Time Square. "Have you been to the ferry and gone over and seen Ellis Island or the Statute of Liberty?" he said.

"I've just seen them from the air."

"Well, then that's a good starting place," and they were off. He tripped the handle and they drove all around the city for about five hours until Charles got tired. His cabbie seemed to have boundless energy and enthusiasm and would have kept going and going, but besides being exhausted Charles was beginning to worry he wouldn't have enough money to pay the fare so he finally said" I think we'd better go back to the hotel." He double checked his wallet just to make sure that he would have enough to pay the cab driver. The cabbie said disappointedly "You've seen enough of it?" Charles replied "Well, you never see enough of New York until you've seen it all, I guess, but I feel a little weak and besides I don't know if I have enough to pay your fare or not." The cabbie brushed that off by saying "Oh don't worry about that. Anything else that you can think of that you'd like to see?" Charles said "No, that's fine." He persisted and said "Can I take you to see diamond alley where they cut and polish diamonds or show you some clothing factories or take you down to Fisherman's Wharf?" "No, no thank you," Charles said. "I think I've had enough."

The cabbie let Charles off at the hotel and Charles asked him "How much?" thinking that he would owe his driver a large amount of money since they'd been out for so long. The cab driver turned around and looked at Charles and said "Buddy, you've paid your fare; it's been a pleasure. Good luck to you,"

"Well, how are you going to square with the company?" Charles asked reaching for his wallet.

"You just let me worry about that. If you need any help getting back to that field—call this number and I'll be there." And then he was gone before Charles could say another word. No one could tell Charles that New York City cab drivers don't have hearts. Charles felt humbled and tremendously impressed by this man's kindness. He had another nice dinner at the hotel that evening, went to bed early again and slept soundly.

The next day Charles went back to the hospital. The nurse in charge said "Are you by any chance Flight Officer Stephens? Where in the world have you been soldier? We've turned this hospital upside down three or four times looking for you? We were wondering how in the world we could have lost a litter patient." Charles laughed and said that he had gone AWOL and had gone into the city to do some sight-seeing. Fortunately the nurse laughed too and said "Quick get back in that bed and I'll try to cover it!" Charles didn't dare go anywhere else after that and spent the night in a hospital bed.

The next morning he was back onto a litter and on to Sedalia, Missouri. They had a six-hour layover in Sedalia, a plane change, and then flew to Denver, Colorado where there was another six-hour layover and another plane change. The next stop and final flight was to Hill Field in Ogden, Utah. At Hill Field there was a welcoming committee with a cheerful little band and women with carts loaded with coffee, tea, sandwiches, and cookies. The soldiers thought they were really special to be getting all that attention.

Chapter 43
Home at Last

The soldiers were taken by ambulance from Hill Field to Bushnell Hospital in Brigham City, Utah. It was about 10:30 in the morning when they arrived at Bushnell and Charles was anxious to be home. He was tired of being a litter patient and tired of traveling. He called the bus station and asked what time the bus left for Logan. The operator at the station told him that there was a bus departing around 12:30 in the afternoon.

Charles immediately got off his litter, dressed in his uniform and walked out of his room. He went straight to the doctor, Captain Swenson. The Captain said quizzically "Can I help you?"

"Yes," said Charles, "I just got in and I want to leave right quick and catch the bus at noon today to go home." Captain Swenson said absent-mindedly "Didn't you just come into the ward?"

"Yah, I did."

"Litter patient?"

"Yah, but I'm a walking litter patient," and Charles told him again that he was ready to go home on leave. Captain

Swenson replied "Not until you've been checked over you're not," and he said that it might take some time after Charles was checked over before he could go home. "What kind of time?" Charles asked. "It may take a couple of weeks before we can let you go on leave." Charles reiterated his position "No, no my war is over. I'll be on that bus going home at noon." The Captain argued "There is no way we can arrange that. You can't go without papers. You'll be AWOL."

"Hey, you think I care about that at this stage in the game? I've been away for almost four years. My war is over. You think I'm crazy enough to sit around here waiting for leave papers within one hundred miles of my home?" Charles told the Captain that if he needed to check him over he'd better make it snappy because he was going to be on that bus going home.

Captain Swenson obliged Charles. He had him strip and set to work checking him over. He said "You're serious aren't you, you mean to go home?" Charles told him he was very serious. Captain Swenson said "Well, you seem all right," and said that the leave was okay but that he couldn't possibly get the papers filled out for Charles to clear the field that soon. The Captain said that he'd have to wait at least another day.

Charles insisted that he didn't care about the leave papers, that the Captain could ship them to him if he wanted. Captain Swenson was taken aback and said "Oh, you can't go without leave papers. We've got to do that. We've got to clear the field."

"Clear the field? Charles hadn't any bills to pay there or any other obligations to fulfill. That's what it meant to clear the field. "Clear the field? What are you talking about? I just got in this morning. I've never even seen where the field is."

Doctor Swenson persisted, "Well, the papers will have to show that you cleared the field." Charles said "Please understand doc, I don't care about the papers. I'm going home!" Seeing Charles's firm resolve the doctor decided not to argue anymore and said "Let's see what we can do." He called an orderly and sent him out with Charles's clearance papers to be signed and then called for a jeep and a driver. Charles was on the bus at noon to Logan.

When Charles arrived in Logan the bus to Bear Lake had just left. He had missed the bus home! Fortunately the man in the ticket window was able to help him find an alternative route. He'd have to take the bus through Grace and Bancroft, Idaho to then catch the Bear Lake Stage to Montpelier. He'd get home around 6:30 that night.

Willard Hansen was his driver on the Bear Lake Stage and he was an acquaintance from home. Charles was thrilled to see a familiar face after so many years of being away. When they got to Georgetown just outside of Montpelier there was a much more wonderful sight to behold! Charles could hardly believe his eyes but, he thought he saw VeNona there waiting for the bus to Montpelier. He said to Willard "Well, wait a minute isn't that VeNona? There's my wife in her blue suit (he'd told her often that he loved that suit)."

"Oh, yah," said Willard "that's VeNona." Charles hadn't sent any word that he was coming home that day so he was truly surprised to see her.

As it turned out VeNona had gotten word from Bushnell that Charles was on leave and coming home. She'd gotten three different reports of his whereabouts that day, the first news that she'd received from the service since his capture. One was a notice from the hospital in England saying that Charles had been released and was being transferred to the United States, but it did not say when he'd be home. Another was a letter saying Charles was being transferred to Burma because there was an urgent need for glider pilots in Burma to fight against the Japanese, and then there was a card from Bushnell Hospital.

VeNona didn't know what to think, but put in a call to Bushnell and found that yes Charles had been there. She remembered that he especially liked her blue suit so she'd hurriedly put it on and walked to the bus stop. She thought that Charles would travel through the canyon from Logan and so she was headed to Montpelier to catch the bus for Logan. She was however, afraid that she was going to miss Charles. As the bus doors opened she immediately set to giving Willard a thorough scolding for being late. She was urging Willard, "Willard you've got to hurry here. My husband's coming home and I've got to get to Logan to try and meet him—so let's move it!"

Boy, that woman could be forceful when she wanted Charles thought admiringly. He just watched her go. Then she looked up startled to see him smiling down at her. Charles said "Hi honey," and before she could say anything more rushed to wrap her in his arms. They laughed and hugged and Willard just sat there with a silly grin on his face.

On they drove to Montpelier together. Willard asked if they wanted him to drop them off at the ranch so that Charles could stop and see his Dad. Without hesitation Charles said "Yes," that he would like that very much. Willard let them out at the ranch and they walked towards the gate. As they opened the gate they saw Charles's Dad.

When John Stephens saw them he stopped dead in his tracks as if he were paralyzed. He stood there his face white, his eyes shining with wonder and love. Finally he dashed forward and threw his arms around Charles and said with a wrenching cry of emotion "Oh son, I thought that I'd never see you again!" And then he just held Charles and sobbed.

That was one of the few times Charles had ever seen his Dad cry. John Stephens could hardly believe that it was Charles standing there. He was so very happy! He said "Son we were afraid that you were dead," and hugged Charles tightly with big tears rolling down his cheeks. Together they finished the milking and went home and surprised Charles's Mother. His parents hadn't known that he would be coming home. Word hadn't gotten to them.

It was wonderful for Charles to be home, but he wasn't able to put Bushnell Hospital and Dr. Swenson completely behind him yet. While at home Charles found that another piece of shrapnel in his hand needed to be removed and his right knee caught and swelled up inexplicably. On returning to the hospital for treatment it was discovered that a piece of shrapnel in his knee joint had cut the cartilage under the knee cap and it too had to be removed. Doctors operated on his hand and knee and removed the shrapnel, but couldn't remove a second piece of shrapnel they found in his knee joint. They felt that if they removed it Charles would have a stiff knee for the rest of his life so they left it to see how it would heal. Charles wore a cast on his leg from his hip to his ankle for four months. When they removed the cast the knee joint was stiff. Charles was given therapy for his knee for another six months and regained partial movement in the knee joint. In all he spent fourteen months at Bushnell Hospital.

During the time Charles was treated at Bushnell he received a purple heart at a special hospital ceremony. Later they said he was entitled to a second purple heart because he was wounded in the air and on the land so he was awarded the oak leaf cluster with a ribbon that serves as a second purple heart.

In addition he received three air medals for the D-Day operation, the Holland mission (Market-Garden) and the Rhine crossing. Shortly after the D-Day mission his whole outfit was awarded the Presidential Unit Citation, a little blue ribbon to put on the side of his vest. Very few outfits received that; Charles's unit received it because they led the invasion.

Charles really didn't know what to do with all of his hardware. He appreciated receiving the medals, but couldn't bring himself to wear them. He gave his son, Craig, his purple heart, and would give his other children: Glenn, Vicky and Lisa, anything that they wanted.

After the war in Japan officially ended in September 1945, the Air Force did away with the rank of Flight Officer and Charles had to decide whether he wanted to take a discharge from the service, or accept a commission. He was told that if he wanted to stay in because of his record and time in grade he would be a First Lieutenant, and if he wanted to accept a teaching position in ROTC and finish his schooling he could probably get a Captain's Commission on a permanent limited disability. Charles could have been assigned most any junior college or high school unit he wanted or he could have chosen from a list of about one hundred different universities throughout the United States. He was told that with his disability he would lose his flying status permanently, however.

Charles chose to be discharged and went before the Army Retirement Board. They recommended retirement, but when his request went to Washington the Surgeon General recommended farther treatment at Fitzsimons Hospital in Denver for another thirty to sixty days and then another evaluation to decide the case or Charles could submit it as it was to the Veterans' Administration for compensation. Charles chose to do the latter as he had been discharged from Bushnell on ninety day terminal leave and was working for San Francisco Chemical Company. Charles was permanently discharged from Bushnell and the army on the 22nd of July 1946, but was on terminal leave and not entirely separated from the service until the end of September 1946.

Epilogue

During the war there were many outside of the service who didn't understand what a glider pilot was and how gliders could be involved in the war effort. Now that the war has long been over and gliders have become obsolete as far as their use in fighting wars is concerned, it is even harder for people to believe that there were WWII glider pilots.

Charles purposely avoided being involved in a lot of veterans groups because of the memories those encounters might stir up; there were things that he'd sooner forget, but when he went to the Veterans hospital for treatment he often saw guys sitting and waiting for the doctors and they inevitably started to talk and ask questions.

They'd ask "What was your job in the service?"

"I was a pilot."

"What did yah fly?"

"Mainly gliders."

"What? What's a glider? Are you one of them damn fools that went in there and cut loose behind enemy lines and fought your way out?"

"Well, if that's a damn fool who done that then I guess I was one of them."

"Boy, why would you ever sign up for an outfit like that?"

"What did you do?" Charles would counter.

And they might say "Oh, I was in the Seabees. We went ahead of the troops and went on an island and I drove a bulldozer and built a runway so that we could get some planes in."

"See any Japs there?"

"Yah, they were sniping at us all the time."

Then Charles would say "What the hell were you doing riding around on a bulldozer without a rifle to be shooting back with?"

"Well, that was my job."

"Okay, that's what I was doing too, my job."

"Hell, you had a choice though, you didn't have to."

Charles would say "Did you have to?"

"It was the best thing in that outfit to do."

"Well, I guess I did it for the same reason." He had lots of conversations like that. They all did their duty then, no matter how risky or difficult; it was what the times demanded.

A few years back one of Charles's old squadron buddies, a fellow named Winkler who'd made good and had become the mayor of a small town in Illinois called him up to talk. After he introduced himself he said "Do you remember me?"

Remember him? Charles said "Of course, how could I forget you? You're my brother." Charles felt a bond with all those who served in WWII, but mostly with his squadron mates and brothers with whom he trained and fought. They lived and died worthy of the "G" on their wings. It was for gliders, and for guts.

Appendix

In 1952 Charles was overseeing the Waterloo phosphate mine and was made supervisor of the Waterloo Mill in Montpelier. Rance Heniwincker, a good friend of Charles and the supervisor of the contracting company, shared this World War II experience while they were out hunting together and swapping stories:

"After the Russians had advanced to Berlin and they were settling the boundaries of German territory and determining which territories the individual so-called Allies would be in control of; Rance was with an infantry company that had been fighting near the south-eastern section of Germany—some of the first to make contact with the advancing Russians. The Russians were holding some German prisoners and Czech and Polish people that the U.S. army wanted back into their zone.

Sergeant Heniwincker and a squad of eight men were assigned to take a train into the Russian zone, and arrangements had been made for the prisoners to be given to them. When Rance and his men got onto the train there was a detachment of Russian soldiers under the command

of a Russian sergeant who were also on the train who knew
nothing of the Americans' mission and were very belligerent
about the Americans being on the train in their territory.
There were about thirty Russian soldiers as compared to the
eight Americans. The Russian soldiers kept heckling Rance
and his men in an attempt to provoke an incident.

Finally the Russian sergeant who spoke English asked
Rance for his rifle. Rance refused to give it to him saying that
the only way they could get any of their rifles was over their
dead bodies. He said the last thing that an American soldier
would do would be to surrender his weapons. The Russian
bragged that they could easily take their weapons by force. In
response to this boast Rance called his squad to attention and
the eight men all backed up to the end of the car and released
the safeties on their rifles. The Russian then said that he was
only joking, that all he wanted to do was look at an American
rifle. When his request was denied again the sergeant then
asked the Americans if they knew how to shoot their rifles.
Rance assured him that they could indeed shoot their rifles.

Several of the Russians took their rifles out to the platform
between the cars and started shooting from the moving train
at the concrete marker posts that were out to the side of the
tracks. Many shots were fired by different soldiers but no
hits were made. Then the Russians invited the Americans to
give it a try. Rance said that they didn't believe in wasting
ammunition. The only time an American soldier would ever
fire his gun while on duty, as they were, was if they wanted
someone to die. The Russians said that they didn't believe
him and continued to try to goad him into it.

Rance didn't like the way that the Russians were looking
at them and feared that they might try to disarm his squad
so he said, "You guys are making me nervous so maybe it will
cause me to miss, but otherwise it would be just too easy of a
shot and I would be going against my orders." They persisted
to the point where Rance felt that he had to fire or they would
have overpowered his squad by their numbers and then taken

their guns. He stepped out onto the platform and took a sight on the next post about fifty yards ahead of them and going at about forty miles an hour he squeezed off a shot and literally exploded the post. It just disintegrated. He then put the safety back on his rifle and walked calmly back into the car. There was complete silence except for the rush of the train. None of the Russians said a word and they all wore a look of astonishment on their faces. Rance said that he'd never seen such a dramatic change of attitude in all his life. Finally after some time had passed the Russian sergeant approached him and wanted to know if all the Americans were as good a shot as he was. Rance told him that most were better and told the Russian to look at the little metal tag on his chest. He said "You see my tag says 'Marksman,' most of them say 'Expert.' That's why we don't waste ammunition on anything we don't shoot at to kill."

Rance said that the Russians didn't trouble them for the rest of that trip. Then he added "I still don't know how I ever hit that post. I've tried several times since and have never hit another, but it sure had its effect on those Russian soldiers."

ENDNOTES

[1] Silent Wings Museum, http://www.lubbockonline.com/silentwings2/pilot.shtml.

[2] Milton Dank, *The Glider Gang*, Philadelphia and New York: J.B. Lippincott Co., 1977, 132-33.

[3] *Tribute to the American Combat Glider Pilots of World War II*, http://www.pointvista.com/ww2gliderpilots/rollof   honor. htm.

[4] *CG-4A Glider, A Brief History of the Combat Glider in World War II*, John L. Lowden, http://www.indianamilitary.org/AtterburyAAF/Gliders.htm.

[5] John L. Lowden, *Silent Wings at War: Combat Gliders in World War II*, Washington and London: Smithsonian Institution Press, 1992, xvii.

[6] Charles J. Masters, *Glidermen of Neptune: The American D-Day Glider Attack*, Carbondale and Edwardsville: Southern Illinois University Press, 1995, 39-40.

[7] James E. Mrazek, *The Fall of Eben Emael*, Novato, CA, Presidio Press, 1999, 39.

[8] Dank, *The Glider Gang*, 51.

[9] *Id.*

[10] Lowden, *Silent Wings*, 45.

[11] *Id.* at 47-48.

[12] Dank, *The Glider Gang*, 58.

[13] Philippe Esvelin, *D-Day Gliders*, Chateau de Damigny: Heimdal, 2001, 53.

[14] Judith St. George, *So You Want to be President*, New York, NY: Philomel Books, 2000, 37.

[15] Mark Bernstein & Alex Lubertozzi, *World War II On the Air*, Naperville, IL: Sourcebooks Inc., 2003, 4.

[16] Masters, *Glidermen of Neptune*, 40.

[17] *Id at 41-42.*

[18] *Id at 42.*

[19] George Brennan, Edward L. Cook, & David H. Trexler, *World War II Glider Pilots*, Paducah, KY: Turner Publishing Co., 1991, 25.

[20] Lowden, *Silent Wings*, 130-31.

Made in the USA